A SOLDIER'S LETTERS TO CHARMING NELLIE

CHARMING NELLIE

A Soldier's Letters to Charming Nellie

BY

J. B. POLLEY
of Hood's Texas Brigade

ILLUSTRATED

Introduction
by
Harold B. Simpson
Colonel, USAF (Ret.)
Special Foreword
by
Robert K. Krick

New York and Washington
THE NEALE PUBLISHING COMPANY
1908

A Soldier's Letters to Charming Nellie

INTRODUCTION

TO THE BUTTERNUT EDITION

Joseph B. Polley, the author of *A Soldier's Letters
to Charming Nellie*, was born on October 27, 1840 in
Brazoria County, Texas. He was one of ten children
born to Joseph H. Polley and Mary Bailey. His father
had originally visited Texas in 1819 with Moses Austin but returned with Stephen F. Austin, Moses' son,
in the early 1820's as one of the original three
hundred colonists who settled in Brazoria County.
His mother's family was equally important in early
Texas history. Mary Bailey was the daughter of Brit-
ton Bailey who had landed at Galveston Island in
1818 and settled in San Felipe. It was reported that
the first Texas Congress met in Joseph H. Polley's
home and that he was instrumental in framing many
of the laws of the Texas Republic. The senior Polley,
following the admission of Texas to the Union in
1846, moved his growing family from Brazoria to
Bexar (now Wilson) County near San Antonio.

When the War Between the States commenced
young Polley had just graduated from a college at
Florence, Alabama. Upon his return to Texas he
immediately volunteered for active service in the
field. He enrolled as a private in the "Mustang Greys"
at Camp Clark, Texas on July 11, 1861. At the time he
was twenty years old; he listed his profession as
"farmer;" he was five feet, eleven inches tall and of
fair complexion with blue eyes and light hair. Camp

Clark, named for Texas Governor Edward Clark, was one of the "Camps of Instruction" set up for training Texas Troops early in the war. The Mustang Greys, commanded by Captain Ed. H. Cunningham, became Company F, Fourth Texas Infantry Regiment, when the Texans arrived at Richmond in late September, 1861. Polley was promoted to third corporal, October 1, 1861 and to second corporal the following month. He was appointed Regimental (Fourth Texas) Quartermaster-Sergeant, November 1, 1862, and continued in this capacity until invalided home in the winter of 1864-1865. Polley was wounded twice, slightly in the head at Gaines' Mill on June 27, 1862, and at Darbytown Road, October 7, 1864. The latter wound caused the amputation of his right foot and subsequent retirement from active military service. Polley always lamented the fact, not that he had lost a foot, but that the loss prevented him from being one of the "immortals who followed Lee to Appomattox and there furled forever the Stars and Bars."

The Fourth Texas Infantry, Polley's regiment, was part of Hood's Texas Brigade. The Brigade was comprised basically of the First, Fourth and Fifth Texas Infantry Regiments. During the war various other regiments and battalions were brigaded with the Texans, including the Eighteenth Georgia Infantry and the Third Arkansas Infantry regiments and the infantry companies of Hampton's South Carolina Legion. During the first half of the war Hood's Texas Brigade was supported by Captain James Reilly's North Carolina Battery. The Texans in Hood's Brigade had a distinct honor: they were the only soldiers from the Lone Star State to fight in the Army of Northern Virginia under Robert E. Lee.

Hood's Texas Brigade fought in all of the major engagements of Lee's army except Chancellorsville. It more than made up for this omission by participating in the battles of Chickamauga and Knoxville with the Army of Tennessee during the fall and winter of 1863-1864, and the Suffolk Campaign in Virginia in the spring of 1863. The war record of this famous fighting brigade was a gallant and a glorious one. It was a record written in blood, battlesmoke and bandages from the swamps of the Chickahominy to the rocks of Devil's Den and to the scrub oaks of the Wilderness. The Brigade was present at thirty-eight engagements that spanned a time period from Eltham's Landng, May 7, 1862, to Appomattox Court House, May 9, 1865.

Polley, fighting with the brigade, participated in six of the greatest battles of the war—Gaines' Mill, Second Manassas, Antietam, Gettysburg, Chicamauga, and the Wilderness and another twenty engagements of less severity. The brigade could count some 3,500 casualties during the war. At Antietam, the First Texas Infantry Regiment lost 82.3 percent of its men for the highest loss suffered by any regiment, North or South, for a single day's fighting during the war. The brigade itself had a casualty rate of sixty-four percent for Antietam. At Appomattox, but 476 members of the Brigade from Texas were left to surrender, a little more than ten percent of those who had served.

Joseph B. Polley kept a diary from the time of his enlistment in Company F, Fourth Texas, in the summer of 1861, until May 11, 1862. He also wrote six letters home to his sister Hattie and to his mother and father between September 20, 1861 and Decem-

ber 21, 1862. These writings of Joe Polley were presented to the Confederate Research Center, Hill
College, Hillsboro, Texas by Polley's granddaughter,
Mrs. G. J. Stewart of Houston, Texas. Mrs. Stewart
was of the opinion that these were the only letters
that Polley sent home to his family during the war.
Also, there were no other entries in his diary after
May 11, 1862. This information would lend credence
to the fact that the *"Letters to Charming Nellie"*
were written and sent to her during the war. Polley
was a prolific writer and apparently Nellie was the
only constant recipient of his wartime writings.

Some controversy has issued concerning the
authenticity of Polley's wartime correspondence
with Nellie. Douglas Southall Freeman, for one, ques-
tioned the genuiness of the correspondence, hinting
that it was probably written as a post war memoir
rather than a wartime correspondence. Was she a
fictitious figure that Polley invented and used as a
vehicle to publish his reminiscences of the war, or
was she indeed a real person with whom he corresponded regularly throughout the conflict? The truth
will never be known for sure; both participants are
dead and Charming Nellie never revealed her identity. Polley would only say that she was "a friend of
one more than a friend" and until his death, insisted
that the correspondence was genuine. Her photo-
graph appears as the frontispiece of Polley's book
and it is simply entitled, "Charming Nellie." Apparently, she started to write the "High Private," as Polley often termed himself, when Hood's Brigade was in
winter quarters near Dumfries, Virginia, January 3,
1862. However, according to Polley, they did not
meet until March, 1865, and on this instance Polley

thanked the lady for keeping him advised of what was happening in Texas in her "charming" friendly way. Nellie might have been a resident of Houston, Texas, as Polley's last letter in the book was written to his friend "Dick" from the Fannin House in Houston, 23, 1865. In 1908, Polley was to write ofMarch her "as a gray-haired wife, mother and grandmother who resides with grace and dignity of the truest womanhood over the home made for her by the gallant officer of the Tennessee Army, her first and only beloved whom she wedded shortly after the close of the war . . . "

The last letter in the book that he addressed to Nellie was dated December 20, 1864, from Botetourt County, Virginia. It was written while Polley was recuperating from his wound received at Darbytown Road. The last letter in the book, as noted previously, was addressed to his friend "Dick" and was written from the Fannin House, Houston. This finished the correspondence part of the book. The last chapter was devoted to a speech which Polley had delivered to the Hood's Texas Brigade Association meeting at Marlin, Texas on June 27, 1903, entitled, "The Fourth Texas at Gaines' Mill." Polley's speech supported the claim that it was the Texas troops that first broke the Federal's line at Gaines' Mill on June 17, 1862. Polley's remarks were in answer to an ariticle in the *Confederate Veteran* that some Virginians were the first to breach the lines at Gaines' Mill.

Polley was a good writer. He had a fine sense of humor, a natural aptitude for story-telling and was a keen observer. His letters are more than mere sidelights to history, they are a record of the brigade in bivouac, on the march and in battle. The latter, how-

ever, is downplayed, probably due to the fact that his
correspondent was a woman and the details of battles make for gory reading. Many of the incidents
written about in *A Soldier's Letters to Charming Nellie* appeared in his subsequent volume, *Hood's Texas
Brigade, Its Marches, Its Battles, Its Achievements*,
but generally in more detail.

Following the war Polley had a full, eventful life.
After returning to Texas he married Martha Le
Grette and took up the profession of law at Floresville, Texas. Four children, three daughters and a
son, were born to the union. He served two terms in
the Texas State Legislature and for years edited a
historical column in the *San Antonio Express* and
was considered an authority on Texas History. Polley
fell on hard times in the later years of his life. In
1914, he applied for and received a Texas Confederate pension. He listed his health as "quite feeble" on
the pension application and declared that his annual
income was not over $300, that he and his wife did
not own property worth more than $1,000, and that
the assessed value of his home was less than $1,000.

Polley was active in Confederate veteran affairs.
The United Confederate Veterans organization was
established in 1890 and soon Texas was honey-
combed with scores of local camps. Joseph B. Polley
joined the Albert Sidney Johnston Camp, Number
144, San Antonio, Texas, and remained a dedicated
member until his death.

Perhaps closest of Polley's heart, however, was his
membership in Hood's Texas Brigade Association,
which was organized in 1872 in Houston. Polley,
although not a charter member of the association,
joined it soon after its establishment. This associa-

tion was one of the most virile of the hundreds of
Confederate veterans unit associations formed after
the war. It met in annual reunions for sixty-two
years, until 1933, except for the two war years of
1898 and 1918. Polley was elected president of the
association in 1896, and was instrumental in bringing the annual reunions of the association to his
town of Floresville in 1897 and 1915. "Judge" or
"General" Polley, as he was usually called in his later
years,and Mrs. A. V. Winkler, widow of Lt.-Col. Clin-
ton M. Winkler of the Fourth Texas, were both sanctioned by Hoods Texas Brigade Association to write a
history of the Brigade. Mrs. Winkler published her
history of the Brigade in 1894. It was entitled, *The
Confederate Capitol and Hood's Texas Brigade* but
was unacceptable to the membership as *the Official
History*. In 1907, the officers of the association met
and sought "a good and able historian" to correct the
"many mistakes and errors of the present [Mrs.
Winkler's] Brigade History." Polley, "with one voice"
was elected historian at the Thirty-Fifth Annual
Reunion held at Navasota, Texas, in 1907. Polley's
book, *Hood's Texas Brigade, Its Marches, Its Battles,
Its Achievements*, was published in 1910, two years
after *A Soldier's Letters to Charming Nellie*.

Charming Nellie's correspondent, never a man to
back down from a fight, was at odds with the Texas
Division of the United Daughters of the Confederacy
over the final resting place for the original colors of
the Fourth Texas. The controversy came to a head at
the 1902 reunion held at Bryan, Texas, when the
United Daughters of the Confederacy requested that
the treasured flag be placed in their museum in Austin. Polley alone took on the Daughters in a lengthy

heated argument, maintaining that the faded, battle scarred emblem of his regiment should be sent to the Confederate Museum at Richmond because "most of the Fourth Texas that had fought under it were now occupying ground [buried] in Virginia." The crippled veteran after a prolonged debate yielded to the pressure from the Daughters.

If the letters, as some historians purport them to be, were reminiscences written long after the war, Polley was most clever in though and skillful in writing not to include a hint of postwar published references in his Charming Nellie correspondence, such as he did in his history of Hood's Texas Brigade. In the latter book it was obvious that he consulted the *Official Records, Confederate Military History, Southern Historical Society Papers, Confederate Veteran* magazine, and the memoirs of various Confederate soldiers and officers. No such references appear in his letters to Nellie.

Joseph B. Polley died at Floresville on February 2, 1918. According to his obituary, he had been sick for several days with bronchial pneumonia. He was buried on February 3, in the local cemetery, with the Confederate flag borne by surviving comrades following his remains. A bulletin issued by the Albert Sidney Johnston Camp, Number 144, United Confederate Veterans stated that,

> His Confederate war record was unsullied, his escutcheon untarnished. . .
> Upon returning to his home in Wilson County, accepting the reult of the war in good faith, he at once, as a good citizen, applied himself to restoring his section to its former state of prosperity,

counseled his people, who still felt that
the South has been grieviously wronged,
to submit to the power of the Government ... He was unobtrusive in his
manner. At all times respectful to the
opinions of others and while decided in
his views, was not dogmatic in expressing them.

A Soldier's Letters to Charming Nellie was originally
published in 1908 by the Neale Publishing Company
of New York City. It is only fitting that the title be
made available again to the readers of the American
Civil War. Thanks to the Butternut Press, this has
now been accomplished. It is a fine addition to the
available literature concerning the Great American
War.

Harold B. Simpson

Hillsboro, Texas
June 1, 1984

J. B. POLLEY, NELLIE, AND THE QUESTION

OF TIMING:

A BIBLIOGRAPHIC ESSAY

Joseph Benjamin Polley was a clever, bright-eyed young man when he served in several of the Civil War's most famous battles. Then and later he wrote about his experiences. High drama, bare-boned information, dry wit, unbridled laughter—all of these things and more mark Polley's accounts of his own war experiences and of the record of Hood's renowned Texas brigade. It is certainly not inappropriate that the more personal portion of his reporting is accumulated in one place, under the title *A Soldier's Letters to Charming Nellie*. A much more objective disquisition came from Polley's pen a few years later as *Hood's Texas Brigade*. Because the first book reflected signs of literary polish, yet was cast in the form of letters directly from the front to a charming Nellie, it has been the victim of casual calumnies over the years. It is my position that this sniping is misbegotten, by and large.

Colonel Simpson's introduction to this new edition supplies some of the background to the controversy. Was there really a Nellie, or was she a phantom foil, produced as a literary device to enliven what is really a memoir? If there were letters, how faithfully did Polley reproduce them? My own belief, offered blandly enough, is that there actually were letters, on which Polley innocently ironed out the wrinkles and burnished the high spots. Thus dressed for public review, they went off to press and into a permanent niche in the war's literature. More firmly than I offer that mild opinion, I would suggest that the existence or nullity of Nellie is all but immaterial.

There is, happily, no need to take anyone's word for any of this. An interested reader may decide for himself by looking at the evidence spread through the pages of early issues of *Confederate Veteran* magazine. Between December 1895 and April 1898, that incomparable treasure-trove-and-rat's-nest periodical carried letters to Nellie submitted by Polley. Only six of the twenty-nine monthly magazines during that period did not include a Polley letter. When the spurt of articles was over, *Confederate Veteran* had published what were in essence twenty-three of the twenty-eight chapters of *Charming Nellie*, a full decade before the Neale house published the book.

Appended to this essay is a listing of the articles in chronological order. They are cross referenced to the equivalent chapter in the 1908 book. Examination will show that the letters as published in the *Veteran* do not differ substantially from those in the later book, with one notable exception which is discussed in the next paragraph. Carrying the letters back another decade closer to the war does not, of course, establish their wartime originality; but it does provide a means of examining Polley's attitude toward working on them. At this late date we are not likely to ever learn whether the changes between the 1896-1898 serial appearance and the 1908 book version were the product of the efforts and desires of the publisher Walter Neale (no shrinking violet) or of J. B. Polley himself.

The one sizable alteration from magazine to book form came in the letter concerning hog hunting. This appeared in the February 1897 *Veteran* and then as Chapter XV in *Nellie*. The letter was very much re-written between the two publications. What's more, Polley appears as the principal actor in the later version, after hiding behind the *nom de plume* "Ben Blank" in the first printing (*nom de guerre* would hardly fit, the foe being nothing more dangerous than pork on the hoof). A detractor might insist that the inconsistency damns the author, but there is also a certain clean vigor that comes through in the image of Polley returning to the first person (as originally written?) in the more solid format of a large single-author book.

An interesting sidelight is the petty quarrel between Polley and a Miss Sue Monroe in the November-December 1896 magazines, over details of an episode at Second Manassas; this sort of quarrel was standard fare in the *Veteran*. That Polley was obviously in error in this particular bit of chivalrous nit-picking is beside the point. His rejoinder gives clear evidence that: (a) he was keeping a regular journal as late in the war as the end of the summer of 1862; and (b) he was accustomed to soliciting corroboration of details from fellow veterans. Both factors bode well for our ability to rely on Polley's writings. The diary which Col. Simpson mentions owning ends in May 1862, so there must be, or must have been, later volumes as well.

Further circumstantial evidence about the antiquity of the letters is sprinkled through the *Veteran* articles. The last two letters published in that format were actually the first two in date. Unless Polley was behaving very disingenuously, the explanation of their earlier unavailability flows naturally. The magazine's venerable editor, Sam Cunningham, implied that he had seen the aging yellowed letters himself. While Cunningham was not entirely above playing the shill, it seems unlikely that he would have casually supplied such overt testimony without cause, and without any substantial gain to be noticed.

If careful use of *Charming Nellie*, and examination of what can be found of its root, does not leave you with the feeling that the book is based quite closely on letters to Nellie, consider this judicious question: So What? There are surviving war letters by Polley to family members; his contemporary journal for part of the war survives, and he clearly had at least one other journal for a later period; he was recognized as his brigade's official historian by its survivors, and communicated with those survivors often on historical questions. Without actually conceding the point, let us stipulate for the sake of argument that the letters are entirely a postwar literary device. Even so, the firm historical bases enumerated above are at least as substantial a foundation as those on which dozens of acknowledged Confederate classics were developed. A comparative list of that sort would be endless, but from Polley's own publisher and from the same or later time period came such familiar classics as those by Worsham, Neese, Moore, Alexander, Sorrel, and Oates— as well as Polley's later widely acclaimed and seldom criticized history of Hood's Brigade.

Forget the salutations, if they befog your vision, and let Joseph B. Polley tell you about war as he knew it.

Robert K. Krick

"Letters"
and
when published
in
Confederate Veteran

Chapters 5, 10, 19, 27 and 28 were not published in *Confederate Veteran.*

CONTENTS

CONTENTS

PORTRAITS

INTRODUCTION

SUCH preface as the following pages require is furnished by the first letter. An introduction, however, will not be amiss.

The body of troops known in the Army of Northern Virginia as Hood's Texas Brigade, as originally organized, was composed of the First, Fourth, and Fifth Texas regiments, the Eighteenth Georgia Regiment and Hampton's South Carolina Legion. In 1862 the Eighteenth Georgia and Hampton's Legion were transferred to other brigades, the Third Arkansas Regiment taking their place in the Texas Brigade, and continuing a part of it until the close of the war between the States. One and perhaps two companies of the First Texas got to Virginia in time to participate in the first battle of Manassas, or Bull Run, as it is called by the Federals. Its other companies arrived in Virginia after that battle, and the regiment was organized with Louis T. Wigfall as colonel, Hugh McLeod as lieutenant-colonel, and A. T. Rainey as major. The companies composing the Fourth and Fifth Texas regiments reached Virginia in September, 1861, the Fourth being organized with John B. Hood as colonel, John Marshall as lieutenant-colonel, and Bradfute Warwick as major; the Fifth with Jas. J. Archer as colonel, J. B. Rob-

ertson as lieutenant-colonel, and Q. T. Quattlebaum as major.

Wigfall was a politician " to the manner born,"
and an " original secessionist." Like many
others of his kind, instead of seeking " the bubble
reputation, even in the cannon's mouth," he
sought it in the civic walks of life.

McLeod had been a valiant soldier in the army
of the Texan revolutionists of 1836, one of the
leaders of the ill-fated Santa Fé expedition of
1841, and one of the Perote prisoners. He died
at Dumfries, Virginia, in the latter part of 1861.

Rainey was a prominent lawyer of Texas, his
home being in Palestine.

John B. Hood was a graduate of West Point,
and had more than once distinguished himself in
service upon the Texas frontier. A native of
Kentucky, he had invested in Texas lands prior
to the war, and by virtue thereof claimed to be
a Texan.

Marshall was a newspaper man, a gentleman
and a scholar, but without a qualification for
command, save his courage.

Warwick was a wealthy young Virginian who
had won a commission from Garibaldi, the Ital-
ian patriot, by his coolness in battle. Although
at first the Fourth complained of his appoint-
ment, because he was not a Texan and was so
young, it soon discovered his merit. He was
mortally wounded at Gaines' Mill, just as he
sprang in front of the regiment to lead it in a
charge upon a death-dealing battery.

Jas. J. Archer was also a graduate of West

Point, and, like Hood, came to us direct from the old U. S. Army. He remained in command of the Fifth but a short time, being then promoted to the rank of brigadier-general and given command of a brigade of Tennesseeans, who under him did magnificent service.

Robertson was a Kentuckian by birth, a Texan by adoption. As captain of a company from Owensboro, Kentucky, he came to Texas in 1836, and, although too late to take part in the battle of San Jacinto, joined in the pursuit of the routed Mexicans, and remained in the Texas army until 1837, when his company was disbanded. In 1839-40 he commanded a regiment raised to repel Mexicans and Indian invaders of the Republic of Texas.

Of Quattlebaum little is known save that he, too, was a West-Pointer. He remained with the Fifth but a few months.

When the three Texas regiments were brigaded with the Eighteenth Georgia and Hampton's Legion, Wigfall was made a brigadier-general and given command of the brigade. In January, 1862, however, he was elected to represent the State of Texas in the Congress of the Confederate States, and on his resignation Hood was made brigadier-general, announcing his promotion and taking command of the Texas Brigade at Fredericksburg in March, 1862.

Until after the battle of Sharpsburg the Texas Brigade and Whiting's brigade formed a division under the command of its senior brigadier-general, Whiting. Whiting's brigade was then

composed of the Fourth Alabama, the Sixth
North Carolina, and the Second and Eleventh
Mississippi regiments. After Sharpsburg, Hood
was made a major-general, Whiting transferred to
another field of duty, E. M. Law made brigadier-
general, and assigned to the command of Whiting's old brigade, J. B. Robertson of the Fifth
Texas made a brigadier-general and given command of the Texas Brigade, Benning's and Anderson's brigades of Georgians attached to the old
Whiting division, and Hood assigned to the command of the division thus organized.

After the battle of Chickamauga, in which
Hood lost a leg, he was promoted to a lieutenant-
generalcy and placed in command of a corps in
the army of General Joseph E. Johnston, General
C. W. Field being, in February, 1864, promoted
to a major-generalcy and given command of
Hood's old division. About the same time General Robertson was relieved of duty with the
Texas Brigade and ordered to Texas, General
John Gregg taking his place as commander of
the Texas Brigade.

Space will not permit mention of the original
captains and lieutenants of the thirty-two companies of Texans in the brigade, or of the numerous changes made in regimental and company
commanders. As usual, the fatalities among officers were greater in proportion to numbers than
among privates. Disabling wounds sent many
home early in the war, but only one of the original captains, prior to being disabled for infantry service, sought and obtained service in

another field of duty. Of the officers hereinbe-
fore named, General E. M. Law only is living.

Whether written in camp, in hospital, or in
hospitable home, the letters tell a plain, unvarnished, and true story of the observations and
experiences, the impressions and feelings, of a
soldier whose only personal regret is that he
could not be one of those whose paroles at Appomattox are patents incontestable that they
fought for the right as they saw it, as long as
there was a hope to encourage them. Though
not intended as history, they are historical in
the respect that they narrate actual occurrences
in camp, on the march, and in the battle. The
lady to whom all but the last were addressed was
no more a myth from 1861 to 1865 than now,
when, a gray-haired wife, mother, and grandmother, she presides with the grace and dignity
of the truest womanhood over the home made
for her by the gallant officer of the Tennessee
Army, her first and only beloved, whom she
wedded shortly after the close of the war. To
her soldier correspondent she was the friend of
one more than a friend. It was not until March
of 1865 that they ever met. Her letters kept him
so well-advised of all that was transpiring in
Texas, and were so friendly, entertaining, and
altogether " charming," that, without leave or
license, he substituted that adjective for the conventional " Miss " to which she was entitled.

THE AUTHOR.

I

EARLY EXPERIENCES IN CAMP

WINTER QUARTERS OF FOURTH TEXAS,
NEAR DUMFRIES, VA., January 3, 1862.

YOUR cordial and flattering acknowledgment
of our introduction at long range is both gratifying and encouraging. It is not only evidence of
the deep interest the ladies of the South take
in our glorious cause, but it also proves that the
humblest Confederate soldier is not friendless,
and thus furnishes him with additional incentives to meet the inevitable trials and dangers
of war with uncomplaining fortitude and courage. While not vain enough to appropriate the
compliment of your letters entirely to myself, I
shall try to deserve them as well, because the
correspondence will be a great pleasure to me, as
for the reason that by showing myself worthy I
may, I trust, count on having a friend "at
court." In that capacity you may prove yourself
of immense service, and earn my warmest gratitude. While it may be true that "absence makes
the heart grow fonder," I fear the statement
applies only to the absent organ, not to the
deserted.   *   *   *

All things considered, our winter quarters are
quite comfortable. They may lack symmetrical

proportions, furniture, and now and then doors
and roofs, but we have expended so much muscu-
lar energy upon them, and have taxed our combined architectural abilities so enormously, that
we are both proud of them and glad to be relieved from further strain of mind.   The responsibility for the cabin which shelters my
mess was impartially and judiciously distributed
among its members.   To the Veteran, Mr. Wil-
liam Morris, whose service in the Mexican War
entitles him to that distinction, was intrusted
the planning and general supervision; to Floyd,
Sneed, and Dansby, the cutting and hauling of
the timbers and the riving of the clapboards
for the roof; and to Brahan and your humble
servant, the digging of a level foundation on the
side of the hill.   Then, when the frame was built,
the pickets set in place, and the roof finished,
there was a reapportionment.   The Veteran volunteered to build the stick chimney, and I to
make and carry the mud (mortar); Sneed and
Floyd took charge of the interior furnishing and
decorating, and Brahan and Dansby daubed up
the cracks.   The product of our joint labors is
a most elegant structure; but, unfortunately for
the Veteran and Dansby, the former made such
a miscalculation of the space required for six
men that, to punish him for his carelessness, he
and Dansby have, by unanimous vote of the
four for whom there is room, been condemned
to sleep in a tent.   It is hard on Dansby, I admit, but he has no business to have a bedfellow
so poor at figures.   *   *   *

The weather has been terribly cold and rainy for the last three weeks. I have suffered from it perhaps more than anybody else in the company; for, to please Brahan's fastidious taste as to soldierly appearance and to keep even with him, I weakly yielded before we left Richmond, to his suggestion that we buy caps, and then foolishly gave the splendid hat I brought from Texas to a darky. The top of the cap tilts to the front at an angle of forty-five degrees, and thus carries water over a visor just big enough to catch hold of with the thumb and forefinger, down on the point of my nose, and the back of it follows the slope of the occiput, and conveys every drop of rain or flake of snow that falls, down my spinal column. Brahan, orderly sergeant; I, a humble private; he stays in camp, while I stand guard, do fatigue duty, and otherwise expose myself. And thus, you see, although I have kept even with him so far as presenting a soldierly appearance goes, he does not near keep even with me in the way of discomfort.

If there is anything else that I have a right to complain of in common with every member of the brigade, it is of the vagaries and hallucinations of the brilliantly astute politician now in command of the brigade. They have been so frequent as to become monotonous. Old Sam Houston must have known whereof he spake when he dubbed him "Wiggletail." Whether it be due to constitutional nervousness, or to that produced by the apple-jack and kindred liquid refreshments of which he is said to be so fond, he has kept us for the last month, and particularly since the Christmas holidays began, in a state of almost constant apprehension. He sees a Yankee in every shadow, hears one approaching in every breeze that rustles and clinks together the ice-incrusted boughs of the pine trees under which the cabin selected for brigade headquarters stands, and no sooner sees or hears one than he takes alarm and orders the long roll sounded by the drummer he keeps close at hand for just such emergencies. The roll, I must inform you, is not the spasmodic rat-a-tat you are accustomed to hear when a company of home guards are drilling in the vicinity of your prairie home, but is a continuous, ear-splitting tat-tat-tat. It is only ordered when danger is too imminent to permit of a moment's delay, and its effect on sleeping soldiers is always startling, and often ludicrous in the extreme. It means that every man must get to the color line without even an instant's delay, fully prepared to resist an attack. The first time I heard it, it awoke me from the profoundest slumber of my life so suddenly, and scared me so badly, that for two minutes I looked under my bed for my gun and out of doors for my pantaloons.

As the First Texas has its winter quarters within a quarter of a mile of the doughty General and his drummer, it has been more frequently robbed of sleep and inspired to profanity than any other regiment of the brigade. Since the first two or three flurries, Colonels Archer and Hood have wisely waited for verbal orders before arousing their commands. Previous to that, Colonel Archer once led the Fifth Texas half way to Cockpit Point before he learned he was on a wild-goose chase. Thank the Lord, say I,—and I know the whole brigade joins me in the thanksgiving,—it is pretty well settled that Wigfall will not long remain in command of us. We are willing to fight the Yankees, but not phantoms; that was Hamlet's task, you know, and my recollection is that he succeeded ill at the business.

Barring guard and fatigue duty and the deprivation of female society, our time passes very pleasantly visiting friends in other companies and regiments and playing checkers, chess, and cards. Whist and euchre are the games most indulged in, but poker has many devotees, and is the favorite with a couple of messes of our company which occupy cabins on opposite sides of the company street and at the lower end of it. Each gives a peculiar but well-recognized notice of its readiness for a game. When the supper dishes are washed and put away Dick S—— steps outside, and cries in his deep bass voice, " Char-c-o-a-l!   char-c-o-a-l!   char-c-o-a-l! " in exact imitation of the venders of that commodity in the large cities. Following him, or perhaps preceding him, the musical tenor of Walter B—— is heard singing the first stanza of an old song known as " Old Mother Flannagan," and ten minutes after either call the dining-table of the mess from which it proceeds is surrounded by as many players as can find room to sit and the cash to venture. No great amount of money is ever won or lost, for our amateur gamblers have not yet acquired the nerve of professionals, and never go beyond " cent ante."

The dailies of Richmond reach us every evening, and from them we learn much that otherwise would remain concealed from us. The great cry and hope is for recognition of the Southern Confederacy by France and England. Every item, argument, and expression on that subject is listened to with an avidity that gives the lie to the loud-mouthed declarations of our fire-eaters, that they are thirsting for Yankee gore, and would be ashamed to go home without a smell of the powder of battle. It may convict me of cowardice, but nevertheless I frankly confess that I would be glad to get home without a single taste or memento of conflict. I am strictly bucolic in temperament, you see; not in the least warlike. Satisfied that

> " The chance of war is equal,
> And the slayer oft is slain,"

and, warned by that truth, I have no desire to experience

> " The stern joy which warriors feel,
> In foemen worthy of their steel."

Still, I propose to take chances with my comrades, and, if there be fighting, do my duty to my country as conscientiously as my legs will permit.

It is really amusing to note the eagerness of some men to hear news. One old fellow of Company F has a habit of listening open-mouthed to what is being told, and then placing a hand to his left ear and saying, " Please tell that over again, will you? " and the boys find great fun in manufacturing sensational news and playing upon his curiosity and credulity.   The professor of Latin for Company F calls him a quidnunc, but whether as a term of reproach or compliment is beyond my ken.   *   *   *

You were kind to wish we had a " merry, merry Christmas."   Every mess had its egg-nog, or a first-class substitute for it, the first thing in the morning, and something better than common for dinner, while after supper, the Veteran says, the whole company became " tangle-footed."   But he must be mistaken; the fellow that is drunkest always claims to be the soberest man in the party.   Anyhow, he and I were at Captain Cunningham's quarters until midnight, and when we left them I found no difficulty in reaching my own.   The Veteran attributes the circumstance wholly to the fact that I went down-hill, but I scorn the base imputation.   The next day headaches were both epidemic and contagious, and I admit that I caught one.

You must pardon the dullness and egotism of this letter.   Only the most trivial incidents occur in these days of waiting and watching.   Had you acquaintances in the regiment, I might entertain you by relating some of their ups and downs.   Deprived of that foundation for gossip, one has to be more egotistic than is in good taste. Sentiment would be dangerous, I fear, in this

stage of our acquaintance, even were it not inter-
dicted by loyalty to " our mutual friend."   If the
war continues—which I hope and pray it may
not—I will likely find many incidents to relate
that will be entertaining to as ardent a Rebel
as yourself.

II

CAMP, NEAR FREDERICKSBURG, VA.,
April 5, '62.

YOUR long delay in answering my letter written at Dumfries last January deserves punishment, and I can imagine none more severe than to compel you to read a lengthier communication.

January and February passed with but two little breaks in the dull monotony of camp life. One was the desperate but successful resistance made on the Occoquan, quite near the enemy's lines, by a party of Texas scouts to the attack of a regiment of Federals. There were only nine of the Texans, and, although the house in which they sought refuge was surrounded, they held the assailants at bay for several hours, and after killing and wounding quite a number, frightened the survivors away by a stratagem which ought not to have deceived a schoolboy.

I shiver at the mere remembrance of the other incident. Company F was sent on a two days' tour of picket and fatigue duty to Cockpit Point, on the Potomac, where an effort was being made to establish a masked battery to play upon shipping on the river. Brahan has become acquainted with my inborn and cultivated aversion to handling pick, shovel, and spade,—in fact, doing any kind of manual labor,—and I shall always believe he arranged with Captain Cunningham the deceptive scheme to call for volunteers from the company for the picket duty that was to be done. Anyhow, such a call was made as soon as we reached the Point, and, glad of an opportunity to escape hard labor, and beguiled to my undoing by a seemingly friendly wink from Brahan, I was one of the first to step to the front in response. For the first six hours I had no reason to regret my rashness. After three months' camp life it was positively a recreation to sit and inhale the salt atmosphere of the tidewater, listen to its music, as, stirred by gentle breezes, it broke in little waves upon the shore; gaze up, down, and across the broad Potomac, and enjoy the life apparent everywhere. Then suddenly and most calamitously a stray norther came sweeping down from the Arctic regions, the hitherto bright sun hid himself behind threatening clouds, and rain, sleet, and snow, in turn, began to beat upon my face and drip unceasingly down the front and rear of my cap. Under these distressing circumstances I awoke to the error of my ways, the foolishness of my choice, and as cheerfully as King Richard would have bartered his kingdom for a horse, I would have given a horse for a man to take my place and let me sneak back to the huge fires which my comrades—who, on account of the rain, had been relieved from their task—had built, and were enjoying in a sheltered place a hundred yards from the riverbank. Convinced that the Yankees would never choose such weather for an attack, I found solace in the fancy that the pickets would also be relieved, but that straw of comfort was too fragile to lean upon.

When dreary night had wrapped its impenetrable mantle over all things mundane the Captain came trudging through the snow to my post, and, with a disgustingly obvious pretense of compassion, informed me that until daylight the safety of the Confederate army would be entrusted wholly to the vigilance of Charley Brown, Berman Gabbert, and myself; and that, as it would be very inconvenient for an officer to tramp from the fire to the post every two hours to relieve us in regular military style, we were expected to sleep near enough to the post to wake each other.

"Bu-bu-but, Gabtain," chattered Gabbert, who is a Dutchman, and was then on post, "how—how—how vill ve know ven der zwei hours is oop?"

"Oh, you can guess at them, I reckon!" responded the officer, who turned on his heel and made what he thought was a bee-line for camp.

Neither of the shivering monuments of man's inhumanity to man whom he left behind felt in the least inclined to apprise him that he was proceeding in the wrong direction, and he had not gone fifty yards when he stumbled over a hidden log and fell headlong into a muddy branch. Rising to his feet, he sputtered entreatingly, "Say, boys! which way is the camp from here?"

"Oh, you can guess at it, I reckon!" I an-

swered instantly, repeating his own words of a
minute before.

But Gabbert, more tender-hearted, shouted:
" Go up mit der grick, Gaptain, und yer fin's her
purty quick, by tam! "

Then we arranged a programme. A bed was
made down, to be occupied by the two not on
duty, while the third kept watch for an hour, as
nearly as he could calculate the time—Brown to
wake me, I to wake Gabbert, and Gabbert, in his
turn, to wake Brown. Fair and equitable as the
plan appeared, there was too much guesswork in
it to be wholly satisfactory, and that was the
longest, coldest, and most wretched night I ever
lived through. Each of us went on duty thirteen
times before daylight; but if there was any miscalculation it was by Gabbert, for Brown and I
were positive we made a liberal estimate on each
hour we were on post. The Dutchman, however,
declared stoutly: " Mine Gott in Himmel! boot
by tam! I schust stand oop effer time more as
von hour und a halluf."

About the 1st of March a rumor went flying
broadcast through the camp that some grand
movement of the army was in contemplation, but
" old Joe " deemed it wholly unnecessary to inform us that it was to be a retreat until the morning of the 8th, and of our departure for this place.

*   *   *   *   *

There is a member of my company whom I
shall dub Jack, lest, by revealing his identity,
the tale I relate should cling to him longer and
closer than did that of his overcoat. Looking

more to his own comfort and sense of the fitness of things than to uniformity of dress and the consequent soldierly appearance for which my friend Brahan is such a stickler, Jack disdainfully rejected the munificent offer of the Confederate States Government to furnish him a gray and strictly military overcoat for $5 on a credit, and expended $25 in the purchase of one of a quality and fashion to commend itself to the most fastidious aristocrat. The first night out from Dumfries the weather was so intensely cold that he decided not to remove any of his garments, and so, wrapping himself in a couple of blankets, he laid down very close to a huge log fire, where, lulled by the genial warmth, he soon fell soundly asleep and began to snore at his liveliest and merriest gait. About midnight Bob Murray's acutely sensitive olfactory nerves were offended by the scent of burning cloth. He had only to look once to discover that as the fire had burned lower and lower, Jack had edged his back nearer and nearer to it, and at last a stray coal had lighted a flame that was playing sad havoc with his blanket and coat. Aroused by Bob's shouts, Jack did some rapid hustling around, but alas! too late to preserve the anatomy, the pristine symmetrical *tout ensemble,* of the cherished garment, and prevent its transformation from an elegant frock into a nondescript, altogether too open at the back to be comfortable, and with two pointed tails hanging in front, instead of in the rear—in short, in two sections, whose only bond of union was the velvet collar. Next morning the crestfallen owner sought to repair the damage by sewing the burned edges together, but that heroic remedy, while reducing the tails to one, and that pointing in the right direction, rendered it impossible to button up the front, and kept him so busy during the day answering questions that when night came he was too hoarse to talk.

A few days ago General Sickles, not content with the fame won in his quarrel with Barton Key, decided to

> " Seek the bubble reputation
> Even in the cannon's mouth,"

and with this laudable object marched his brigade of negroes in the direction of Fredericksburg. Barker, of Company G, Fourth Texas, one of the first Confederates to discover the movement, came near paying dearly for the information. While on a scout in the vicinity of Dumfries he caught sight of a couple of darkies in blue uniform, armed and equipped for battle. Never a slave-owner but always wishing to be, he decided then and there to make use of his opportunities and capture and confiscate both of the likely fellows, and immediately began a stealthy approach. But, like the milkmaid with her basket of eggs,—vide Webster's " Elementary Spelling-Book," last page,—who counted her chickens before they were hatched, Barker counted his " niggers " before they were caught; for, when he got within fifty feet of them, and stepping from behind a tree, called on them to surrender, they instantly dropped their guns, and took to their heels. Afraid to shoot, lest he should depreciate the value of the chattels, Barker set off in chase, and, stimulated by thought of the prize at stake, gave his whole mind to the race to such purpose that he was reaching out his hand to grasp the collar of one fellow, when pursuer and pursued entered open ground, upon which, fifty yards distant, was Sickles's guard detail, and two hundred yards beyond that, the camp of his brigade. Taking in the situation at a glance, Barker came to an abrupt halt, while the officer of the guard shouted, "Turn out the guard! turn out the guard!" as loudly as he could. The darkies were too badly frightened by the appearance of a Rebel in hot chase of their comrades, to obey orders, and Barker took advantage of the general confusion to regain his breath. Then, just as order began to resolve itself out of chaos, he saluted, in exact imitation of an officer of the day, and saying, politely, "Never mind the guard, sir," turned on his heel and was soon out of sight.

General Hood—our late colonel, you must know, has been promoted to the rank of brigadier-general—no sooner heard that Sickles was on the war-path, than he determined to gratify the gentleman's bellicosity, and at the same time win honors for himself and the Texas Brigade. The members of the command, rank and file, manifested a spirit and zeal largely due, I fear, to the report circulated by some mischievous

fellow that all prisoners taken were to be held
as the private property of their respective captors. At any rate, on the march toward Dumfries there was not a single laggard, and so rapid
was our advance that we reached the ground
where Barker had discovered the darkies, about
two o'clock in the afternoon of the day we
started. But, alas! Greatly to our regret and
disappointment, the doughty Sickles and his
" nigger " compatriots were *non est inventus.*
Whether frightened by Barker's impetuous
charge and cool retreat, or terror-stricken when
notified of the approach of our Texas regiments,
they had ingloriously fallen back to a point
nearer the Potomac and reinforcements than,
reckless and anxious to confiscate a batch of con-
trabands as we were, we dared to go. Properly
supported by other troops, we could easily have
marched ten miles farther in pursuit of laurels
and Ethiopians, and not a man have fallen lame :
wholly unsupported, though, and without hope
of either glory or plunder, privates and officers
alike became foot-sore and weary. And to add
to our woes, snow began to fall, and by night lay
three inches deep on the ground. It was on the
bleakest hillside in the whole country that we
sought to rest our tired bodies that night. General Hood said we were bivouacking, but if our
experiences that night are fair samples of that
performance, I beg to be excused from further
indulgence in the pastime—camping will be more
to my taste and comfort. Next morning, standing little on the order of our going, so only we

went, we straggled back to our camp near Fredericksburg.   Some of the boys disobeyed orders,
and seduced by the thirst produced by intense
cold, halted in Falmouth long enough to be captured by the provost-guard.   As a result, they
are each wandering up and down the color line,
toting a rather heavy log.   I was too high-toned
to risk such a punishment.   But as one of my
messmates not only was not, but evaded capture,
I had no lack of liquid refreshments to complain of.

I am much obliged to you for the hint I read
between the lines of your last letter.   But it will
do me little good, I am afraid, as long as that
cavalry company is allowed to stay out of danger.   Observation has already taught me how attractive the uniform of an officer is to the ladies.
Privates are nobodies up here, when a fellow
with bars on his collar and " chicken-fixens," as
the boys call them, on his arms, comes in view.
But I'll not despair; my lady's last letter was all
it should be.   Optimism is a fellow's best hold
when his patriotism denies him certainty.

NOTE 1—In common with most of his comrades, the author
implicitly believed the report, originating, he supposes now,
in the mind of some reckless wag, that General Sickles commanded a brigade of negroes.   The scout Barker insisted
that he chased negroes, and when he had run them into their
camp was confronted by negroes.   Whether his assertions
were true or false, they corroborated the report.   We were
as credulous then in respect to the Northern people as they
were with regard to us.   As a historical fact, negroes were
not organized into military commands until late in the year
1862.   If Barker really chased negroes, they were probably
mere individuals of the race who had been permitted to
enlist with a white company.

III

AROUND YORKTOWN

CAMP NEAR RICHMOND, VA.,
May 19, 1862.

ARRIVED at Yorktown, we camped about a mile and a half to the rear and right of that dilapidated old town. It was here, you know, that Cornwallis surrendered. The embankments thrown up during the Revolutionary War are yet in a fair state of preservation, and would likely have been exceedingly interesting to me had not the present war—in the shape and terror of bombs from a Federal battery—furnished a more practical and exigent subject for reflection. Some of my comrades grew quite enthusiastic over the fact that we were on historic ground, made sacred by Washington's great victory, and eloquently insisted that the scene should inspire us with extra courage and patriotism. Suspecting that the larger part of their enthusiasm originated in the canteen of whisky they bought from a blockade runner, I tasted it, but it aroused no corresponding sentiments in my pacific bosom.   *   *   *

About two o'clock on the morning of May 4th the pleasing information was communicated to the Texas Brigade that to it had been granted

the proud distinction of serving as the rear-guard
of the Confederate army in a retreat from the
Peninsula. In fact, all the other troops of our
army had already folded their tents, and, without
giving us the slightest hint of their intention, had
hours ago marched away toward Richmond, and
under these circumstances even the compliment
paid the brigade by giving it the post of honor
failed to relieve us of a feeling of lonesomeness
and insecurity. Just as day appeared we took
up the line of march, and anxious to put as
much ground as possible between us and the
presumably fast following Yankees, stepped out
in our very liveliest manner. But either because
they knew that Texans were the rear-guard, and
feared to attack such desperadoes, or were not
fleet enough of foot to overtake us, we went
peacefully on our way and overtook the main
body of our army about four miles from the old
colonial town of Williamsburg—with the proud
and inspiring consciousness thrilling our patriotic bosoms of duty well performed by heroic
efforts to get beyond reach of a dastardly enemy.
Yet although terribly tired by the rapid march
over eight miles of the muddiest road imaginable,
we halted not an instant, and leaving Williamsburg to our left, hurried rapidly on toward York
River. We were in good luck, for after an hour
or two of tramping, the roar of artillery and the
roll of musketry—fortunately many miles behind
us—smote upon our unaccustomed ears, and we
could reflect exultingly, that while the honor and
glory of having been the rear-guard was ours

beyond dispute, we had yet escaped all the dangers of that distinguished position. General Hood neither halted, changed the course of the march, nor furnished us with a single particular as to his intentions, but hastened us on with a speed which appeared to indicate so strong a desire to reach a haven of complete safety that the proceeding met our most hearty approval and co-operation; not a man straggled —not one lagged in the rear. As a result of this unanimity of purpose we were soon beyond recall and sound of the battle and made camp that night in the heavy timber about four miles from Eltham's Landing.

Here we remained until the 7th, when at dawn we advanced nearer to the landing and the enemy. General Hood and his staff were a hundred yards in advance of the Fourth, Company F next to the leading company, and we were approaching a large deserted house situated on an eminence overlooking the wide valley of York River.

Between us and the mansion were some cavalry pickets, who, like veritable dummies, had sat on their horses and permitted a company of Yankee infantry to shelter itself behind the building. Hood reached the picket post scarcely a hundred yards from the house, and immediately a squad of bluecoats stepped out in plain view and poured a volley into us—doing no greater damage, however, than to give us a terrible scare. We had been marching at will and in column, and except that of John Deal of Company A, not a gun was loaded. It was a complete surprise. We were in a newly cleared field full of pine stumps, and, with the instinct of self-preservation suddenly aroused, every man except Deal—who immediately knelt, fired and mortally wounded the sergeant of the attacking force—hastily sought the protection of a stump, loading his gun as he ran. Hood came dashing back, shouting to the regiment to fall into line, and as every stump I made for was appropriated by a quicker man, and I had managed to load my gun, no option was left me but to be among the first to obey orders and place myself in approved battle array.

Not half a minute elapsed, though, before every man of the regiment was in ranks, and then came the order to charge. Rushing bravely and furiously to the crest of the eminence, we were overjoyed at seeing the enemy fleeing across an open field to a skirt of timber half a mile away—their precipitate flight availing them little, however, for not a man of the fifty or more in sight and range escaped wounding or death.

To the right of the house grew heavy timber, and there after we had deployed into skirmish line a number of Yankees were killed and captured. After a while the brigade moved forward across the field into the woods beyond, but the enemy was driven back so rapidly by our skirmishers that not a single one capable of doing duty came within my view. I made no complaint, and as long as I kept out of their sight was thoroughly

content. The other two Texas regiments—the
First and the Fifth—had hot fights which they
won by gallant charges, and in two hours or so
the Yankees were forced to take refuge in trans-
ports protected by gunboats, which shelled the
woods until night.

Thus, Charming Nellie, began and ended your
friend's first experience under fire. He did not
distinguish himself, it is true, but he finds great
consolation in the fact that neither did the enemy
nor the Virginia cavalry, who, by their carelessness, almost caused the Fourth Texas to show
" the white feather " in its first engagement.
Here I looked for the first time on the dead and
wounded of a battle. After the fighting was over,
Jack Sutherland and I went to a poor fellow
who was mortally wounded, and filling his canteen with water did what else we could to make
him comfortable. He admitted being from Wis-
consin, but absolutely refused to name the particular command to which he belonged, saying
it was against orders. He was just about my
age, and it was not a pleasant thought that some
day soon I might, like him, be mortally wounded
and left in the hands of the enemy. I do not
often indulge in such grim fancies, but in his
presence could not avoid them.   *   *   *

Three days' rations were issued to us the day
before we left Yorktown, and on the morning of
the 8th, our haversacks being again empty, four
ears of corn were dealt out to each man. When
parched it was not at all bad eating to hungry
soldiers, and we soon became genuine Cornfeds.

About two o'clock on the morning of the 9th the regiment was aroused and informed that it was to be carried out of very dangerous quarters, right under the noses of the enemy, and that the most profound silence must be maintained, and not even a cup suffered to rattle. Thus enjoined, we marched out of camp as quietly and stealthily as Arabs, taking the road to Richmond through an open country enveloped by a dense fog.

To the right and very near the line of march could be distinguished the shadowy forms of horses and their riders, standing silent and motionless—cavalry pickets, whose close proximity to the road should, according to military usage, have indicated that the enemy was but a short distance away; when, however, it was learned that the pickets were ——, our fears instantly subsided, for we felt confident the gallant sabreurs of that State would keep too careful a lookout for their own safety to permit an enemy to approach within shooting distance. Nevertheless, the speed of the march suffered no abatement until broad daylight, and the lifting of the fog furnished ocular demonstration of safety. Then I drew a long and heartfelt sigh of relief, being philosopher enough to derive much comfort from that soul-inspiring sentiment of the poet,

> "He who fights and runs away
> Will live to fight another day."

At ten o'clock A. M. we passed the White House,

the home of the Lee family, and the place where General Washington " caught a Tartar " by marrying the widow Custis. But as no member of the brigade cared just then to make any historical researches, we pushed on and on until fully assured that half of the Confederate army lay between us and the Yankees, and then— about noon—won our most appreciated laurels by camping in a thicket of those shrubs. In truth, we deserved them, for little gallantry as we displayed at Eltham's Landing, the Yankees displayed less, and our bold front had prevented the debarkation of Franklin's corps and the capture of our immense wagon trains.

What do you think? After going into camp in the laurel thicket I witnessed the performance of a strange feat by a sleeping man—he caught a live rabbit with his hands. It is a solemn, undeniable fact which can be proved by a hundred men who failed to capture the little animal. It was this way: The rabbit jumped out of a hollow stump which some soldier wanted for firewood, and the moment it was seen an immense shout went up and half a thousand men began chasing and grabbing at it. It ran hither and thither, and finally jumped squarely on Dansby's breast just as his hand, moved unconsciously, descended to rest on the breast. The two acts— that of the rabbit and that of the man—were so nearly simultaneous that the rabbit evidently imagined it had found a hiding place, and made no effort whatever to escape. Dansby drew a long breath, opened his eyes in astonishment, looked a moment at the captive, and then sprang to his feet, saying with a smile of delight, "By gum, boys, but I'm hungry!" In less than five minutes the trusting little rabbit was stewing on the fire, and ten minutes later Dansby was eating it.

What a long letter I am writing—or rather have already written! Luckily I am at no expense for postage, having, in common with members of Congress, the franking privilege. You may find the reading a sore tax on your patience, but I must bring my story up to date, nevertheless.

There is no telling how long we will remain here or when I will again be as comfortably fixed for annoying you. I have driven four stakes into the ground in proper position to hold a board, covered by a blanket, at the right height to allow me to make a chair of Mother Earth. Another reason for not closing and marking at the bottom "to be continued" is that I may not live to do the continuing. Ever since I received your last letter the child's prayer paraphrased to read "If I should die before I write" has been ringing in my head. I am not silly enough to fancy it a premonition, I assure you. On the contrary, I feel certain of escaping death. But I know that is a possibility, and so, holding a letter received as an obligation to be honorably met only by a full and complete answer, I will trespass on your endurance and fortitude a while longer.

We rested in the laurel thicket several days,

during which the recruiting officers who left us at Dumfries rejoined the brigade with batches of raw recruits and many letters from home folks. When the order at last came to march it was raining heavily and it continued to do so until midnight. Troops had been passing for five or six hours before we moved, and we began to fear that General Johnston intended to make us the rear-guard again. It was a great relief therefore to be marched a half mile farther from the enemy, even if then left standing in mud and water for two full hours. After that we began a system of alternate marching and standing still, which continued until after midnight. Order and discipline came to an end, and it was "every man for himself and old Nick for the hindmost."

Nobody could say who was next to him, the different commands of the army having become inextricably intermixed in the darkness, rain and mud. Officers on horseback rode back and forth along the road begging, praying, and ordering the men to move forward as fast as possible and get across the Chickahominy, and determining that if that was all they wanted me to do, it should be done, I resolved myself into an independent command and set out for the bridge. Near it and stretching across the road was an immense and apparently unfathomable mudhole. Some provident fellow had hung a lantern to the limb of a tree, and its light disclosed not only the length and breadth of the obstruction but a narrow and dry way around it, and that way was being taken by the soldiers. General Whiting and I reached the loblolly about the same time. I was much the wiser man of the two, though; I followed the current, he endeavored to change it. "Wade right through that mud, men," he commanded; "it is not deep." Whereupon a fellow who was marching in single file in the narrow way around, said in the sarcastic tone so easily adopted by the most timid man in a darkness and confusion which prevents identification, "You go through it yourself, Mr. Little Man, if you're so sure it ain't deep." "Do you know, sir, you are talking to General Whiting?" angrily demanded that officer. "Maybe so," responded the unknown, now almost around the mudhole, and at any rate too far away to be identified, "but d——d if I believe a word of it. You are more likely one of his couriers, taking advantage of this dark night to play the general and order your betters around. Anyhow, if you are a general, you are a d——d small one." "Arrest that insolent fellow!" shouted Whiting furiously—so beside himself with rage that he spurred his horse into the mudhole and was splashed from head to foot with its contents. "Oh, dry up, you d——d old fool!" came echoing back through the black darkness into which the daring fellow plunged; and in a moment more Whiting was laughing heartily at the ridiculous position and plight in which his hastiness had placed him.

While this colloquy was taking place I was tramping around the mudhole, and a few minutes

later arrived at the bridge. " Get across at once,
men, and get out of the road," was the constantly
reiterated order of the field officer who stood
there, and obeying it I marched across, then
turned out to one side, and half a mile farther
on dropped down on the first moderately dry
spot I could locate by guessing. When I awoke
the sun was shining upon thousands of men who,
like myself, had sunk down exhausted. Within
three feet of me lay Brahan fast asleep. Neither
of us could tell who got there first, or where anybody else was. But the still forms around us at
last began to move, order to resolve itself out of
confusion, and by ten o'clock the Fourth Texas
was again a regiment under control of its officers.
That was day before yesterday, and on the same
day we made this camp. Yesterday I received
your letter and one from my mother, and having
already answered hers, have only the conscience
to add to this a postscript.   *   *   *

A great deal is being said in the papers about
England and France recognizing the Confederacy. I do not admit being less brave and patriotic than others, but I frankly acknowledge that
if recognition will bring peace and give me the
privilege of going home, the announcement of the
fact will be the sweetest music on earth to my
ears. A little while back I was foolish enough
to nurse in my bosom a few dreams of military
glory and distinction, but hard rubs against the
realities of soldiering have reduced them into the
thinnest and most unsubstantial nothingness. If
permitted, I shall go home resolved to be con-

tent, hereafter and forever more, with such triumphs as are to be won in " the piping days of peace." Chief among these, and that which will most contribute to my happiness, will be the winning of a wife in the person of our mutual friend.

NOTE 2—It was on the 8th of March, 1862, that the Texas Brigade abandoned its winter quarters and joined in the retreat of the Confederate forces from the lines they had held since the battle of First Manassas to the line of the Rappahannock. Three days later it established camp near the city of Fredericksburg. Here remaining until April 8, it began on that day a long and tiresome march down to Yorktown on the Peninsula, arriving there, I think, on the 13th of April, 1862.

IV

In Camp Somewhere, June 24, 1862.

Hood's Texas Brigade and Jackson's troops are lost in the wild, tangled wilderness surrounding Ashland, the birthplace of Henry Clay. We have been here a couple of days, but when and where we are going next, only the Lord and General Jackson can form any definite idea. There may be free agency in religious matters, but experience teaches a private soldier there is none in military affairs—to him. He is an automaton, guided, directed, and controlled by wires pulled by superiors.   *   *   *

While never confronted by a body of the enemy, the Fourth Texas was actively engaged during the better part of the two days' battle of Seven Pines, dodging Minie and cannon balls and shells fired by the Yankees. Webber, a German of Company F, was the only man of the regiment who actually refused to duck his head at every invitation. " Vat for doadge? " he would say. " Ven ze time coom, ve die any vay—ven ze time no coom, ze ball, he mees." However, we were double-quicked back and forth from one end of the battleground to the other, in futile effort to reach the enemy. The ground was low and

44

swampy, the rain fell in torrents, and when night came he was a lucky man who found a rail or log on which to sleep and keep out of mud and water.

During the engagement, the Sixty-first Pennsylvania was driven so hurriedly out of its well-appointed camp as to leave all of its baggage and commissary stores. Fortunately for the Texans, the troops who did the driving were denied time to take possession of the captured property, and it was promptly confiscated to our use and benefit. Someone looted the tent of Major G. F. Smith of the aforesaid Sixty-first, and seized upon his commission and a bundle of letters—among them one of recent date from his sister. In the division of the spoils this fell to me, and was so charming and homelike that I read it over and over again, and then, lest it should fall into unappreciative hands, burned it. Judging from the letter, the writer is a highly accomplished young lady—a daughter of a member of the Legislature from West Chester County, Pennsylvania. It differed essentially from the others I read from Northern ladies, for it contained but one allusion to the Rebels, and that by no means bitter. It would please the gallant Major, no doubt, if he survived the discomfiture of his regiment, as well as his lovely and lively sister, to be assured of my gratitude for the pleasure afforded me; the Major, by a hasty retreat, and the lady, by writing a letter so interesting, newsy, and humorous as to charm a stranger and Rebel and remind him of his own loved ones in

far-off Texas. While perusing it the Rebel sat
on a chunk of wood at the foot of a tall pine tree,
with his feet in the water. A heavy shower had
just fallen, and dry places were not easily to be
found. Every now and then a cannon ball or
shell, fired from a Federal gun, would crash
through the top of the tree; but he was inside of
the range of the gun, and any damage done by it
was to people far back in the rear.

On the eleventh of this month the Texas Brigade was ordered to Staunton to reinforce Stonewall Jackson. The day after reaching Staunton,
however, it marched back across the Blue Ridge
toward Charlottesville. Early in the day General Hood halted each regiment in turn, and
gave his orders. To the Fourth he said, " Soldiers of the Fourth: I know as little of our destination as you do. If, however, any of you learn
or suspect it, keep it a secret. To everyone who
asks questions, answer, ' I don't know.' We are
now under the orders of General Jackson, and I
repeat them to you. I can only tell you further,
that those of you who stay with the command on
this march will witness and participate in grand
events."

Such an address, such orders, and such a pre-
diction, not only astonished the soldiers, but in-
flamed their curiosity to the highest pitch. Many
were the conjectures—some sensible, some ludicrous, but none probably near the truth. There
were many stills in the sequestered nooks of
the mountains, and by noon quite a number of
the men were in an exceedingly good humor—a

few staggering—and apple-jack and peach brandy could be had out of hundreds of canteens. To prevent the men from getting liquor, General Hood authorized a statement, which was industriously circulated and really believed, that smallpox was raging among the citizens. Whether true or not, it had a good effect; I did not straggle.

Riding along by himself, half a mile in rear of the brigade, General Hood discovered, lying in the middle of the road and very drunk, a soldier of the Fourth. Checking his horse, the General asked, " What is the matter with you, sir? Why are you not with your company? " The stern and peremptory voice sobered the man a little, and rising to a sitting posture and looking at the General with drunken gravity, he said, " Nossin' much, I reckon. General—I just feel sorter weak and no account." " So I see, sir," said Hood; " get up instantly and rejoin your company." The victim of John Barleycorn made several ineffectual attempts to obey, and some men coming along just then, Hood ordered them to take charge of him and conduct him to his company. But as they approached with intent to carry out the order, the fellow found voice to say between hiccoughs, " Don't you men that ain't been vaccinated come near me—I've got the smallpox—tha's wha's the masser with me."

The men shrank back in alarm, and the General, laughing at the way his own chickens had come home to roost, said, " Let him alone, then —some teamster will pick him up," and rode on.

General Jackson gave strict orders against depredating on private property. Apples were plentiful, and it was contrary to nature not to eat them. Jackson saw a Texan sitting on the limb of an apple tree, busily engaged in filling his haversack with the choicest fruit. He reined in his old sorrel horse, and in his customary curt tone, asked, " What are you doing in that tree, sir? " " I don't know," replied the Texan. " What command do you belong to? " " I don't know." " Is your command ahead or behind you? " " I don't know." And thus it went on— the same " I don't know " given as answer to every question. Finally, Jackson asked, " Why do you give me that answer to every question? " " 'Cause them's the orders our Gineral gin us, this mornin', an' he tole us he got 'em that er way, straight from ole Jackson," replied the man in the tree, and disgusted with a too literal obedience to his own commands, but yet not caring to argue the point, General Jackson rode on.

Our camp is in an extensive grove of oak and pine. Far as one's eyes can reach are standing, sitting, recumbent, and moving men, with not a woman in sight to relieve the sameness and exercise a softening influence. Within a hundred feet of me religious services are being held. Looking at the portly, well-fed body of the chaplain officiating, and remembering my fondness for chicken, I am tempted often nowadays to wish I were a Methodist preacher myself. Honestly, I have not had a chance at a chicken in a month of Sundays. I used to prefer it in the shape of pie, but would take it now in any style that came handy to the cook. However proverbial Virginia hospitality, it draws the line, according to my observation, at that kind of poultry. At any rate, at every house whose surrounding premises have come under my inspection, all feathered bipeds are kept under lock and key at night. Otherwise, my mouth would not be watering at the mere thought of a Methodist preacher, for, though I am yet too high-toned to rob a hen roost myself, I have a messmate of venturesome spirit, and, when favorable opportunities fall in his way, few scruples. But *revenons à nos moutons*—the mutton, or subject, being the aforesaid preacher, and my mind being called back to him by the loudness of the prayer he is now offering in behalf of the sinners of the brigade. He appears to have forgotten that he himself is the greatest sinner of the crowd.

As perhaps you know, Mrs. Mollie J. Young recently succeeded in raising thirty thousand dollars in gold for the purpose of establishing an exclusively Texas hospital in Richmond. But just when every arrangement was made with the Catholic sisters in charge of the Infirmary of St. Francis de Sales to take care of our sick and wounded exclusively, and nothing remained but to sign the papers, this same loud-mouthed chaplain became a stumbling-block. Going to the infirmary one day, after many of our sick had been sent or transferred to it, he had the shameless effrontery to hold a Methodist service there, without the consent of the Sisters and against their indignant but polite protest. It was such an insult to the faith of the Sisters and the Roman Catholic Church, that although assured the chaplain should be muzzled, the bishop in charge of the diocese absolutely refused to consider the project any longer. As a result of this overbearing Methodism, more men will die for lack of the careful nursing of the Sisters than will ever become professors of religion under the ministrations of the chaplain. Men go to hospitals to save their bodies, not their souls. The Sisters would not have objected to any private religious talks the chaplain chose to make, but they had a right to forbid any public service not sanctioned by their Church.

To take the bitter taste of this incident out of my memory, I must go to Texas in thought, if not in person. I regret that your kind invitation to attend the ball and dance with you came too late for acceptance, even had my superiors consented to the long absence necessary. It reached me just after General Hood had assured us that grand events were impending and near at hand. While at the time I had no greater real hankering for a fight than the old farmer had for the crow he ate in order to prove to his hired hands that he could eat anything set before him, I was so anxious to witness grand events that I determined to risk being compelled to take an active and perilous part in any battle necessary for their accomplishment. Hence, I made no application for a furlough to Texas. That I now wish I had, only shows how near approach to danger

MRS. MAUD J. YOUNG
OUR FRIEND IN NEED

—it is in the air, that the Yankees are close at hand and waiting for us—dissipates enthusiasm, dampens courage and weakens the patriotism that would gladly die for its country. The "light, fantastic toe" having already been "tripped," it will be in order, I reckon, to express a hope that the cavalry present enjoyed it more than they would a battle. But while I felicitate them, my heart is full of regret; my bosom, of envy. With nothing to do and a horse to do it on; with every delicacy to tempt the appetite, and with starched linen to wear; with a servant to wait on him, and, while he takes a post-prandial siesta, fan the flies off his noble brow and away from his soft, white hand; with ladies to look at and walk with, listen to and talk to, and dance with and make love to, and with only a lazy gunboat in the hazy distance to affright his heroic soul by an occasional shell—who, oh who, wouldn't gladly risk his life in arduous service on the Texas coast? Show me the man who wouldn't, and I'll shoot him. But, alas, a stern and unaccommodating fate denies the crown to my ambition that such a service would be; it is only here in Virginia I may hope to win laurels.

V

CAMP NEAR RICHMOND, July 12, 1862.

CROSSING the railroad at Ashland on the morning of June 26, a large force of skirmishers was sent forward. I was one of them, and the distinction cost me the hardest day's work I ever did. We were formed in line, twenty feet apart, and admonished to keep the line well dressed, to maintain the intervals between us, and to keep a sharp lookout for the Yankees. You can imagine how difficult this was in the wilderness of pine timber and matted undergrowth into which we plunged. The most important duty seemed to me to keep watch on my front for the enemy, and if I gave my whole mind to that, I was certain to get behind or ahead of my comrades, or to join forces with the man to my right or left. I managed somehow, though, not to get lost, and to be on hand about 11 o'clock A. M., to assist in driving an outpost of the Eighth Illinois Cavalry from its camp in such haste that it left cooking utensils, provisions, and forage. Luckily, a halt was called here, and we made good use of the time dining at the enemy's expense. A cup of well-cooked rice and the best half of a ham fell to me in the distribution of eatables. The rice had just been taken from the fire, and was too warm to carry in my haversack, and as the last thing a Confederate soldier can afford to do is to waste provisions, I immediately sat down and downed the rice.

Then noticing a party of men sitting on their horses in the road near me, I sauntered down to interview them. I was on the point of making some impertinent remark—inspired by the contempt infantry soldiers feel for cavalry—to a particularly seedy, sleepy-looking old fellow, whose uniform and cap were very dirty, and who bestrode a regular Rosinante of a horse, when an officer, all bespangled with lace, came up in a gallop and, saluting, addressed my man as General Jackson. At first I was disposed to doubt, but being convinced by the deference paid him that it was really old Stonewall, I congratulated myself for not disturbing his meditations as I had intended. No one offered to introduce us to each other, and, as we were both bashful, we lost the best chance of our lives to become acquainted.   *   *   *

That night we camped within hearing distance of musketry and artillery firing on both right and left; that on the left being between Ewell and the enemy, and that on the right, away off in the direction of Mechanicsville. Friday morning, June 27, we again advanced. The Yankees fell back until they reached a strong, almost impregnable position on the ground in the vicinity of Gaines' Mill. They occupied a ridge overlooking the Chickahominy and between us and that stream, their artillery being massed behind three lines of breastworks so constructed along the side of the ridge next to us that firing from one could be done over the heads of the troops in the other. All the force of the enemy on our side of the Chickahominy was concentrated to check the advance of Jackson. The Confederates began their assaults on this position about noon, but were constantly beaten back. Brigade after brigade had been ordered to charge. They had charged and met repulse before Whiting's division—which consists, you know, of Law's brigade and ours—reached the scene of action at 4 o'clock in the evening. *   *   *

Said General Whiting to General Hood, pointing to a battery that was doing tremendous execution in the Confederate rank, "That battery ought to be taken, General." "Then why has it not been done?" asked Hood. "Because the position is too strong," answered Whiting. "My brigade is composed of veterans, but they can do nothing with it." "I have a regiment that will capture it," said Hood; and, galloping to the Fourth Texas, dismounted and called it to attention. Then marching it by the flank to an open field, he gave the orders to bring it into line of battle, and shouted, "Forward!"

Shot and shell began to come thick and fast as, surmounting the rise of the hill, we arrived in plain view of the Yankees, and half way across the field men began to drop, wounded or dead, from the ranks. We passed over two regiments —said to have been Virginians—who, protected by a depression of the ground, were lying down, apparently afraid either to advance or retreat. At the crest of the hill Hood shouted rapidly the orders, " Fix bayonets! Make ready! Aim! Fire! Charge!" The timber between us and the enemy hid them from view, but we pulled triggers nevertheless, and rushed down the hill into and across the branch, at the Yankees in the first line of breastworks. They waited not for the onset, but fled like a flock of sheep, carrying with them their supports in the second and third lines. Reaching the road which ran along the summit of the hill beyond the branch, and looking to our left, we could see large bodies of the enemy in full retreat, but they were so far behind us that, mistaken for our own troops, not a shot was fired at them.   *   *   *

Just across the road from us was an acre lot inclosed by a rail fence. In its center stood a log stable, and from behind this an armed Yankee peeped out. Stringfield, of Company A, saw him, and mounting the fence in hot haste, ran toward the stable, determined to capture the fellow. Lieutenant Hughes, of Company F,—a mild-mannered gentleman who never really takes the name of the Lord in vain, but comes perilously near it sometimes—sang out, " Go it, Stringfield, go it! Kill him, dod dam him, kill him!" But just as he reached the stable Stringfield was confronted by the muzzle of a loaded gun, and had it not been for Wolfe, of Company F, who instantly aimed, fired, and killed the Yankee, would have been killed.   *   *   *

The regiment had more work to do, and gallantly did it. Hood formed the remnant of the command in an old apple orchard while exposed to a terrific fire from the batteries, and once more gave the order to charge. Lieutenant-Colonel Warwick sprang to the front, shouting, "Wait, General, until I get ahead of them," and fifty yards farther fell mortally wounded. The Fourth rushed down into a ravine and up the steep bank to find that instead of one battery, there were three so disposed as to attack from the front and on the flank. The enemy made no stand at the first, but supporting the second were eight companies of the Second United States Cavalry— among them the very company in which Hood had served as a lieutenant. A squadron of this command charged upon the Fourth, but more than half of it were killed and wounded, and the balance forced to retire in disorder. This was the last organized resistance, the third battery being easily captured and the enemy driven a mile beyond it. Then night came on and human slaughter ceased.   *   *   *

After the fighting I was surprised to learn how little of it I had really seen and participated in. It is only the General, who stands back in the rear and directs the movements of an army, who is able to take note of all that occurs. We privates look only to our immediate front, right, and left, and are not permitted to stand on eminences which overlook the whole field of battle. Therefore you must bear in mind that much of what I relate comes from the lips

ALBERT POLK BROWN
Sergeant, Co. A, Fourth Texas Regiment
LYCURGUS MCNEAL BROWN
Private, Co. A, Fourth Texas Regiment

of others. Caesar could say, " *Veni, vidi, vici,*"
but the privates of his army had to speak in the
first person plural, and say, " *We* came, *we* saw,
we conquered."

General Hood kept the promise made to us
when he was promoted to be brigadier-general,
and commanded the Fourth in its first fight. He
exposed himself most recklessly, but was not
harmed. The Veteran said to me yesterday. " I
tell you what, Joe, I got mighty nervous and
shaky while we were forming in the apple orchard to make that last desperate charge on the
batteries. But when I looked behind me and saw
old Hood resting on one foot, his arm raised
above his head, his hand grasping the limb of a
tree, looking as unconcerned as if we were on
dress parade, I just determined that if he could
stand it, I would."

The Texans feel very proud, for they have been
complimented from all sides. In general orders
the credit of being the first to break the enemy's
lines on the 27th has been given to the Fourth.
Yet, elated as we are by that fact, we willingly
admit that either the First or Fifth Texas would
have done as well if the same opportunity had
been theirs. Why the troops failed to take the
position earlier in the day is very strange to me,
for, judging from the speed with which the
Yankees fled at our approach, they would have
been equally courteous to any other Confederates
who made a determined dash upon them.

The Fifth Texas captured two whole regiments
of Yankees—the Fourth New Jersey, raised in

Newark, and the Eleventh Pennsylvania, raised in Philadelphia—whose officers insisted on surrendering their swords, in a body, to Colonel Upton, and were so prompt in the duty that he was compelled to lay down the frying pan which he carries in place of a sword and hold the weapons presented in his arms. Just when the Twentieth was being rendered to him, he noticed a commotion at the far end of the captured regiments. That was near the timber, and a squad of the prisoners were making an effort to pass by " Big John Ferris," of Company B, who stood there unaided endeavoring to intercept them. Springing upon a log, the armful of swords dangling about in all directions, Upton shouted, " You John Ferris! What in h—— and d—— are you trying to do now? " " I'm trying to keep these d——d fellows from escaping," returned Big John, in a stentorian voice. " Let them go, you infernal fool," shouted back Upton. " We'd a d——d sight rather fight 'em than feed 'em.   *   *   *

That was my first real experience of battle, Charming Nellie. As you know, I have been under fire on the picket and skirmish lines, and with my regiment several times, but on this occasion there was genuine fighting to be done— enemies in plain sight to shoot at and to be shot by. I frankly admit that when I first knew we were going in I trembled, and my heart seemed to be palpitating away down in the region of my boots. I was in the same condition of mind as the Tennesseean at Manassas. As his regiment advanced on the enemy a little cotton-tail rabbit ran through the Confederate lines and sped away to the rear. The Tennessee man watched it a moment or two, and then exclaimed, in accents which betokened heartfelt sincerity, " Run, cotton-tail, run! If I had no more reputation to maintain than you have, I'd run, too." When I got fairly on the way I felt that it was either fight or run, and as soon as the orders to fire and charge were given, dragged my heart up from its hiding-place to its proper position. This done, I became a trifle anxious to return the compliments our blue-coated friends showered incessantly upon us, and lost all sensation of fear, although fully conscious of the danger. The most singular sensation I experienced was when my comrades to the right and left began to drop, dead or wounded. Then a strange curiosity assailed me to know how soon a bullet would hit me, what part of my body it would strike, and how I should feel as I sank to the ground. My curiosity was fully gratified a little later. Something, which I thought to be a ball, struck me fairly in the center of the forehead and sent me backward, flat on the ground and unconscious. In the instant between blow and unconsciousness, though, I had time to think that it was death. I had been kneeling, and just behind me crouched Lieutenant Barziza, of Company C, both of us waiting for the command to go forward. When I came to, my first act was to feel for the hole I was sure was in my head, and Barziza's first remark was, " They would have

got you that time, Polley, if your head hadn't
been so hard." It was only a splinter, however,
from a rail struck by a solid shot, but it placed
me *hors de combat* for the balance of that day,
and will leave a scar that I fear will mar the
beauty of my frontispiece.

I will not distress your gentle heart by an account of the horrors of the battlefield after the
fighting was over and it was occupied by the
wounded, the dying, and the dead. In time, perhaps, I will grow accustomed to such scenes, or
perhaps in the very next battle may become one
of the horrors myself. Who knows but God?
But, understand, I do not expect to be killed,
and am not going to be if I can honorably avoid
it; too much happiness awaits my return to
Texas " when this cruel war is over "—that is,
provided I am not anticipated by the cavalry.

L. A. DAFFAN
Private, Company G, Fourth Texas Regiment

VI

BATTLE OF SECOND MANASSAS

CAMP NEAR WINCHESTER, VA.,
October 8, 1862.

MY last letter to you was mailed at Richmond, some time in July. Since then we have been so steadily on the go that I have only been able to write the briefest of notes to inform friends of my continued existence and good health. From the newspapers you will by this time have placed yourself *au courant* with all important events. To relate my personal experiences and observations will require a longer letter than I usually have the heart to inflict, even upon a lady.   *   *   *

I overtook the command on the south side of the Rappahannock—the five regiments in bivouac, side by side, on an open hill, and all out of tobacco. So too was I within five minutes, for not suspecting the condition of affairs, I entered camp smoking, and was at once relieved of my superabundance of Zarvona, and even of the small sack of Lone Jack which in a moment of aristocratic extravagance I had purchased in Richmond for almost its weight in Confederate money. But about sundown Commodore Dunn appeared with a whole wagon load of the weed, and then happiness prevailed and clouds of fragrant smoke ascended in spiral wreaths toward the blue heavens.

At two o'clock of the 26th day of August we began the longest and most fatiguing march we have ever made. All that evening, all that night and all the next day until sundown, it was tramp—tramp—tramp. Jackson was up at Manassas Junction, had captured an immense amount of commissary and quartermaster supplies, but was about to be surrounded and wanted help. * * *

A couple of hundred yards from the road the body of a man dressed in the uniform of a Confederate officer swung from the limb of an oak tree. The story, as I heard it, was this: A message, purporting to be from General Longstreet, was delivered by an officer to General ———. Obeying it, the latter instantly halted his command, but, suspecting treachery and seeing Longstreet approaching, detained the messenger. "Why have you halted, sir?" demanded Longstreet angrily. "By your order, sir?" replied General ———. "Who delivered the order?" "That officer on the sorrel horse." "Who authorized you to deliver the order, sir?" demanded Longstreet of the officer. "General Longstreet," replied he without a moment's hesitation, and looking Longstreet full in the face. "Do you know General Longstreet?" "I do, sir." "Is he present?" "He is not, sir." "Arrest that man," said Longstreet, turning quickly to the officer in command of his bodyguard; "then detail an officer and six privates to carry him to that tree

over yonder and hang him—he is a spy." The
fellow acknowledged that he was a Federal officer and had been offered an immense sum of
money if he would delay the march of Longstreet's corps long enough to enable Pope to capture Jackson. He had played for a big stake and
lost, but, asking neither trial nor mercy, met his
fate like a man.   *   *   *

On the evening of the 28th we passed through
Thoroughfare Gap, and at sundown camped on
the side of an open hill. Near the top of it the
commissaries were busy issuing hard tack. Some
idlers gave a couple of empty barrels a twirl and
a kick that sent them racing down the hill with
a racket like the charge of a regiment of cavalry,
and instantly, while many of our men sprang
for the guns stacked on the color line, hundreds
sprang to their feet intent on seeking safety in
flight. I did neither, I am proud to say. Happening to be standing close to the only tree
within three hundred yards, I stood my ground
like a man. "It's nothing but barrels, you
fools!" shouted some cool, observant fellow, and
thus checked an incipient stampede.

At daylight of the 29th we were awakened by
the noise of musketry and artillery firing. It
was several miles away, but still loud enough to
convince us that a terrible battle was in progress
between Jackson and Pope. At sun-up we were
on the way to relieve old Stonewall, the brigade
marching in column, but with skirmishers—your
humble servant one of them—under Colonel Upton, in advance. No enemy appearing to check

us, we made rapid progress, and about ten
o'clock in the morning took position on Jackson's
right, a mile or more from the scene of the matu-
tinal battle—the regiment lying comfortably and
at ease in line on one edge of a narrow skirt of
timber, the skirmishers standing behind and ar-
dently hugging the trees on the other edge. In
front was a gently undulating meadow, probably
a quarter of a mile wide, stretching to right as
far as the eye could reach, and to the left to the
railroad cut from which Pope had been trying
all the morning to drive Jackson's men. On the
opposite side of the meadow from us was another
skirt of timber, and here were posted Yankee
skirmishers. But as neither they nor we were so
desirous of cultivating an intimate acquaintance
with each other as to make ourselves conspicuous, the day passed with but occasional inter-
changes of hostile compliments.

Indeed, Yankee thirst for gore was so fully
and early satiated by Jackson's brave Louis-
ianians and Virginians, that both armies appeared to have regained their good humor and to
be enjoying an interregnum of what Caesar,
Cicero, or some other great and famous Roman,
denominates as " *otium cum dignitate.*" Deceived
into carelessness by these apparently amicable
relations, Jack Sutherland and I, about three
o'clock in the evening, were finding ease for our
weary limbs at the foot of a tall tree at the extreme outer edge of the timber; he, resting his
head against its trunk; I, sitting crosslegged a
few feet from him; our guns held in our laps.

Jack was at the most interestingly philosophical part—to him—of a long dissertation on social etiquette, when the boom of a cannon broke upon our ears. The sound came from the right, and, looking in that direction, we became witnesses of a seemingly desperate cavalry battle, but at such a distance from us that we were unable to distinguish Confederates from Federals. Dense black clouds of dust and smoke marked the points where charges and countercharges were made and repulsed, lurid flashes of fire from the mouths of cannon leaped now and then into sight beneath the overhanging pall, while an incessant rattle of small arms and roar of artillery greeted our ears. Wholly absorbed in watching that scene, it was startling to hear the simultaneous crash of a dozen batteries on our left. This latter demonstration was an effort of General Pope to demoralize Jackson's troops preparatory to charging and driving them in confusion from their position in the railroad cut. This was not more than half a mile long, but running diagonally across our line of vision, we could only see the red banks of clay behind which crouched the defiant Confederates. The Federals, however, forming in battle array, and with flags waving proudly in the breeze, moved forward, a dark and threatening line of blue, in plain view. Advancing to the crest of the hill within a hundred yards of the cut, they halted a second, as if to perfect their alignment, and then, as if moved by a single impulse, sprang forward, with a long-drawn " huzzah " ringing from their ten thousand throats. On they went until half the distance to the cut was covered, and then the smoke, flash and roar of four thousand well-aimed guns burst from the Confederate intrenchment, and a wild, reckless, and terrifying Southern yell echoed and re-echoed over the hills and hollows and through the woodlands. And scarcely had it ceased to reverberate, when the smoke lifted and disclosed the survivors of that murderous volley fleeing for dear life back to their own lines, its victims lying, dark blots on the greensward, writhing and struggling, dead, dying and wounded. That infantry struggle lasted scarcely five minutes, but a thousand men were killed and more than twice as many more wounded! The cavalry fight on our right continued an hour, but only five men were killed and seventeen wounded. No wonder all want to "jine the cavalry"!

Three such assaults were made on the railroad before the Yanks, on that part of their line, decided they had enough. About the time they reached this wise conclusion, half a dozen bullets pattered on the ground and against the trees around me and Jack. Someone said, "Jack, you and Joe had better get behind a tree; those fellows are shooting at you two." The advice seemed so sound that I immediately sought the protection of an adjacent tree. Being much lazier than I, Jack did not move as quickly. But when, half a second after he had summoned up energy to let his head drop forward toward his knees, a ball struck the tree on the very spot where his cranium had rested, he displayed an activity truly wonderful!

Ten minutes afterward, orders came to the skirmishers to drive the Yankees out of the timber beyond the meadow. Casting a look behind to assure ourselves that our respective regiments would follow closely enough to enable us to give them prompt warning of danger, we moved forward, the light of battle in our eyes—I reckon—and the fear of it in our hearts—I know.

Much to our delight, the enemy was as swift in retreat as we in advance. They did not even fire on us as we crossed the meadow, and once in the timber, our courage returned in full vigor. It is really surprising how comfortable even a sapling is to a fellow on a skirmish line. But by this time it was getting dark, and before I reached the open field beyond the timber it was not only quite dark, but the skirmish line had melted into utter nothingness. There was no severe fighting going on anywhere, so far as sight and hearing enabled me to judge, but I was alone, not a friend near to advise me, and bullets were whistling around me in such threatening superabundance and from so many directions, that I felt very much as I used to when my mother compelled me to sleep in a room all by "my lone self." Besides, I was getting very tired of dodging.

Just when my patriotism had sunk to the lowest ebb, I heard the command, "Forward, Eleventh Mississippi! Guide center!" and saw a long, straight and dark line moving, apparently sidewise, down the hill in the direction of where I supposed the enemy to be. Following it, I soon overtook the rash fellows, and when the regiment halted at the bottom of the hill to recover the breath it had lost in descending, placed myself in position to support its right flank. I thought the colonel in command would be too wise to proceed farther. But again his hoarse voice shouted " Forward! " while a captain close behind me declared he would shoot the first man who attempted to skulk. Thus you see, Charming Nellie, danger not only confronted me, but lurked in my rear. Rapid thought was a necessity. The Fourth Texas was certainly entitled to the credit of any gallantry I might accidentally or otherwise display. Knowing that I was not with the regiment, Colonel Carter would naturally conclude I was at the front, and would come immediately to my relief with the whole regiment at his back. Obviously the Eleventh Mississippi was going into danger, and it was better to risk the captain's pistol than the thousand and tens of thousands of guns which would be turned against me if I went forward. Thus reasoning, I permitted my Mississippi compatriots to proceed without me. The captain immediately rushed at me, pistol in one hand and drawn sword in the other, shouting, " Move forward, sir—move forward! " so fiercely that I was almost tempted to take him at his word. But better counsel prevailed. " I belong to the Fourth Texas, Colonel," I explained hastily; whereupon, cajoled by my flattery into returning it, he exclaimed,

B. P. FULLER
Captain, Fifth Texas Regiment

" That's all right then, Captain—nobody would be so far in front but a Texan."

My trust in Colonel Carter was speedily justified by the approach of the Fourth. But we had not gone a hundred yards after I dropped into the ranks of Company F, when we heard the report of half a hundred muskets in our rear. Halting and looking back, we saw a line of camp fires spring up as if by magic on the top of the hill at the edge of the woods, while the tall silhouettes of many men and horses flitted around them and between them and us. Half an hour later the brigade faced to the left, and the First Texas leading, marched toward the lights. Suddenly a loud voice cried " Halt! " a single gunshot rang out on the still night air, and the command came whispered back, " Silence! we are surrounded by the enemy."

VII

(Letter of October 8, 1862, continued.)

"SILENCE!" We could well observe the command. "Surrounded by the enemy!" It was a pretty tale to be told on Texans, who had come two thousand miles to capture the Yankee nation and force it to terms, that they had carelessly walked into a trap and surrendered without firing a gun in defense of the flags they had sworn to bathe in floods of glory. Chagrined and mortified, Texas pride humbled into the dust, who wanted to talk? These were, of course, first thoughts; second ones embraced the difficulties and exigencies of the situation and the chances of escape, but were far from pleasant and comforting.

But the humiliation we felt was self-inflicted, the fears idle, the difficulties imaginary. Within an hour General Hood found a gap in the circumvailing lines; then he rode, first to Longstreet's headquarters, and next to Lee's, and asked leave to remain where he was, and begin the attack at daylight. He argued that the enemy, imagining they had cooped up only one regiment, would be demoralized, and easily routed when attacked by two such brigades as his and Whiting's. Overruled by his superiors, however, he returned to the command, which, led by him, marched in darkness, with bated breath, and without the rattle of a cup or a canteen, between two Federal brigades, and at daylight confronted the foe whose clutches it had so narrowly escaped, in the same position it had occupied the day before.

Had I been consulted previous to learning of the getting out place, I should certainly have indorsed Hood's plan; but not after the avenue of escape was not only pointed out, but we had availed ourselves of it. Then I joined most heartily with my comrades in congratulating ourselves on having, as an illiterate fellow said, so skillfully " unsurrounded " ourselves.

The day and night's work cost us the slight wounding of a few men and the capture of Bill Calhoun, of Company B, Fourth Texas. This Bill Calhoun is an oddity of whom we are very proud. Always sad of countenance, there yet dwells in the recesses of his bosom a spirit of constantly effervescing drollery which now and then, and when least expected, bubbles over and explodes. His messmate and bedfellow is Davidge. Carrying out their plan of an equitable division of labor, Davidge, on the day we passed through Manassas Gap, was intrusted with the blankets, while Bill charged himself with the transportation of the provisions and limited culinary apparatus. Davidge straggled, and, when camp was reached at night was *non est inventus*. Confident he would come soon, Bill prepared supper, and, Davidge still not appearing, ate it all himself, lighted his pipe, smoked and chatted awhile; and, then remarking that Davidge would be along soon, stretched himself out on the bare ground to rest. But here in Virginia the nights are cool enough even in July to make covering acceptable, and though Bill endured the hardness of his couch and the chilliness of the night with unbroken placidity until midnight, he could stand it no longer. Rising and standing erect in the midst of five thousand recumbent forms darkening the moonlit hillside, he broke into magniloquent apostrophe: "O Davidge, Davidge! friend of my bosom and possessor of my blanket, where art thou, Davidge, this cold and comfortless night? Art thou indeed false to thy many professions—false to the sacred obligations of true and loyal friendship thou hast sworn—oblivious of duty, and forgetful of the friend who hath confided to thee even the blanket on which he dependeth for protection from the chilling blasts of winter? Art thou now reclining peacefully and blissfully on some hospitable feather bed dreaming of the joys that will come when this 'cruel war is o'er,' or art thou, beguiled and betrayed by the demon of intemperance and a damnable thirst for apple-jack, wallowing like a hog in the dust before the door of some disreputable mountain stillhouse; while I, thy friend and messmate, thy boon companion in happiness and adversity, stand here alone—a homeless, houseless orphan, his wandering footsteps guided only by the pale light of yonder refulgent orb of night, his shivering body covered

A GENUINE SOLDIER BOY OF 1861

16 Years Old
(Taken in Richmond, Va., 1861)

Co. H
4TH. TEX. REGT.
HOOD'S TEXAS BRIGADE

HOUSTON ENG CO

F. B. CHILTON
Company H, Fourth Texas Regiment, Hood's Texas Brigade,
Army of Northern Virginia; later Captain C. S. A.

A Confederate Veteran of 1907

62 Years Old
(Taken in Houston, Texas, 1907)

Captain Frank Bowden Chilton

Houston, Texas

President Hood's Texas Brigade Monument Committee
Monument to be erected on Capitol Grounds, at Austin, Texas.

only by the blue canopy of the sky, and his restless slumber watched over only by the myriads
of twinkling stars that shine in the heavens above
me? Alas! Davidge, thou trusted friend, companion, and confidant of my youth and manhood,
thou hast been weighed in the balance and found
wanting. The surrounding and circumambient
circumstances are proof strong as Holy Writ that
I have been duped, deceived, outwitted, and un-
gratefully left to encounter the slings and arrows of misfortune alone and unsustained by
any human aid." And dropping from the sublime to the ridiculous, Bill nudged the nearest
man with his foot and said in a voice of entreaty
that would have melted the hardest heart, " Say,
Val Giles, let me get under the blanket with you;
if you don't, I'll be a standing monument, before
morning, of man's inhumanity to man."

I have told you this story to prepare you for
that of Bill's capture, as related by a Confederate who was near enough to see and hear everything, but laid low and kept dark lest he, too,
should be captured. It is so in keeping with
Bill's unique character that no one doubts it.
Bill was on the skirmish line, and, like myself,
lost sight of his Confederate friends, and got too
far to the front. Carrying his gun in both hands,
with a finger on the hammer ready to cock it at
the first glimpse of an enemy, he was suddenly
brought to a halt by the harsh and totally unexpected command, " Surrender, you d——d Rebel;
throw down your gun and surrender! " Such language, followed as it was by the threatening click

of half a dozen gunlocks, was not to be treated lightly. Bill's fingers simultaneously released their grip on his Minie rifle, and it dropped, clanging to the hard, stony ground; then he looked to his right and saw, behind a clump of bushes he had almost passed, a squad of Yankees. They were within twenty feet of him, and one of them stood with cocked and leveled gun pointed directly at his breast. Bill was no fool; the enemy had the drop on him, and any appearance of hesitation on his part might be unhealthy. Therefore, he made haste to say, in a voice pitched at a key plainly to be heard, " Of course, I surrender. Who the devil is talking about not surrendering? " The celerity with which the gun was dropped, the odd manner of surrendering, and the absurd question asked, set the Yankee to laughing at such a rate that he forgot to lower his weapon, but kept it pointing in the general direction of the captive as warningly as his shaking sides would permit. Noticing this, Bill protested earnestly, " See here, mister; please quit p'inting that gun at me. I've done surrendered, and the darned thing might go off unbeknownst to you." " Oh," answered the Yankee between bursts of laughter, but still failing to lower his gun, " I ain't a-goin' ter shoot you." " Mout as well shoot a feller at once as to scare him to death with a wobblin' gun," rejoined Bill. " D——d if I wasn't always afeard of a wobblin' gun; it's just as apt to hit as to miss."   *   *   *

It was not until four o'clock on the evening of

the 30th that our brigade again sought the foe. The same meadow was to cross, the same skirt of timber to pass through. As the Fourth emerged from the latter, the Fifth New York Battery, commanded by Captain Curran, and stationed on a commanding eminence on the other side of a deep hollow, devoted its whole attention to us, and to show our appreciation of the courtesy, we made directly for it. A Federal regiment between us and the battery fired one volley at us and fled as fast as legs could carry them. Another regiment that had been placed in a pine thicket immediately in rear of the battery as a support to it, followed suit, but, undismayed, gallant Captain Curran fired his guns until every artillerist was shot down, and he himself fell as he was in the very act of sending into our huddled ranks a charge of grape and canister that would have sent the half of us to kingdom come. A braver spirit than his never dwelt in the breast of man. " You would never have captured my battery," said he, as at his request a Texan laid him under one of the guns and placed a knapsack under his head, " if my supports had been men instead of cowards." We fully agreed with him. * * *

Looking up the hill, a strange and ghastly spectacle met our eyes. An acre of ground was literally covered with the dead, dying, and wounded of the Fifth New York Zouaves, the variegated colors of whose peculiar uniform gave the scene the appearance of a Texas hillside in spring, painted with wild flowers of every hue and color.

Not fifty of the Zouaves escaped whole. One
of their lieutenants, who had lost an arm, told
me that they were in the second line of the breastworks which the Fourth Texas had carried at
Gaines' Mill a month before; that in the mad
retreat of the first line of Federals they had been
swept away, and that, on learning the position
in the Confederate line occupied by our brigade
here at Second Manassas, they had made a special request of General Pope to be permitted to
confront us on the 30th, and regain the laurels
lost at Gaines' Mill. There they met the Fourth
Texas and suffered ignominious defeat—here,
they came face to face for a minute only with
the Fifth Texas—and suffered practical anni-
hilation.

The Zouaves, it seems, were posted just under
the crest of the hill, and a hundred feet from
the edge of the timber, and fired the moment the
heads of the Texans showed above the crest. Of
course they aimed too high, and before they could
reload the Texans poured such a well-directed
and deadly volley into their closely formed ranks
that half of them sank to the ground, and the
balance wheeled and ran. Not waiting to reload,
the Texans rushed after the fugitives, and, club-
bing their muskets, continued the work of destruction until every enemy in sight was left
prone upon the ground. Then, as General Hood
said, the Fifth Texas "slipped its bridle and
went wild." Had they not been recalled, they
would have gone right on to the Potomac. That
night I was aroused from deep slumber by the

sound of merriment. Rising to a sitting posture, I asked my disturber, "What in the name of common sense are you laughing about at this ungodly hour, Jim?" "About those d——d Zouaves," said he. "You know that Belgian rifle with a bore almost as big as a cannon that I showed you this morning? Well, I was with the Fifth when it struck those fancy-dressed fellows. I didn't shoot when the balance did, but just waited until the scoundrels got well huddled together as they ran down the hill, and, getting about twenty of them in line, I put my gun to the back of the nearest one, and pulled the trigger; and d——d if I don't believe I killed the whole *posse comitatus.*" Honestly, I shuddered with horror and disgust. The idea of such bloodthirstiness as would permit a man to laugh over the slaughter of so many men is repulsive.

I am not writing history, Charming Nellie; only endeavoring to paint a few scattering lights and shadows of this terrible war. The anecdote I have just told is a darker shadow than usual; so let me lighten it by another. Jim Ferris, of the Fifth Texas, found himself at Second Manassas in a dilapidated condition externally. The legs of his pants lacked several inches of the proper length, and in the absence of a pair of socks his ankles had been sadly lacerated by the briars and brambles through which he had been compelled to scramble in skirmishing. While running wild with his regiment when it slipped the bridle on the 30th, it occurred to his mind that he might supply deficiencies in his raiment

by administering on the estate of some dead
Yankee. A pair of leggins to button around the
calves of his legs would answer his purposes
admirably, he thought, and he resolved to have
them. It was midnight, though, before he began
operations. Being a very large man himself,
only the body of a large man could be depended
upon to supply Jim's need; and in the search
for such a one he wandered to and fro over the
silent field of the dead until, awed by the solemnity of his surroundings, cold chills began to
run down his back at the least noise; and he
expected every minute to encounter a ghost.
Finally he found a corpse of apparently suitable
size, and, hastily turning back from its legs
the oilcloth which covered it from head to foot,
began with no gentle hand to unbutton a leggin.
At the first jerk the supposed deadest of all the
many dead flung the oilcloth from his head, and,
rising to a sitting posture, exclaimed, "Great
God alive, man! Don't rob me before I am dead,
if you please!" In horrified amazement, Jim
sprang twenty feet at one bound, but, knowing
no ghost would speak so sensibly, natural politeness prompted instant apology. "Indeed,
Mr. Yankee," said he, in the most gentle and
winning tone he could assume, "I hadn't the
least idea you were alive, or I never would have
been guilty of the discourtesy of disturbing you.
Please pardon me, and let me know what I can
do to make amends for my rudeness." "I would
like a drink of water," said the revived corpse.
"Take my canteen, sir," rejoined Jim, instantly

D. C. FARMER

Captain, Fifth Texas Regiment

offering it, " and please oblige me by keeping it; I can easily get another."

After this experience Jim decided that, rather than risk waking another corpse, he would do without leggins; but on his way to camp he came across a stalwart form lying at full length on the ground, and at the very first glance saw that here could be obtained the needed articles. No mistake must be made, though; and so, laying his hand on the shoulder of the Yankee, he gave him a shake, and asked, " Say, Mister, are you dead or alive? " There was no response, and next morning Jim Ferris strutted about the camp in a magnificent pair of linen leggins.   *   *   *

NOTE 3—Following Gaines' Mill, Hood's brigade was under heavy fire at Savage Station, Fraser's Farm, and Malvern Hill, but not being actively engaged, its casualties were trifling. A few days after the last of these engagements it went into camp near Richmond, where it rested for something over a month. Marching thence about the 10th of August, it participated in fierce skirmishes at Kelly's Ford and Freeman's Ford and in a sharp battle at Hazel River, losing, however, few men. These actions are not mentioned in any of the letters for the double reason that the author was not then with the brigade, and the engagements in themselves were unimportant. At Thoroughfare Gap, mentioned in Letter 6, but two regiments of the brigade did any fighting of consequence—the Fourth Texas, fortunately, doing none.

VIII

CROSSING OVER INTO MARYLAND

(Letter of October 8, 1862, continued)

" Ugh-igh! " exclaimed Bob Murray on the morning of September 5, with an emphatic crescendo inflection on the last syllable. " Darned if I don't believe all the ice houses in western Maryland were emptied into this river last night." We were wading the Potomac, bent on effacing the print of the " despot's heel " from " Maryland's shore," and Bob had just stumbled over a rock in the middle of the channel and gone under, head and ears. With less reason than he, I was of the same opinion. The coldness of the water, however, was more than equaled by the frigidity of the welcome extended. Not even the dulcet strains of " Maryland, My Maryland," evoked from half submerged instruments by Collins' band aroused the enthusiasm of the people; no arms opened to receive, no fires blazed to warm, and no feast waited to feed us, as wet, shivering and hungry, we stepped out of the water and set our feet on Maryland's soil.

*　　*　　*　　*　　*

That day Jack Sutherland and I straggled; he, because of a sore heel, and I to escape the heat and dust I should encounter if I remained in the ranks. Next morning, on our way to rejoin the

R. W. MURRAY

Private, Company F, Fourth Texas Regiment

command on the Monocacy, near Frederick City, we ran across three Georgians butchering a beef. Being totally ignorant of the deliciousness of a cowboy's tidbits, the sweetbread and marrowgut, they generously consented to our appropriation of those rare and dainty gastronomic delicacies.   *   *   *

On this occasion, if never before, Jack was a trifle too greedy, and, to use a bit of slang, the singularly exhaustive expressiveness of which justifies a departure from the rules of rhetoric, " cut off more than he could chaw." The marrowgut is never over three feet long—the art in securing it consisting of knowing where to begin and where to stop. Much practice when I was a cowboy, which I wish I was now, has made me an adept in the art. Jack is not an adept, but as he insisted on doing the carving, I had to let him do it. He began with commendable discretion, and, having stripped out about eighteen inches of the entrail, bade me take hold of the end of it, and proceeded with his carving. At what I judged to be three feet, I suggested a halt. " Dry up!" said he testily; " don't you s'pose I know what I'm about? " Figuratively extinguished, I stood mute, and Jack continued cutting until he reached the six-foot mark. Whacking it off there and rising to his feet with his end firmly clutched between his fingers, he asked how we should divide it. " Just cut it in two in the middle," said I, knowing that thus only could I hope to get the only eatable part. He did so, and then, each of us taking half the sweet-bread,

and smacking our lips in anticipation of the
treat in store for us when we reached the frying-
pan of our respective messes, hastened on to
camp. But, alas! while neither I nor my mess
had the least cause for complaint, Jack and his
did, and he was denounced by his messmates in
terms more forcible than elegant for his carelessness in both selection and division.

Leaving the Monocacy on the 9th, we moved
on to Hagerstown, and encamped on the grassy
banks of a beautiful clear stream of water
*   *   *   With trembling pen and an
ashamed heart, I must confess that at that particular juncture in my career as a soldier I was,
according to the polite but graphic language of
our camp Chesterfields, "quite insectuous."
Only persons who have been similarly afflicted
can realize the joy I felt when a happy chance
—an apparently providential interposition in
my behalf—furnished me, from the crown of my
head to the soles of my feet, with a change of
raiment. The clear stream of water came in
then most handily for the extensive and laborious
ablutions rendered obligatory by my keen sense
of the fitness of things.

Being in a portion of Maryland never before
depredated on by an army, rations were abundant, even if evidences of the good will of the
people were few and far between. Willingly
would we have remained longer at Hagerstown,
but it was not to be. " Grim visaged war " again
showed " his wrinkled front," and blew his blasts
in our ears. The sound of cannon back in the

direction of Frederick City proclaimed that
" Little Mac " was coming after our scalps, and
within an hour our brigade was on the march
to Boonesboro Gap.

The desire of General " Shank " Evans to
have his brigade of South Carolinians assigned
to Whiting's division, on the day after the enemy
was routed at Second Manassas, was, at first
blush, a compliment; we had no objection to
sharing the honors of the future with a brigade
which had gained renown at Ball's Bluff. But
the desire appeared so soon to be wholly self-
serving that we regretted our complaisance, and
would willingly have foregone the flattery.
Evans's commission as brigadier-general ante-
dated that of Hood, and this gave him command
of the division in the absence of General Whiting. When, therefore, Evans's first act of authority was an unwarranted demand on Hood
to turn over to Evans's quartermaster a lot of
nice ambulances Texas scouts had captured, and
which had been appropriated to our use and
benefit, and when Hood, refusing, was placed
under arrest by Evans and deprived of command,
the indignation of the Texans was all the deeper
because of the necessity of suppressing it. Nor
did it find audible expression until the sound
of the enemy's guns on the 14th of September,
and the sight of our beloved General riding, with
bowed head, in the rear of the men who trusted
him, emphasized the outrage, and forced an appeal to supreme authority. General Lee sat on
his horse by the side of the road, almost within

reach of the enemy's guns, and each Texan as
he passed joined in the meaning refrain to the
deep-seated resolve, "If there's any fighting to
be done by the Texas Brigade, Hood must command it." Understanding the full significance
of the demand, Lee raised his hat courteously,
and replied laconically, "You shall have him,
gentlemen," and immediately dispatched an aid
to inform Hood of his release from arrest. The
men began to cheer, but when our gallant General, his head uncovered and his face proud and
joyful, galloped by to his rightful place at the
head of the column, the cheers deepened into a
roar that drowned the volleys of the hundred
cannon that were even then vengefully thundering at the Gap.   *   *   *

Mounted on a good horse, I turned short to
the right, and, after riding all night, crossed the
Potomac at Williamsport, whence I proceeded
up the Shenandoah Valley to Staunton. Having
so far devoted this letter exclusively to "feats
of broil and battle," "little would I grace my
cause" by descending to a monotonous story of
traveling among a friendly and hospitable people. Indeed, the trivial incidents of that journey
would afford but slight entertainment, even were
this a time of peace, much less when every Southern heart is enlisted in the great and glorious
cause for which our soldiers are laying down
their lives. Nor shall I attempt any description
of a battle in which I did not participate.
        *   *   *   *   *

When I rejoined the brigade, it was encamped

EDWARD BUCKLEY
Private, Company L, First Texas Regiment

here near an immense spring of clear, cold water. Looking about me for the faces of men endeared to me by common suffering and danger, I missed many. Some of them were killed outright at Sharpsburg; many were wounded, and of a few, the best and worst that could be said was that they had been reported as " missing."

The brunt of the battle on that part of the Confederate line occupied by Hood's brigade at Sharpsburg fell upon the First Texas, and they bore it like the heroes they are. Even if they did lose their flag—their color-bearer being killed at a time when the enemy was pressing the regiment too vigorously for its members to attend to any duty but shooting—they proved by their unflinching gallantry that, given the same opportunities, either one of our Texas regiments could be depended upon to do all that mortals may to win victory and punish a foe. Using the expressive nomenclature of camp, I may say that at Gaines' Mill it was the " Hell-roaring Fourth " that carried off the honors; at Second Manassas it was the " Bloody Fifth," and at Sharpsburg it was the " Ragged First."

Anent the matter of that lost flag. It was a long, lean private of the Sixth North Carolina who administered a retort courteous to a would-be wag of the First Texas. The regiments were passing each other, two or three days after the battle, and the representative of the Lone Star State, with more wit than discretion, sang out of the Sixth, " Halloa, fellers! Have you a good supply of tar on your heels this morning? "

"Yes," answered the long, lean man pleasantly, but too pointedly to be misunderstood, "and it's a real pity you'uns didn't come over and borrow a little the other day; it mout have saved that flag o' your'n."

Nearly two months of incessant marching and battling in heat, dust, mud, and rain, and of exposure to all the perils of active campaigning in front of a largely outnumbering enemy, have made this rest at Winchester a very pleasant one. We have little to do but eat, drink, sleep, and talk. The officer who would suggest drilling the veterans of the brilliant campaign just ended would merit summary dismissal from the service.

    *   *   *   *   *

Their fond mothers are sensible in keeping your friend and his cousin John so near home as to be constantly within reach. While those two bravest of the brave were dancing attendance on the ladies, eating fried chicken, and drinking pure coffee three times a day, sleeping under mosquito bars at night, and taking noonday siestas in hammocks, with a darky on either side to brush away the flies, I footed it from Richmond to Manassas, and from Manassas to Hagerstown, carrying an average weight of forty pounds, sleeping on the ground, often wet to the skin, sometimes choked by dust, always hungry, generally tired, and on various occasions gave the Yankees, whom they so bitterly hate, every opportunity to kill me that a fairly expert marksman could ask. But, while I have not yet "shuffled off this mortal coil," there is no tell-

ing when I may, and it seems to me I would take
the risk twice as willingly if Tommie and Johnnie
were only here to share it. My experiences are not
singular; every man in Lee's army has done as
much, and the majority of them a great deal
more in the matter of hard and dangerous service, than I. Pray, do not mention what I have
said to the gentlemen named. They might think
me envious of their good luck, and I am. Can't
you persuade the one my lady likes the better
to exchange places with me? Should the other
choose to follow, I have a messmate as willing
as myself to get back to Texas. But I must close.
Some movement is in contemplation, for aides
and orderlies are hurrying in all directions.

Note 4—From Winchester, where the foregoing letter is
dated, and where it remained fully four weeks, Hood's brigade marched across and to the eastern slope of the Blue
Ridge, camped near Culpeper Court House a couple of
weeks, moved on to the south side of the Rapidan and
camped there three weeks, and then proceeded to Fredericksburg, arriving but a few days before the battle fought
there.

IX

CAMP NEAR FREDERICKSBURG, VA.,
                    December 20, 1862.

AN hour before daylight on the 11th of this
month the thundering boom of two heavy guns
awoke the sleeping Confederate army. Scarcely
had its echoes ceased to reverberate through the
wooded hills and hollows south of the Rappahannock River when every Southern soldier was
on his feet, armed and equipped to meet the
enemy whose coming it announced. Not a
thought of defeat disturbed the minds of the
tried veterans who had driven McClellan's vast
and well-appointed army from the gates of
Richmond, routed Pope's at Second Manassas,
and sent it a mass of demoralized fugitives to
the shelter of the intrenchments around Washington City, and had held their own at Sharpsburg against the doubly outnumbering forces
commanded by McClellan " *redivivus.*" The battle had been promised by Burnside to the Northern people; Lee counted on, and made arrange-
ments for it, and not a brigadier-general of the
Confederates but knew his place in the lines of
defense.

When the dense fog that laid low over the

E. S. JEMISON
Captain, First Texas Regiment
Taken during the war

E. S. JEMISON
Captain, First Texas Regiment

wide, level valley on the south side lifted on the morning of the 12th, and the sun of a cloudless sky touched the earth with its sheen of light, the scene had changed. The ground next to the river, which the day before was yellow with the stubble of grass and grain, was now blue with Yankee uniforms, the monotony relieved only by the glistening of burnished arms and the bright colors of a hundred flags. Massed between railroad and river, division behind division, artillery in front, cavalry in rear, and infantry in the center, and protected by the heavy siege guns planted on the low range of hills crowning the north bank of the stream, Burnside's army was an imposing, awe-inspiring spectacle. * * * Marye's Hill is a spur of high land that approaches within half a mile of the river and terminates in a bluff overlooking the little city nestling between it and the stream. At the foot of this bluff runs a narrow wagon road parallel with the river, and on the side of the road next to the city is a low fence built of stone.

At nine o'clock on the morning of the 14th the battle began in earnest. On the top of the hill, and close to the edge of the bluff there was a battery, and behind the stone fence crouched Cobb's brigade of Georgians—one of the regiments being the gallant Eighteenth, which, when in our brigade, complimented us by its willingness to be known as the Third Texas. * * * To assault this position was a desperate undertaking, and it would seem that the calculating, death-fearing, simon-pure Yankees shrank from it with a dread that even unlimited supplies of whisky could not abate. Foreigners, though, were plentiful in the Federal army, and the loss of a few thousand more or less would break no Yankee hearts; therefore, I imagine, Meagher's Irish Brigade was selected for the sacrifice. But even Irish hearts had to be tempered for the ordeal, and to this end it was necessary not only to appeal to their love for "ould Ireland," but to imbue them with a supplemental fictitious courage. Only when a sprig of arbor vitæ, stolen from the deserted yards of the town, was pinned upon their caps to remind them of the shamrock of their native Isle, their throats moistened liberally and their canteens filled with liquor, did they become ready to move forward as an initiatory forlorn hope. * * *

Between the last houses of the town proper and the stone fence stretched a piece of level, open ground about two hundred yards wide. Entering this, the Federals halted a second or two to reform their lines; and then, some shouting, "Erin go bragh!" and others the Yankee huzzah, they rushed impetuously forward against a storm of grape and canister that, as long as the guns on the hilltop could be sufficiently depressed, tore great gaps in their ranks. But, wavering not, they closed together and rushed onward until within fifty yards of the stone fence, when in one grand, simultaneous burst of light, sound, and death, came the blinding flash, the deafening roar, the murderous destruction of two thousand well-aimed rifles, the wild, weird, blood-curdling Confederate yell, and two thousand Irishmen sank down wounded or dead, and a cowed and demoralized remnant sought safety in inglorious flight.

Seven assaults were made on the stone fence during the day, and five thousand men were sent to eternity before Burnside convinced himself that the position was impregnable. Only two regiments of our division were engaged in any undertaking that might be called a battle. These were the Fifty-seventh and Fifty-fourth North Carolina regiments, composed of conscripts— young men under twenty and old men—all dressed in homespun, and presenting to the fastidious eyes of us veterans a very unsoldierly appearance. But we judged hastily. Ordered to drive the enemy back, they not only charged with surprising recklessness, but kept on charging until, to save them from certain capture, General Hood peremptorily recalled them. As they passed our brigade on their return, one old fellow halted, wiped the powder grime from his weather-beaten face with the sleeve of his coat, and wrathfully exclaimed, "Durn ole Hood, anyhow! He jes' didn't have no bus'ness ter stop us when we'uns was ah-whippin' the durn blue-bellies ter h—ll an' back, an' eff we'uns hadder bin you Texicans, he'd never o' did it."

It was, I think, on the 14th that our brigade was lying—presumably on its arms—in a forest of tall timber, but near enough to the front to get into line at a moment's notice. A blanket

had been spread on the ground and four or five
men were seated around it playing poker. A
hand was dealt and Bill Smith felt happy; he
held four sixes. Two of his companions were
also lucky, and when one of them bet fifty beans
—they were playing cent ante—the other raised
him two hundred. Confident of winning—for
two hands of fours are seldom held in the same
deal—Bill, with a fine pretense of bluffing, looked
over his cards long and anxiously and finally
said, in a trembling voice, " I see your bets, gentlemen, and go you five hundred better." Scarcely
were the words out of his mouth, when a shell
from a long-range cannon struck the dead limb
of a tree near by and sent a piece of it against
Bill's breast with such force as to knock him
backwards to the ground, the cards flying from
his hands, each in a different direction. Jumping to his feet and glaring wrathfully on everybody in sight, he exclaimed, " D——d if I can't
whip the cowardly whelp who threw that chunk!
Now's his time to cheep, if he's got any sand in
his craw." But nobody " cheeped." Bill meant
every word he said, and was well known as a
man who could not be insulted with impunity.
And it took quite a while, and considerable argument, to persuade him that the person responsible for his loss was on the other side of
the Rappahannock, fully two miles away.

The battle of Fredericksburg has been no exception to the rule in furnishing us with a feast
—lots of pure coffee and unlimited quantities
of desiccated vegetables. Soup made of the lat-

ter has been the first, last, and sometimes middle
course of every meal I have eaten for a week.

*   *   *   *   *

Confident that the Yankees will be in no hurry
to risk a repetition of the drubbing they have
received, we are making preparations for the
winter. Snow has fallen to the depth of several
inches, but wood is plentiful—and most of us
drew an extra supply from the Yankees in the
way of blankets. I sleep in a tent with our
adjutant, but mess with my German friend,
Webber. He is not only a good and economical
cook, but is willing to act in that capacity without relief, and this last consideration appeals
strongly to my keen sense of the fitness of things.
While our alliance as messmates began only a
few days ago, our friendship dates from the retreat from Yorktown. He is the happy possessor
of a huge pipe as German as himself, the bowl
of which, lined with iron, holds fully an eighth
of a pound of tobacco. For facilities of transportation as well as because he loves the weed,
the pipe is always hanging from his mouth on
the march, and within reach of it when he lies
down to sleep. Coming up from Yorktown, everybody's tobacco except Webber's got wet, and
Webber refused peremptorily to divide with several who at different times applied to him. It
was a case of wet or dry tobacco with me, and I
schemed. Catching the old fellow off to himself,
I said, " Give me some dry tobacco, Webber,
please; mine is wet and won't smoke." He
glanced around at me quickly and suspiciously

and answered gruffly, " I giffs not mooch tubacca
avay." " I know you don't," said I, " and I
don't blame you for refusing to divide with everybody; but give me some now, and when we get
to our knapsacks I'll give you half of mine."
" Vell, den," he replied, opening his heart and
tobacco pouch simultaneously, and beaming
upon me with the first smile I ever saw on his
face, " dat vash goot." And not only then, but
until I had a chance to dry my own tobacco,
Webber's pouch was constantly at my command.
Of course, I made my word good when I got to
my knapsack, and since then tobacco is common
property between us.

" Why did you join the Confederate Army,
Webber? " I asked one day. " It vash my beezness," replied he. " I vas been a solcher in Char-
many all ze time." " You would have joined the
Northern Army, then, if you had been in the
North, wouldn't you? " I asked again. " Oh,
yah," he answered. " Vot ish der defrance?
Vat ish got to coom, vill coom anyvay, und to be
a solcher vash my beezness."

While I write, some of my comrades are ex-
changing compliments with half a regiment of
cavalry that is marching by, which incident reminds me of another. One day on the trip from
Winchester, while our brigade was encamped
near Culpeper Court House, a lone Virginia cavalryman came wandering in an offensively lordly
way through the camp. Had he come afoot, little attention would have been bestowed on him
and he would likely have been suffered to depart

in peace and happiness. Presumptuous enough, however, to bestride a gallant steed, whose hoofs stirred up more or less dust, he promptly became the cynosure of all eyes. About the strongest feeling infantry and cavalry have for each other is that of contempt. Down in the bottom of his heart the foot soldier nurses an idea that his mounted comrades lack a great deal of doing their whole duty in killing and taking the chances of being killed, while from his elevation on the back of a horse your cavalryman feels himself a superior being, and looks down with an air of humiliating pity upon an arm of the service which must depend on its own legs for transportation. When, therefore, it appeared that this particular gentleman had no other object in view than to gratify an idle and impertinent curiosity concerning a people of whom he had heard the most wonderful tales, the Texans, not being in holiday attire or in the humor to be closely inspected by strangers, determined to trade a little upon their reputation for bloodthirstiness.

A fair opportunity was given them, for it happened that for the purpose of solving some doubt which a cursory view failed to settle or remove, the visitor came to a temporary halt in the middle of the camp and proceeded to look, at his leisure, on the strange surroundings. Immediately encircled by a dozen or more Texans, several of them with their guns, others with pistols belted around their waists, and all wearing, either naturally or intentionally, the most reckless and dare-devil airs imaginable, he suddenly lost his look of unconcern, and began to glance uneasily around in search of an avenue of escape from his admirers. One fierce-looking fellow stepped to the side of his horse, and, assuming the manner of a sick man just out of the hospital, laid his hand on the Virginian's scabbard, and, in a whining voice, asked, " Couldn't you pull your jobber out for a minute, Mister, just to please a sick man? " The laugh that followed the request caused a flush of anger to overspread the countenance of the horseman, and he was about to make an angry reply, when his attention was arrested by a colloquy between two of his entertainers, which, although not at all personal in character, was not calculated to reassure its hearer and object—the tone, manner, and looks of the speakers indicating something more than mere idle banter.

" How much is it, Tuck," asked the one, with a significant glance at the Virginian, " that Longstreet offers for the body of a dead Virginia cavalryman? " " A thousand dollars in gold," answered Tuck, " and if a feller wasn't partickerly squeamish, it'd be powerful easy to git the body." " Why, Tuck," protested the first speaker, " you wouldn't think of killing this feller, would you? " " Why not? " replied Tuck, looking at his gun, apparently to see if it was capped. " That's the only way I know of to git the money, fur none of these d——d cavalry fellers ever git close enough to a live Yankee to be killed."

The gallant Virginian lost not a word or a

movement of the participants in this conversation, and, knowing Texans only by repute, deemed it prudent to work himself and steed to the edge of the crowd, experiencing just enough difficulty in this undertaking to increase his very natural apprehensions of bodily harm. Once there, he bestowed a hurried but tremulously polite "Good-mawnin', gentlemen," on the party assembled in his honor and went off at a brisk trot. He was allowed to reach the outskirts of the grove without molestation—then a gun cap snapped behind him, and even his iron nerve could not restrain him from glancing back, and —when he discovered Tuck on his knees, gun in hand, hurriedly fumbling in his cap-box for another cap—from clapping both spurs and whip to his steed and disappearing in a cloud of dust, amid the derisive shouts and jeers of the brigade.

X

IN AND AROUND RICHMOND

FALLING CREEK, VA., March 20, 1863.

IT was with deep regret and a noticeable temporary increase of profanity that the Texas Brigade moved out of its winter quarters at Fredericksburg. Rudely fashioned and half-finished in many respects as they were, they offered comforts and conveniences that were not only restful, but made us feel just a little as though we were "sorter at home." Having an idea that the order to abandon them, and come down here to bivouac in the near vicinity of Richmond, emanated more from the silly fears of the original secessionists who so much prefer legislating for the Confederacy to defending it from its enemies, we found a large measure of appositeness in the words that Shakespeare puts in the mouth of one of the characters in King Lear—

"Thou hast seen a farmer's dog bark at a beggar
And the creature run from the cur; there,
There, thou might'st behold the great image of authority;
A dog's obeyed in office."

We left Fredericksburg on one of the coldest days in February, coming by railroad to Richmond, and thence, meandering from one side of the road to the other, out to this camp, four miles from the city. I use the word "meandering" advisedly. You may be able to guess why, when informed that, since a learned justice of the peace decided that our military authorities had fractured the constitutions of both the State of Virginia and the Confederacy when they prohibited the sale of ardent liquors by the drink, saloons have become plentiful in Richmond, and the man with the cash need not long remain thirsty. Let me forestall, however, the unkindly suspicion which may creep into your mind that I was one of the meanderers, by stating on my soldierly honor that I went astride of a horse, and that, given a loose rein, the sagacious animal swerved neither to right nor left, but carried me straight to camp.

Whatever the alarm that brought us down here, it subsided the moment it was known in the city that two divisions, Hood's and Pickett's, had come to defend the Capital and the trembling lawgivers assembled there. The Union forces which had disturbed the serenity of these statesmen retired in haste, and much to our delight we have had but one tramp since arrival at our present quarters. That was out to Ashland. Some timid cavalryman had come on an almost exhausted horse to Richmond with the report that the Yankees were moving in force toward that place, and to meet them and drive them back ere they approached near enough to the city to prevent our Congressmen from continuing their weighty deliberations on the conscript act which was to force every man of the South except themselves and their kind into the army, we pulled down the few tents we had, and loading them on the wagons, marched rapidly to the probable theater of hostilities. But it proved a false alarm, and, halting in a veritable wilderness of pine, we sought a much-needed rest. Next morning we set out on the return march in a blinding snowstorm that held on all day. Its demoralizing effect, however, was first visible only when we reached the city. Then, in a manner, the brigade disintegrated, every man of it, save the small minority of teetotallers, making a flank movement, and going in search of warming liquid refreshments. So sudden, surprising, and inexplicable was the depletion in the ranks that when General Robertson, our present commander, looked back through the darkening mist of falling snow, and down the long, straggling, and attenuated line of shadowy, moving figures, he could only give expression to his consternation by exclaiming, " Where in h—ll is the Texas Brigade? " He was about to send details in search of the absconders, but luckily General Hood, who was riding near enough to overhear all that was said, and who, although a West-Pointer, is fairly well acquainted with the Texas and Arkansas temperament and taste, thoughtfully interposed, " Never mind, General—never mind," he said ; " you'll get them all back in the morning, or at any rate in time to lead them into the next fight."

The fact that General Hood and I were that night both the guests of Mr. John James of San

Antonio, Texas, a warm and highly valued friend
of my father, must serve to avert any suspicion
that I was one of the absconders.   Mr. James
brought me letters from my home folks, and a
fairly good and much-wished-for, but not really
needed, supply of cash. He also secured permission from General Hood for me to stay with him
at the hotel during the few days he remained
in Richmond.   Boarding at a stylish hotel was
a novel experience to me, and as Mr. James
kindly paid all the bills I made the most of the
picnic by indulging my appetite to its limit.   A
hearty eater is usually an excellent listener.
A Virginia officer who sat near me one day in
the dining-room related an anecdote that so
amused me, and so well illustrates the unwilling-
ness of some people to confess themselves the
victim of a practical joke, that I must repeat
it.   Colonel M., commanding a regiment in Pickett's old brigade, is an excessively dignified gentleman.   But, though a brave and capable officer,
he is to the rank and file of his regiment what
the representative of the Confederacy to the
Court of St. James (for all the good he has done
us, or is likely to do us) might as well be to the
English Government, that is, *persona non grata*.
His war-horse is his wife's favorite buggy-horse,
and was named by her Ossawatomie. The Colonel was one day informed that on the next he
was expected to ride at the head of his regiment
through the principal streets of Richmond, and,
as that was the home of himself and most of the
men, and he desired his command to appear at

its best, he notified the company officers of the
intended movement in ample time for all needful preparations. That very night some grace-
less reprobate shaved Ossawatomie's tail, leaving not a hair on it. At the hour when Colonel
M. was informed of the shearing it was too late
for him to secure another mount, and he had,
perforce, to ride the bob-tailed steed. The laughing and raillery of the riff-raff, the street gamins
and adult idlers, he met with disdain, not appearing to notice them. His wife, however, had
rights which ten years of matrimony had taught
him it was not wise to deny. The estimable lady
stood among a crowd of distinguished people,
and no sooner discovered the disfigurement of
the horse than at the top of her voice and in the
shrillest of its tones, she cried, " Why, Robert,
my dear, who in the world shaved Ossawatomie's
tail off that way? "

To have such a question asked at such a time
and place was horribly embarrassing to the
doughty officer, and for two seconds he remained
silent. Then, casting a sternly reproachful look
at the partner of his joys and sorrows, he replied, " It was done by my order, Madam—it
was done by my order."

In my haste to tell you the reasons for our
change of base and what has transpired since
we arrived here, I have omitted to mention the
great snowball battle in which practically the
whole of Longstreet's corps participated. It
occurred at Fredericksburg, the day after a very
heavy fall of snow. What company or regiment

initiated the affair, I do not know. The first
intimation given me of its progress came in the
shape of a snowball that, judging from the way
it hurt me, must have been left out in the cold
so long as to become solidified. It was thrown
by a little bandy-legged Georgian of Benning's
brigade, whose good marksmanship was doubtless due to the practice indulged down in the
" Goober Grabbling State " of knocking chickens'
heads off with rocks. To add insult to the injury
done to the back of my head by the first snowball, the impudent fellow threw another, twice
as hard, which hit me in the same place. Do
not imagine I was running, though, for I was
not—I was only taking longer and faster strides
than usual. In self-defense, as soon as I regained my feet and saw he was preparing to continue the contest, I dived into the adjutant's
tent, and within its protecting walls administered a soothing rubbing to the fast swelling
bump on my occiput. The battle was a long and
hard-contested one, and lasted nearly all day.
Field, staff, regimental, and company officers, as
well as privates, figured conspicuously in it, and
even a general or two took a hand. Although no
serious wounds were inflicted, black eyes, bloody
noses, ragged ears, and sadly disfigured phys-
iognomies were abundant after hostilities ceased.
The Texas Brigade, as usual, was in the thickest
of the fray; that is, all of it except myself and
a few others who, because of the inclemency of
the weather, and after the first few volleys,
deemed it imprudent to remain outside of a tent.

Such, indeed, was the din and racket created, so loud and long-continued was the shouting and the yelling, that imagining our army preparing for an immediate advance, the officer in command of the Yankee cavalry doing picket duty on Stafford Heights ordered his men into the saddle.   *   *   *

One of my comrades, whom for convenience I will call Jack, has great faith in Providence. Ask him when he is hungry and his haversack empty, where he expects to get his next meal, and he invariably answers, "Providence will provide." He has aired that faith and said those words so often that he is becoming known to some of the boys as "Old Providence." A few days ago he was entirely out of meat, and had been for the better part of two days, having devoured the three days' rations issued to him in one. The five dollars in Confederate money that yet lingered in his pocket, a sad and lonely remnant of the twenty-two in the same currency that was paid him the day after we got to this camp in compensation for two months' service, could purchase nothing for him in a camp where there was nothing to sell, and going to Richmond was out of the question, for he had exhausted for a long while his right to a pass. While endeavoring to allay the cravings of his inner man by tightening his belt, he gave his mind to reflection, and judging from the alacrity with which he donned his cartridge-box and shouldered his gun, and the speed at which he struck off down the railroad track, a more than usually brilliant idea had illumined his mind. Half an hour later he returned to camp, a smile of triumph on his hitherto gloomy countenance and half a side of bacon dangling from the bayonet end of his gun. But not a word did he utter till he had hung the meat on a limb, set the gun against a tree, and divested himself of the cartridge-box. Then, turning to the envious comrades who in surprise had gathered near and silently watched his every movement, he said,

"Haven't I told you, boys, time and again, that if you would only cultivate the proper kind of faith, Providence would provide all that you needed? Indeed, I have, and as many times you have laughed at and derided me, and held me up to scorn. But, gentlemen and fellow-soldiers in the holy cause of the South, there is the proof that I knew whereof I spake," and with the air of a conqueror he pointed to the bacon. "If there is one among you who doubts its being a genuine article of fat, juicy, sugar-cured, and hickory-smoked bacon, he is at liberty to smell it and be forever convinced."

"Where did you get it, Jack, and by what peculiar *modus operandi?* " instantly asked Bill Calhoun. "That is the burnin' question that is most fiercely and voraciously agitatin' the moral and intellectual faculties of this present enthusiastic gathering of your friends and well-wishers."

"I got it out in the woods yonder, and just as easy as falling off a log," replied Jack, as with deft strokes of a sharp knife he began to cut thick rashers from the middling. "If a man wants Providence to help him, he must put himself in the way of Providence. That's what I did, and this meat is the result. Feeling hungrier and having less to eat than usual, I set off down the railroad with my gun, hoping that by some fortunate chance I might get a shot at a rabbit or a squirrel, or, perhaps, run across a terrapin. But the squirrels were all asleep, the rabbits visiting distant neighbors, and the terrapins *non est inventus*. Feeling that luck had deserted me, I sat down at the foot of a tree, and bless God, hadn't been there more than a minute when a darky came along with a big middling of bacon. Thinking it a special interposition of Providence in favor of a starving man, I proposed to buy a piece of the meat, and the darky willingly sold me the half of the middling for five dollars."

"Willingly, Jack—willingly?" queried Calhoun, a suspicion of doubt apparent in tone and look. "Did I hear you use the word 'willingly,' my boy?"

"Of course you did," replied Jack, as he carefully laid a couple of slices of bacon, each a foot long, into the half of a canteen which served the purpose of a frying-pan. "But I would have come nearer the mark had I said 'gladly,' for the poor devil was actually staggering under the weight of the whole middling, and was really glad to sell me half of it at so fair a price."

"Ah, me—ah, me!" sighed Calhoun, his eyes dreamily wondering. "Ah, me, boys, when, after

lis'ning to our beloved and respected comrade in
arms, and hearing him use the word ' willingly '
in connection with his sudden acquisition of a
piece of bacon that can't weigh a pound less'n
forty poun's averdepaws, an' also an' likewise
hearin' him insist he oughter of said 'gladly,'
I take a squint at the tablets of memory an' see
norated on 'em in shinin' letters that 'cordin'
to this mornin's papers the partikalar kin' of
internal refreshments our afo'said comrade is a
statin' he give five dollars fur the whole she-
bang of, is sellin' at sixty cents a poun', an'
mighty little to sell at that, my overweenin' an'
trustin' faith in human natur' sorter weakens
an' gits sour, an' I feel like sayin' with the poet,

> " ' Can such things be
> And overcome us like a summer's cloud,
> Without our special wonder? ' "

Jack had continued too intent on a speedy
appeasement of his ravenous appetite to listen
to Calhoun's remarks.   Conscious of this and
knowing I must have heard all he said, Calhoun
came over to where I sat against a tree, about
thirty feet distant from Jack, and in an aggrieved
tone said,
   " The only time a feller has a God-given right
to tell a darn no such a thing, Joe, is when he's
jus' got to tell it, or go to the guard-house.
Then it's natteral an' proper, 'cause it's self-
defense, an' you know the Bible says, ' All a man
hath will he give fur his life,' or words to that
effeck.   But a feller hasn't got any business lyin'

to his comrades. What sits most uneasily on my sensations of morality in Jack's story is his sorter reckless use of the words ' willingly ' and ' gladly,' fur there wan't a bit o' willingness an' gladness in the poor nigger's bosom after he run afoul of our high-minded and distinguished fellow-soldier. Jack seen him first, an' knowin' he'd robbed some ole citizen, got the drop on him with his gun, an' commanded him sternly an' vociferously to surrender.   Then, Jack whacked the middlin' in two, give him the five dollars, an' choosin' the bigges' half, toted it into camp.   That's the truth, the whole truth, and nothin' but the truth, so help me Moses, an' all the holy prophets and disciples! "

I declined to express any opinion on the subject—it was none of my business, I thought; besides, I felt sure Jack would invite me to supper or breakfast. My faith in his hospitality was not misplaced, and I do not mind confessing that the bacon, which proved the main staple of the meal, tasted sweet enough to have been first stolen by the darky, and then confiscated by my host.

*   *   *   *   *

All the odd characters in the Texas Brigade are not members of the Fourth Texas, by any means. The " Ragged First " has many on its muster roll, and among them, a tall, powerfully built and red-faced corporal whose name escapes me at this moment. The corporal was on the picket line one day down at Yorktown, and, being both hungry and ragged, decided to venture

beyond the line in search of something he might
eat or wear. He had not gone fifty yards to
the front when he discovered the body of a well-
dressed and splendidly equipped Yankee lying
behind a little thicket of sassafras which concealed it from the view of anybody in the
trenches. That he might the more exhaustively
and leisurely administer on the dead man's estate, the corporal carried the body and all its
attachments and belongings to the shelter of the
breastworks. The inventory justified the rash
venture of the self-appointed administrator, the
corpse yielding a pair of extra good shoes, a suit
of first-class clothing, a well-filled haversack,
sixty dollars in gold, and, best of all, a canteen
two-thirds full of excellent whisky. Having
swallowed a good four fingers of the whisky, the
corporal wiped his lips with the sleeve of his
coat, put on a long, solemn face, and, looking
down at the corpse, said in mournful accents,

" Poor fellow, poor fellow! Like the many of
your tribe that have gone before, their departure
from this vale of tears hastened by well-aimed
Confederate bullets, you have gone to your
eternal home in the lowest depths of that other
world whose fires are never less than red hot.
But, though I mourn your untimely demise, it
is not with a grief that is without consolation.
That you were a gentleman and not a vagabond
is evident—your boots and your coat, your pants
and your liberal supply of filthy lucre, in short,
your whole *tout ensemble*, stamping you as that
beyond any controversy. But, had I a shadow

of a doubt of your being a gentleman in every sense of the word, the quality of the liquor in your canteen would resolve it in your favor by an overwhelming majority. So here's to you, Yank! Living, though an enemy of my country and therefore deserving of death, you must have been a jolly good fellow—dead, you'll soon return to the dust whence you sprang, and that you may the sooner do the returning act, my comrades and I will lay you under the sod of old Virginia just as soon as we have emptied your canteen."

The corporal was as good as his word, and, assisted by his comrades, dug a grave in the sand and buried the body.   *   *   *.

NOTE 5—The Texas Brigade remained at Falling Creek until about the 1st of April. Thence it went to Petersburg and camped in that vicinity three or four days, when, taking the Jerusalem Road, it passed through the town of the same name, and crossing the Blackwater River, arrived at Suffolk about the 6th day of April. Here it and the other forces along under command of Longstreet pitted themselves against gunboats, big and little, holding the Federals closely within their lines until a large amount of quartermaster and commissary stores could be hauled out of the country south of the city. At the time Longstreet was notified that a battle was impending at Chancellorsville all his wagon-trains were away on foraging expeditions, and it was impossible to recall them in time to enable him to reach Lee and take part in the battle of Chancellorsville. The troops under his command, however, recrossed the Blackwater, going north on the day or may be the day after that battle was fought and won, passing through Petersburg and Richmond again, and in the vicinity of Orange Court House and near the Rapidan rejoining the main army between the 10th and 20th days of May.

XI

CAMP NEAR RICHMOND, May 10, 1863.

THE battle of Chancellorsville has been fought and won, but it has cost us the life of Stonewall Jackson. It is the only great battle General Lee has fought without Longstreet. McClellan, Pope, McClellan again, Burnside, and Hooker have each been pitted against our peerless chieftain. Who will be the next is both an interesting and vexed question with us Confederates. Confident of the superiority of our commander over the very best material the Yankees can find, we prefer that he should meet a foeman worthy of his steel. But while there is little credit to be gained, either by army or commander, in opposing such vainglorious boasters as Pope, Burnside, and Hooker, there are more rations, and these are getting to be a consideration of no small importance. Why we cannot be better and more regularly supplied, is a problem beyond our solution. Perhaps we are expected to live off of the enemy; if so, we protest. When fighting ceases to be a matter of pure, self-sacrificing patriotism, and degenerates into a mere business, we Texans will ask discharges. We are getting homesick, anyway, and nothing in the world

111

increases the severity of that complaint more than hunger. Apropos to nothing, apparently, except the communings of his own inner man, a comrade said the other day, " I wish to God I was at home." " Oh, yes," I replied, " you want to see the girl you left behind you, don't you? " " No, indeed," he blurted out, " but I want something to eat," and, hungry myself, I unanimously acquiesced in the sentiment.

It is not so much at the quantity of rations we grumble, as at the intolerable sameness of bread and meat. Such a limited variety gives us, by the rule of permutation, only two changes; if coffee were added to the menu, we could have nine, and if sugar also, no less than twenty-four. As Bill Calhoun says, " This thing of having bread for the first course one day, and meat the next, and so on, *vice versa* and alternately *ad infinitum et nauseam,* has an excessively depressing effect upon a fellow's patriotism."

Writing of Bill reminds me of his generosity at Suffolk, where, in order to accomplish any good, our men would have had to be amphibious. One day while the brigade was there, General Hood halted for a moment at the Fourth's camp to speak about some matter to Colonel Key. While talking, the General noticed Bill standing a little way off, and, knowing his character, with a view to sport, said in a voice loud enough to be heard by the whole regiment, " Detail an officer and twenty-five of your best men, Colonel, and order them to report to me at once at my quarters. I have set my heart on one of those gunboats down on the river, and I know that many men of the Fourth can easily get it for me."

Bill heard and accepted the challenge. Stepping to the side of Hood's horse and laying one hand on the animal's neck, while with the other he touched the brim of his hat in respectful salute to the rider, he said: "Now look ah-here, General, if you've just got to have a gunboat, whether or no, speak out like a man and the Fourth Texas will buy you one, but we don't propose to fool with any of them down yonder in the river. They say the darned things are loaded, and, besides, there's only a few of us fellers can swim."

Not being with the brigade at Suffolk, I can tell you little of its performances there. I was more pleasantly engaged hunting for rations and forage in the section of North Carolina lying near the coast between the Pasquatank and Chowan rivers, where the only obstacle to rapturous enjoyment of life was the invariable monotonous diet of salted shad. Intensely Southern in sentiment, and within the Yankee lines quite long enough to delight in the sight of a Confederate soldier, the people were lavish in their hospitality to us, and the young ladies everything that was kind and charming. But, while at first almost captivated, the exclusive fish diet demanded such watchfulness and operated so adversely against any indulgence of a naturally æsthetic temperament, that I insensibly acquired the habit of looking more carefully for bones than for aught else. Indeed, toward the last I not only began to feel fishy, but imagined that my entertainers regarded me with fishy stares. These, however, may have been caused by my strict and undeviating adherence to the soldierly principle of eating everything in sight—a course in which, by the way, I was ably seconded, if not outdone, by my comrades for the time being, Captains Jimmie Littlefield, Jimmie Rust and Walter Norwood, each of whom, and especially the last named, is a trencherman of unsurpassed capacity, spirit and persistence.   *   *   *

Where we are going now is a question concerning which a private soldier can only surmise. Camp rumor saith that the time has come to offer the Marylanders another chance to flock to the Confederate standard, but of the truth of the report or even of the probability of a movement at all, I must absolutely refuse to vouch. While protesting vigorously against the inaction which denies me access to the Federal commissary department, I have long ago gratified my once inordinate thirst for gore and glory. Sometimes I feel inclined to echo the desire expressed by Jackson's man, who, reprimanded by his General for running out of the fight " like a baby," broke into a big boohoo and exclaimed between sobs: " I don't care what you say, sir, but I wish I was a baby, and a gal baby at that! " Not for the world would I cast the faintest shadow of a slur upon the manly characters of my comrades here in the Army of Northern Virginia, but we are all human beings, and I honestly believe there is a whole lot of the bravest and most gallant of them

W. N. NORWOOD
Captain and A. Q. M., Fifth Texas Regiment

who would at times be glad of a chance to return
to babyhood, even at the risk of a change of sex.
With their easy access to Europe, the plagued
Yankees have such an ability and habit of outnumbering us, that we are not prompt to join in
any severe censure of the Fifth Texas Irishman,
who, sent out on the skirmish line, came back on
a treble quick, and when told by his lieutenant,
" I'd rather die, Mike, than run out of a fight in
such a cowardly manner," fixed upon the officer
a witheringly sarcastic look and replied, " The
hail you would, Leftenent—the hail you would,
sor, whin there was only a skimmish line of us
boys, an' two rigiments and a batthery of thim ! "

Still, their numbers furnish a certain class of
our soldiers with grand opportunities for killing.
Charley Hume, of the Fifth, tells an amusing
story about a member of that regiment, whose
name he will not mention, but whom I shall call
Dick.   Dick is something of a braggart and is
wonderfully assisted at times by a vivid imagination.   On the day after the Yankees recrossed
the Rappahannock at Fredericksburg, Hume
found him snugly and safely ensconced behind a
huge rock on the south side of the river, apparently busy in death-dealing warfare.   " What
are you doing here, Dick? " inquired Hume.
" Doing? " repeated Dick, as if surprised at being asked so foolish a question, " what am I doing? Well, sir, I'm killing Yankees, if you must
know.   Don't you see those fellows over yonder
on the side of that hill?   I've just set here by my
lone self and killed every son of a gun of 'em."

Hume looked, and, sure enough, there on the hillside, half a mile away, were twenty or more bodies dressed in blue, lying silent and still. But while he was wondering at such wholesale destruction of human life and framing a suitable compliment to the fell destroyer at his side, first one and then another of the presumed dead rose to his feet, and, picking up gun and accouterments, sauntered carelessly up the hill without once glancing behind to indicate that he was aware of having been shot at. Hume's wonder and admiration evaporated instanter, but when he turned to apprise his companion of the fact and suggest that the corpses were a little too lively to be those of dead men, Dick was out of sight and hearing.

To make honors easy between me and Dick, I must relate a joke that I can now laugh at, but for obvious reasons, personal to myself, have carefully concealed from my comrades. While moving from Winchester to Fredericksburg last fall, I straggled one morning, and about nine o'clock knocked at the front door of a handsome residence on the Orange Plank road. It was opened by a hospitable old lady whose first inquiry was whether I had been to breakfast. Conscience prompted an affirmative and truthful answer, but appetite overruled it, and I replied in the negative, and for reward was ushered into a spacious dining-room and delivered over to the tender mercies of two young ladies, while my hostess gave necessary orders to the cook. One of these girls was a Texan, and both were so entertaining and witty that I was at once put fairly on my mettle, joining forces with the fair Texan in defense of our State against the jocular but vigorous attacks of the equally fair Virginian. After a long, lingering breakfast of fried chicken, hot biscuit, fresh butter, and potato coffee, we adjourned to the sitting-room, where two old gentlemen—the host and a visitor—were keeping themselves warm before a bright wood fire. Texas being still the subject of conversation, the right of the Southern States to secede was incidentally adverted to, and, strengthened wonderfully by the breakfast, encouraged by the presence and bright smiles of my Texas compatriot, and foolishly presuming upon the ignorance of the gentlemen, I boldly asserted that Texas had a right to secede superior to that of any other State.

"Ahem!" said the host, straightening himself up in his chair and looking at me with the air of a man ready for an argument. "Upon what fact, sir, do you base that claim?" Surprised by the prompt challenge and disconcerted by the intelligent look of my interrogator, I forgot the reason generally advanced—that Texas was an independent republic when she entered the Union—and answered, "Upon the well-known fact, sir, that when Texas became a State of the Union she expressly reserved the right to secede whenever she chose." I spoke so confidently that the Texas girl gave me an admiring look and an encouraging smile. But, to my dismay, my antagonist returned to the charge. "Ahem!

ahem!" said he. "Really, sir, I fail to recall any such reservation, although I was a member of Congress from the time annexation was first proposed until it was consummated." And then, as if determined to rout me "horse, foot and dragoon," he turned to the other old fellow, saying, "You were my colleague in Congress, Judge; do you recollect any such reservation?" "No, sir, I do not," replied the Judge emphatically. "I recall nothing of the kind. Our young friend is certainly mistaken, for I distinctly remember——" But I was too utterly vanquished to care to listen to reminiscences, especially when the Virginia girl seemed to take keen delight in my discomfiture, and the Texas maid to have lost faith in me; so, seizing my hat and bidding the party a rather hasty and awkward adieu, I made my exit, vowing to myself never again to take part in a political discussion without first learning how many of the persons present had been members of Congress.

XII

NEAR FREDERICKSBURG, July 30, 1863.
"GRIM - VISAG'D war hath smoothed her wrinkled front" temporarily, and I am sitting in a chair and writing on a table to-day, Charming Nellie, under the grateful shade of a wide-spreading maple and amid surroundings so pleasantly peaceful that the scenes recently witnessed, the adventures experienced, and the hardships, privations, and dangers undergone, seem like

"Dreams which, beneath the hovering shades of night,
Sport with the ever restless minds of men."

But alas! the present can only be an interlude between the acts of this terribly real and bloody tragedy of war. Another day may never come to me, and, to make the most of this, I devote a part of it to your entertainment. Don't imagine that because I am so happily situated I am not on duty; for I am. Ostensibly, I am protecting the premises of an F. F. V.—a gentleman of the old school, the paternal ancestor of a pretty and vivacious daughter, and the host of a prettier and more vivacious friend of the daughter. Under the humanizing influence of the fragrant roses that bloom in the yard and those animate flowers who, flitting from room to room and from piazza to porch of the house, come within range of my greedy eyes whenever I raise them from the table, my warlike spirit has been tamed into the peacefulness and timidity of "Mary's little lamb," and, were it not for the conflict between obligations that distresses my tender conscience, would be as sportive.

The trouble is this: In exchange for three substantial daily meals, and the blessed privilege of flirting *ad libitum* with the young ladies and sleeping at night in the front yard, I am expected to protect my host's roasting-ears, watermelons, pumpkins, apples, and the like from the depredations of my comrades, encamped three miles away in the direction of Fredericksburg. At the same time, my duty to these comrades is to afford them every possible opportunity to follow the advice of Jim Sanders of the Fifth. Catching sight of a terrapin one day, he captured it, saying, "A man orter vairegate his eatin' every chance he gits." Considering that Jim has been a man of mark ever since he awarded to the Enfield rifle the palm of superiority over the Mississippi Yager, on the sensible ground that the "chronic" ball carried by the former was much more destructive than the round ball of the latter, the Texans are not to be censured for following his wise counsels. This granted, I do not feel called upon to be an obstacle to "vairegation" as long as I can keep myself out of the sight and hearing of the boys.   *   *   *

Crossing the Potomac on a pontoon bridge, at noon we halted in the outskirts of the town of

Williamsport, Md., and, *mirabile dictu,* drew
rations of whisky. There was only about a gill
to the man, but as the temperance fellows gave
their shares to friends, the quantity available
was amply sufficient to put fully half the brigade
not only in a boisterously good humor, but in
such physical condition that the breadth of the
road over which they marched that evening was
more of an obstacle to rapid progress than its
length. At an early hour John Brantley, of
my company, became so exhausted by his lati-
tudinarian tendencies as to prefer riding to walking, and perceiving that Colonel Key was in an
excellently good-natured condition, took advantage of a momentary halt to approach that gallant officer, and, slapping him familiarly on the
leg, remark, " Say, Kunnel! I'm jes' plum' broke
down; can't you walk some an' lemme ride a
while? " Bending forward over his horse's neck
and grasping the pommel of his saddle with both
hands to steady himself, the old Colonel looked
pityingly down at Brantley and, between hiccoughs, replied, " I'd do it in a minute, ole feller,
d——d if I wouldn't, but I'm tired as h—— myself, ah-sittin' up here an' ah-hol'in' on."

Just after crossing the boundary line into
Pennsylvania, I went to a farmhouse in sight of
the road and inquired if the owner had any
bacon for sale. Answered in the affirmative, I
asked the price, and was told " fifteen cents a
pound." Reflecting that in Virginia the price
was two dollars a pound, and bacon almost impossible to buy at that, I determined to lay in

a good supply. So selecting from his well-filled smoke-house two sides which weighed exactly eighty pounds and were streaked with lean and fat in exactly the right proportion to be exceedingly toothsome, I tied them together with a piece of old rope, and, throwing them across the loins of my horse, handed the farmer a twenty-dollar Confederate bill. "Oh!" said he, as he took it gingerly between thumb and forefinger, and eyed it as if suspicious it were unclean, "I can't pass this kind of money here in Pennsylvania." "Yes, indeed you can, my dear sir," said I, speaking with the fervor of absolute conviction. "Can't you see from the army passing by that we intend to take possession of this little neck of the woods? You will need our money to pay taxes and for many other purposes, and you had better begin to get hold of it." "But I can't change this bill, for I haven't got any of the same kind," he whined. "Oh! that's a small matter," said I; "just give me greenbacks—I ain't afraid of them." "I'll see what I can do," he answered, after a moment's hesitation, and walked into the house. In less than a minute I heard the shrill voice of an angry woman scolding vigorously, and, guessing that the farmer was encountering opposition that might interfere with the trade, deemed it prudent to mount my steed and be prepared for emergencies. I had scarcely settled myself in the saddle when the farmer appeared, and, extending the bill toward me, said, "Here, Mister, give me back that ar bacon and take your money—I can't

make the change, for I ain't got eight dollars
in the house." Fully equal to the imperative
demands of the occasion, and, assuming the most
lordly Southern air of which I was capable, I
said, "Then just keep the change, sir," touched
my weather-beaten hat with the politeness of a
Chesterfield, and, giving free rein to my horse,
soon overtook a wagon and unloaded my prize
into it.

There are men in the Fourth Texas endowed
with as keen a scent for food as any animal,
and Dick Skinner, of Company F, is one of them.
Excepting the driver, whom I swore to absolute
secrecy, not a soul saw me put that bacon into
the wagon, and yet, within twenty minutes after
we went into camp near Greencastle, Dick approached me with as bland a smile as he wears
when asking a comrade to hold his gun while
he takes a drink of water, and said, "See here,
Joe, I hain't had a bite to eat for three days, and
I'm gettin' too weak to serve my country. Can't
you lend me about ten pounds of that bacon you
got this evening? I'll make it even with you
within the week." Devoting one minute to wondering how in the world Dick had learned of my
purchase, I gave another to rapid reflection.
While the fellow lied like a trooper about his
starving condition, he was obviously too hungry
to be a good Christian and obey all of God's ten
commandments, and especially those against
covetousness and stealing; therefore, solely out
of regard for his moral welfare, I placed temp-
tation out of his reach by lending him the bacon.

But, although I adjured him with tears in my eyes not to think of making things even until he could buy as I had, I am satisfied that when, two or three days later, he settled the account by sending me a couple of fat chickens, somebody's henroost had been robbed.

*   *   *   *   *

Horses were needed to move the artillery, and, to obtain them, the non-combatants of the Q. M. Department were ordered to scout through the country and pick up as many as possible. Always ready to serve our country in its time of need, we set out as blithely as schoolboys on a frolic, our cheerfulness wonderfully increased by timely information that we would not be expected to penetrate the mountain fastnesses where guerrillas were supposed to be lying in wait for the unwary, but, on the contrary, were to confine our researches to the open country between Longstreet's corps and Ewell's, then far up the Susquehanna toward Harrisburg. Shortly after noon of the first day's scout we caught sight of two colts feeding on a hill a mile to the right of the road. Knowing their dams must be near them, we cut across the country, and, tied to a hedge, found two splendid young mares. I took the bay, while Captain Cussons (or Cozzens), of General Law's staff, who had joined our party, took the sorrel. The poor animals kept up such a constant and increasing racket over the separation from their offspring that when night came, and we encamped in a grove some distance away from any road, an expert at milking was in demand. Far away from the protection of friendly infantry, in an enemy's country and armed only with pistols, we felt unpleasantly lonesome, insecure, and forlorn. It was recklessly imprudent, therefore, to run the risk of having our presence betrayed to passing foes, as it might be, unless the uneasiness of our captives was speedily allayed. Having graduated in the art of milking when a boy, I lost no time in practicing it on the animal chosen by me. Captain Cussons, however, had more difficulty. It was his first essay as a milkmaid, and, although under my laughing tuition he finally succeeded, it was at the cost of infinite travail and labor, and he carried away in his eyes and mouth, and on his face, long flowing beard, and new uniform far more milk than fell upon the ground.

An old Dunkard gave us such an early breakfast next morning that when at noon we halted before a large and elegant mansion, surrounded by beautiful grounds, we were as hungry as bears. It fell to my lot to ask for entertainment, and, dismounting, I rapped gently at the front door. Waiting a reasonable time and hearing no sound from within, I rapped again a little more vigorously than before, and, after another interval of absolute quiet, a third time. Then a well-preserved lady of fifty opened the door, and, her face as white as a sheet, looked silently at me. Raising my hat in acknowledgment of her presence, I stated my errand. Not a word fell from her lips until she had looked at me from head to

foot, and glanced in the direction of my companions, then she said, in a tremulous voice, " You
are Rebels, are you not? " " That is what you
call us, Madam, I suppose, but we call ourselves
Confederates," I explained. " Orders have been
published," said she, " prohibiting citizens from
giving any aid or comfort to the Confederates."
" I shall regret very much, Madam," I rejoined,
" to have the orders obeyed in our particular
case, for in that event we will have to ask elsewhere for food, and we are quite hungry, I assure
you." " That alters the case," she replied
quickly, smiling for the first time. " The Bible
commands us to feed the hungry, and it is of
higher authority than the orders of man. Ask
your friends in—I will give you dinner." The
smile and the spirit of genuine Christian hospitality which spoke in the lady's sweet voice and
shone in her still bright eyes captivated me, and
I suggested carrying my party around the house
to the back door, rather than have them tramp
through the spotlessly clean hall. She smiled
again, gratefully this time, saying, " Thank you,
sir. You have been trained by a careful mother,
I see. It will please me very much to have your
friends conducted directly to the back porch—
they will find water, towels, and a comb and
brush there, should they need them."

To make a long story short, within half an
hour eight Confederates sat around a long table
in a spacious dining-room, eating huge slices of
light bread, cold ham, corned beef, and roast
mutton, interspersed liberally with sweet pick-

les, jam, jelly, and apple butter, drinking genuine coffee and the richest of milk, and, between sups and bites, chatting as merrily with our hostess, her three handsome daughters, and an old gentleman whom the girls called "Uncle John," as if they were acquaintances of long and intimate standing. Stray whithersoever he might in the delightful fields of literature, prose, poetry, the arts, and the drama, the disputatious, critical, and sarcastic Captain Joe Wade, of the Fourth Texas, found his match in the well-informed, bright-minded elder sister; for every one of our many crude essays at wit or humor, Captain Walter Norwood, of the Fifth, and your humble servant, the writer, received an ample *quid pro quo* from the next in age of the girls, and Captain Mills, of the First—a Chevalier Bayard *sans peur et sans reproche,* although quite an old bachelor—and the others of the visitors, found ample entertainment in lively, laughing converse with our hostess, her youngest daughter, and "Uncle John."

We sat there fully three hours; then Captain Mills suggested departure, and, calling me to one side, quietly dropped a treasured five-dollar gold piece into my hand, saying in a low voice, "Here, Joe, pay for our dinner with this. They have been too kind to us to be offered Confederate money." Turning to the hostess, I offered the coin and asked if it would satisfy her for her trouble. "Yes, sir, it would, were I willing to accept pay," said she, drawing back rather indignantly. "But I am not. We have heard horrible stories of the treatment we might expect from Confederates, but if all are gentlemen like yourselves, I will make them as welcome to my house and table as you have been. Won't you stay longer? It is early yet." The invitation declined, each of us expressed our thanks for her hospitality and took leave. It was my youthful appearance, I reckon, that gained me the compliment, but when I said good-by, she clasped my hand warmly, and, looking at me with eyes that reminded me of my own good mother in faraway Texas, said, " Good-by, my dear boy, and remember if you get sick or are wounded, and will only let us know where you are, you shall be brought here and nursed until you are well again."   *   *   *

Rejoining the brigade late that night at its camp near Chambersburg, and being very tired, I laid down near the wagons and went to sleep. Awakened next morning by Collins's bugle, and walking over to the camp, I witnessed not only an unexpected but a wonderful and marvelous sight.   Every square foot of half an acre of ground not occupied by a sleeping or standing soldier was covered with choice food for the hungry. Chickens, turkeys, ducks, and geese squawked, gobbled, quacked, cackled, and hissed in inharmonious unison as deft and energetic hands seized them for slaughter, and scarcely waiting for them to die, sent their feathers flying in all directions; and scattered around in bewildering confusion and gratifying profusion appeared immense loaves of bread and chunks of corned beef,

hams, and sides of bacon, cheeses, crocks of apple-butter, jelly, jam, pickles, and preserves, bowls of yellow butter, demijohns of buttermilk, and other eatables too numerous to mention. The sleepers were the foragers of the night, resting from their arduous labors—the standing men, their messmates who remained as camp-guards and were now up to their eyes in noise, feathers, and grub. Jack Sutherland's head pillowed itself on a loaf of bread, and one arm was wound caressingly half around a juicy-looking ham. Bob Murray, fearful that his captives would take to their wings or be purloined, had wound the string, which bound half a dozen frying chickens, around his right big toe; one of Brahan's widespread legs was embraced by two overlapping crocks of apple butter and jam, while a tough old gander, gray with age, squawked complainingly at his head without in the least disturbing his slumber; Dick Skinner lay flat on his back—with his right hand holding to the legs of three fat chickens and a duck, and his left, to those of a large turkey—fast asleep and snoring in a rasping bass voice that chimed in well with the music of the fowls.   *   *   *
The scene is utterly indescribable, and I shall make no further attempt to picture it. The hours were devoted exclusively to gormandizing until, at 3 P. M., marching orders came, and, leaving more provisions than they carried, the Texans moved lazily and plethorically into line—their destination, Gettysburg.

XIII

GETTYSBURG

(Letter of July 30, 1863, Continued)

HERETOFORE, Charming Nellie, it has been my privilege and delight to boast of victory—acknowledged and glorious victory. I know the Northern people claim that Lee's army met defeat at Sharpsburg—Antietam, they call it—but the calm, unbiased judgment of the future will never sanction the claim. Considering that the Federal army outnumbered ours fully two to one, that Lee held his ground against all assaults, that he stood ready to receive an attack for one whole day, and then retired slowly, deliberately, without molestation and without additional loss, certainly only the partisan swayed and blinded by prejudice, passion, and pride can refuse to him the laurels of the victor. An army knows when it is whipped, and when, after a hard-fought battle, brave men still wear confident smiles and cheer their general as he passes —as Lee's army did him the day after its return to Virginia soil—it is because they know they have won the fight. But, alas! Sharpsburg furnishes but little of compensation for Gettysburg, for here defeat—bloody, terrible, and disastrous defeat—stared us in the face at the beginning of the conflict, and swept down on us, an overwhelming pall of gloom, at its ending. At Sharpsburg McClellan attacked, and Lee held his ground; at Gettysburg, Lee made the assault, and Meade, the successor of McClellan, held his ground. At the one place the Federals met withering, deadly repulse—at the other, the Confederates.

While at Gettysburg the Confederates fought heroically; while Pickett's charge on Cemetery Heights has never been equaled in vigor, dash, and reckless daring; while every division, brigade, and regiment of the Southern army did its duty nobly and well, the odds, both in numbers and position, were against us—the God of War hostile, and inevitable, crushing defeat fell to our lot. Nor did it come at Gettysburg only, for on the same day Pemberton surrendered, Vicksburg fell—the news of that companion disaster reaching us almost simultaneously with the knowledge of our own misfortune.

That a mistake was made at Gettysburg is admitted by all; who made it it is now too late to inquire. The cavalry out of place and reach, General Lee lacked the exact information requisite to successful generalship. Fighting where we did—assaulting heights defended by superior numbers and difficult to scale even by unarmed and unopposed men—it seems now impossible to have won. Had we moved to the right across the Emmitsburg road, and, selecting our position, awaited the attack Meade would have been compelled to make, the result might have been different, the Confederates now singing the songs of victory instead of doing their best to keep out of the slough of despond.

Why we did not move to the right, General Lee only knows, and defeat—novel and humiliating as it is—has not shaken our confidence in him and his subordinate commanders. The rank and file of the army did its whole duty and absolutely refuses to admit that, either through carelessness or intention, its generals did less. We are not such hero-worshipers as to believe even Lee infallible, especially when we remember his noble and magnanimous words, " It is all my fault, men, it is all my fault." Self-respect would have prohibited that admission had it been wholly untrue.

Butler says in Hudibras:

> "In all the trade of war, no feat
> Is nobler than a brave retreat."

That is biting, subtle irony in the connection in which it appears, but might be written seriously and truly of the retreat from Gettysburg —of the endurance of the Confederate army, the brave front ever turned upon the pursuing enemy, and the generalship of Lee. Beaten and crushed, decimated by death and wounds, gaunted by hunger and footsore with marching as was that army, Meade, although elated by victory, dared neither to follow it closely nor attack it when, like a lion in his path, it stood at bay; and at Hagerstown it lay in defiant but restful security long enough to build pontoon bridges, send across them its immense train of wagons, and follow at its leisure. Let the Yankees boast as much as they please over this their first success. We have met repulse, but, God willing, will yet win freedom, independence, and separate nationality. Given a fair field, our disaster will be retrieved, and the Yankee nation taught that "one swallow does not make a summer."

I can tell you little of the battle of Gettysburg, for, luckily or unluckily—just as one chooses to regard it—I was not a participant. In the attack, on July 2, on Little Round Top the brigade was exposed to a terrific fire of shot, shell, and canister, and lost many of its best men.

Among the many daring acts of which the boys speak in warm admiration is that of George Branard, color bearer of the First Texas, who bore his flag so far and gallantly to the front that the Yankees, in recognition of his bravery, shouted to each other, "Don't shoot that color bearer—he is too brave!" It appears that in the unavoidable confusion incident to an attack by several brigades upon a common point, the colors of several Georgia regiments and those of the First Texas came so near together behind a natural breastwork of rocks that they not only drew the concentrated fire of the enemy, but made it difficult to determine which flag was farthest in advance. To settle the question beyond dispute, Branard called upon his color guard to follow him, and, mounting the rocks,

dashed forward toward the Yankee lines. It was
here the Federal infantry sought to spare him;
their artillery, however, could not be so magnanimous, and the bursting of a shell carried
away all but the lower part of the flagstaff, and
laid Branard unconscious upon the ground. At
first it was thought he was killed, but that was
a mistake. He revived in a few minutes, and, if
his friends had let him, would have attempted
to whip the whole Yankee nation by himself—he
was so mad.   *   *   *

It is only of the lights and lesser shadows of
this cruel war I care to write; its horrors I
avoid, as well because, soldier-like, I try to forget them, as because it is unkind to shock your
womanly sensibilities with things so revolting
and gruesome. But, fortunately, there are few
amusing incidents to record of the battle, and
to delay saying, " Farewell! Othello's occupa-
tion's gone," and closing this already lengthy
epistle before the boys from camp have had time
to make their daily raid on the corn patch, I
must perforce descend to egotism; so *" revenons
à nos moutons"*—which means, translated under stress of the present emergency, let us return
to our wagons.

After night descended on the 4th day of July
and concealed our movements from the enemy,
they were loaded with those of the wounded who
could stand rough transportation, and ordered
across the Potomac. It rained heavily all night
long, and right gladly would I have crawled beneath the sheets of a wagon and found protection

J. C. MURRAY
Private, Company F, Fourth Texas Regiment

from the storm. But my steed refused to lead and I was forced to take the rain and be content with such cat-naps as occasional halts permitted. Just before daylight I called at a house by the roadside, and, although the sour and forbidding countenance of the proprietor indicated no anxiety to cultivate amicable relations, persuaded him to fortify my inner man with two cups of coffee and a proportional share of bread and butter.

Daylight brought with it the dread fear of pursuit, and the teams were pushed rapidly on. But, on arriving at Williamsport, what was our surprise and consternation to find the Potomac conspiring with the enemy, and so swollen as to be impassable in the absence of pontoons! To add to the Iliad of our woes, the Yankee cavalry came swooping down on us at noon, and the dire and deplorable misfortunes of capture and captivity stared us broadly and unwinkingly in the face. Still, just as a mouse will fight when cornered, so will commissaries, quartermasters, and their immediate subordinates, and the small cavalry force escorting the train was at once reinforced by a body of men who, however non-combatant ordinarily, on this occasion faced danger gallantly and—although sadly out of practice—used the few weapons to be had with a deadly skill that soon put the foe to flight.

Fortunately, too, just when the Yankees were fairly on the run, General Imboden came creeping up with a brigade of Confederate cav-

alry, and, without a blow to win them, coolly
appropriated all the honors of the engagement.
I am glad he was so generous and considerate;
the last thing the gentlemen officiating in various
capacities in the quartermaster and commissary
departments desire is a reputation for courage;
that fastened upon them, they might have more
fighting to do.

While endeavoring to keep out of the reach of
death-dealing missiles at Gettysburg, and at the
same time watch the progress of the battle, I
took advantage of a lull in the firing to ride down
the main street of the little town. Discovering
a lot of shoes—cloth gaiters such as ladies wear
—scattered in confusion over the muddy floor of
a cellar and, without apparent ownership, I selected a pair of No. 3's and brought them away
with me. Really, I had as little idea what I
wanted them for as the soldier had with respect
to the grindstone he stole. However, I soon
learned there was a demand for just such articles.

On my way to Staunton with the wounded
I espied three persons—a mother, father, and
daughter—standing in the doorway of a residence close to the highway, whose surroundings
and air of elegance pronounced it the abode of
wealthy and refined people. An uncontrollable
desire to smoke immediately assailed me, and,
dismounting at the gate, I filled my pipe, and,
approaching the party, requested a light. While
a little darky was bringing a coal of fire, the
ladies and I fell into conversation.

While thus pleasantly engaged, an ambulance, to the roof of which were tied a half dozen sets of hoops, such as you ladies use, came within view. Catching sight of them, the two ladies left me in the lurch, and, accosting the driver of the vehicle, insisted that he should sell them at least one set. But, although they offered an extravagant price, and to pay in gold, silver, Confederate money, or greenbacks, the driver remained faithful to his trust—the articles belonging, he said, to Dr. ———, who was sending them to lady relatives near Staunton. Tears, prayers, and entreaties were alike wasted upon his obdurate heart, and the would-be purchasers returned empty-handed, angry, and the younger actually in tears. "The mean old thing!" began the old lady, and was proceeding to give vent to her wrath and " Hail Columbia " to the driver, when her daughter reminded her by a glance that a stranger was present. Then she explained that hoops had been absolutely unobtainable since the war began, and would have furnished me a long list of facts concerning the deprivations her sex was subjected to, had I not fortunately remembered and mentioned the pair of shoes then in my knapsack and on the way up the Valley. Thus far, I had been merely a private soldier—entitled as such to kindness, but not to any special consideration—but the possession of a pair of shoes, number threes, lifted me at once out of the vale of obscurity and made me a personage of high and mighty consequence; the young

lady just must have them—they were her exact
number, and a man like me had no use in the
world for them. What could I do, Charming
Nellie? My right to the shoes questionable, conscience forbade their sale, while economy prohibited an absolute giving away. The gentle zephyrs
which floated through the wide hall wafted to
my keen-scented olfactory nerves the delightfully
appetizing and tempting odors of a frying
chicken; the red lips of the fair pleader seemed
not less inviting and tantalizing; a piano, visible through the open windows of an elegantly
furnished parlor, promised music. All things
considered, the quickly formed wish to strengthen
my corporeal system by a square meal, gratify
my taste for sweets by a kiss, and please my
ears with dulcet strains of melody, were not, I
hope, a boldness and impudence for which a poor
soldier all the way from Texas should be censured.

But, whatever it was, I got a good dinner, enjoyed the most deliciously entrancing
music, but, too diffident to suggest osculatory
exercise in the presence of the old folks, com-
promised on permission to lace the gaiters on
the lady's feet. "Why, that's nothing, Mollie,"
said the sensible mother, when her daughter,
startled by the proposal, would have refused.
"You never object to clerks tying your shoes,
do you?" Under such willing maternal sanction, a fair and positive bargain was made; and
I reckon would have been consummated and the
lovely maiden now be wearing the gaiters, had

the old lady been at home when I returned from Staunton, instead of three angular and squeamish aunts—all old maids. As it was and is, I have the shoes yet, and, for all I know, the young lady is going barefooted.

Note 6—Even when assured, as was claimed after the battle of Gettysburg, that "the backbone of the Rebellion had been broken," Gen. Meade, who continued in command of the Federal Army until succeeded by Grant, did not deem it prudent to again offer battle to Lee during the year 1863. Though he followed Lee into Virginia, it was at a respectful distance, and the march of Longstreet's corps south was leisurely. The Texas Brigade rested from the march for a week or more at Raccoon Ford on the Rapidan, and thence proceeding toward Fredericksburg, arrived in the vicinity of that city about the 25th of July, remaining in camp there until about the last of August, when it moved down to Port Royal, some twenty miles below, on the Rappahannock. Thence, with McLaws' division and under command of Longstreet, it went to the aid of Bragg's army, joining that army in time to participate in the two days' battle of Chickamauga.

XIV

CHATTANOOGA, TENN., October 1, 1863.

I WROTE to you last from Fredericksburg, Va.
Then I sat in a chair by the side of a table and
under the shade of a maple—sore and downcast
over disastrous defeat, but doing my best to
"keep a stiff upper lip," and make light of it;
now, elated by a glorious victory, I sit in the
shadow of Lookout Mountain, with my back
against a tent post, writing on a wide board
held on my lap.   *   *   *

With the details of the long and tiresome journey in boxcars from Virginia, I will not weary
your patient soul—remarking, however, by way
of parenthesis, that somewhere on the route I
not only lost my knapsack, but also the pair of
No. 3 cloth gaiters which, as I wrote you, I
refused to give to the young lady in the Shenandoah Valley. You may think it just retribu-
tion, but I impute the happening to the meanness
of the fellow who did the stealing.   *   *   *

The battle of Chickamauga was fought, as you
know, on the 19th and 20th days of last month.
The Texas Brigade got into position early on
the morning of the 19th, and, during the balance of that long and struggling day, the boom-
ing of artillery and the roar of small arms on

its right and left was incessant and terrific. Judging alone from the noise, it appeared to us that every man of both armies must soon be wounded or killed, and we wondered much why the sound of the firing seemed neither to recede nor advance, and why there was none of the yelling to which we had been accustomed in Virginia. And when at last it was learned that the opposing lines were simply standing two or three hundred yards apart, firing at each other as fast as guns could be loaded and triggers pulled, comments were many and ludicrous —the consensus of opinion being that such a method of fighting would not suit troops which in Virginia were accustomed to charge the enemy at sight. One brave fellow said, and voiced the sentiment of all, " Boys, if we have to stand in a straight line as stationary targets for the Yankees to shoot at with a rest, this old Texas Brigade is going to run like h—ll! "

It is said that when Longstreet, on this second day, heard the shouts of his men as the Yankees were being driven back, suggested to Bragg that a general and simultaneous attack should be made all along the lines. " But I have no assurance that the enemy has begun to retreat," objected Bragg. " Well, I know he has," replied Longstreet, " for I hear my men yelling, and can tell from it that they are driving the enemy before them." But Bragg was skeptical and waited for actual reports from the front, and these came too late for a movement which would have forced Rosecrans beyond the Ten-

nessee River and given us possession of Chattanooga almost without a struggle. As it is, the
Lord only knows when, how, or whether we shall
ever capture it; for there is no rainbow of promise yet in the sky of war that points in the direction of that "devoutly to be wished" consum-
mation.   *   *   *

The part of the lines around Chattanooga occupied by us begins at a point half a mile from
the foot of Lookout Mountain; the picket line,
as first established, resting its right on Chattanooga Creek, and stretching across a wide bend
to that stream again. General Hood's loss of
a leg at Chickamauga has devolved the command
of our division upon Brigadier-General Jenkins,
whose brigade of South Carolinians joined us at
Chickamauga. This brigade is composed of a
magnificent body of men whose brand-new Confederate uniforms easily distinguish them from
the members of other commands.

I was lucky enough to be on picket duty a few
nights ago with my friends Will Burges and
John West, of Companies D and E of the Fourth,
each of whom is not only a good soldier, but a
most entertaining companion. As the night advanced, it became cold enough to make a fire
very acceptable, and, appropriating a whole one
to ourselves, we had wandered from a discussion of the war and of this particular campaign
that was little flattering to General Bragg, into
pleasant reminiscences of our homes and loved
ones, when someone on horseback said, "Good-
evening, gentlemen." Looking hastily up, we

discovered that the intruder was General Jenkins, alone and unattended by either aide or orderly, and were about to rise and salute in approved military style, when, with a smile plainly perceptible in the bright moonlight, he said, "No, don't trouble yourselves," and, letting the reins drop on his horse's neck, threw one leg around the pommel of his saddle and entered into conversation with us.

Had you been listening for the next half hour or so, Charming Nellie, you would never have been able to guess which of us was the General, for, ignoring his rank as completely as we careless Texans forgot it, he became at once as private a soldier as either of us, and talked and laughed as merrily and unconcernedly as if it were not war times. I offered him the use of my pipe and smoking-tobacco, Burges was equally generous with the plug he kept for chewing, and West was even polite enough to regret that the whisky he was in the habit of carrying as a preventive against snake bites was just out; in short, we were beginning to believe General Jenkins of South Carolina the only real general in the Confederate service, when, to our surprise and dismay, he straightened himself up on his saddle, and, climbing from "gay to grave, from lively to severe," announced that at midnight the picket line would be expected to advance and drive the Yankees to the other side of the creek. We might easily have forgiven him for being the bearer of this discomforting intelligence had that been the sum total of his offending; but it was not; he rode away without expressing the least pleasure at having made our acquaintance, or even offering to shake hands with us—the necessary and inevitable consequence of such discourtesy being that he descended at once in our estimation to the level of any other general. But midnight was too near at hand to waste time in nursing indignation. Instant action was imperative, and, resolving ourselves into a council of war with plenary powers, it was unanimously decided by the three privates there assembled that our recent guest was an upstart wholly undeserving of confidence; that the contemplated movement was not only foolish and impracticable, but bound to be dangerous; and that, if a single shot were fired at us by the enemy, we three would just lie down and let General Jenkins of South Carolina do his own advancing and driving. Being veterans, we knew far better than he how easy it was at night for opposing lines to intermingle with each other and men to mistake friends for enemies, and we did not propose to sanction the taking of such chances.

All too soon the dreaded and fateful hour arrived; all too soon the whispered order "Forward" was passed from man to man down the long line, and, like spectral forms in the ghastly moonlight, the Confederate pickets moved slowly out into the open field in their front, every moment expecting to see the flash of a gun and hear or feel its messenger of death, and all awed by the fear the bravest men feel when confronting unknown danger. Not ten minutes before, the shadowy forms of the enemy had been seen by our videttes, and if the line of the creek was worth capturing by us, it surely was worth holding by the Yankees. But all was silent and still; no sight of foe, no tread of stealthy footstep, no sharp click of gunlock—not even the rustling of a leaf or the snap of a twig came out of the darkness to relieve our suspense and quiet the expectant throbbing of our hearts. Under these circumstances, West, Burges, and your humble servant, like the brave and true men they are, held themselves erect and advanced side by side with their gallant comrades until the *terra incognita* and impenetrability of the narrow but timbered valley of the stream suggested ambush and the advisability of rifle-pits. Working at these with a will born of emergency, we managed to complete them just as the day dawned, and jumping into them with a sigh of inexpressible relief—our courage rising as the night fled— waited for hostilities to begin. But the Yankees had outwitted us, their withdrawal, by some strange coincidence, having been practically simultaneous with our advance—they taking just start enough, however, to keep well out of our sight and hearing. West remarked next morning, " It's better to be born lucky than rich," but whether he referred to our narrow escape, or to that of the Yankees, he refused to say. *   *   *   Soon afterward, a truce along the picket lines in front of the Texans was arranged; that is, there was to be no more shoot-

ing at each other's pickets—the little killing and
wounding done by the practice never compensat-
ing for the powder and shot expended, and the
discomfort of being always on the alert, night
and day.

But the South Carolinians, whose picket line
began at our left, their first rifle-pit being within
fifty feet of the last one of the First Texas, could
make no terms whatever. The Federals charge
them with being the instigators and beginners
of the war, and, as I am informed, always ex-
clude them from the benefit of truces between
the pickets. It is certainly an odd spectacle to
see the Carolinians hiding in their rifle-pits
and not daring to show their heads, while, not
fifty feet away, the Texans sit on the ground
playing poker, in plain view and within a hundred yards of the Yankees. Worse than all, the
palmetto fellows are not even permitted to visit
us in daylight, except in disguise—their new
uniforms of gray always betraying them wherever they go. One of them who is not only very
fond of, but successful at, the game of poker,
concluded the other day to risk being shot for
the chance of winning the money of the First
Texas, and, divesting himself of his coat, slipped
over to the Texas pit an hour before daylight,
and by sunrise was giving his whole mind to the
noble pastime.

An hour later a keen-sighted Yankee sang
out, " Say, you Texas Johnnies! ain't that
fellow playing cards, with his back to a sapling, one of them d——d South Carolina se-

cessionists? Seems to me his breeches are newer'n they ought to be." This direct appeal for information placed the Texans between the horns of a dilemma; hospitality demanded the protection of their guest—prudence, the observance of good faith toward the Yankees. The delay in answering obviated the necessity for it by confirming the inquirer's suspicions, and, exclaiming, "D——n him, I just know it is!" he raised his gun quickly to his shoulder and fired. The South Carolinian was too active, though; at the very first movement of the Yankee, he sprang ten feet and disappeared into a gulch that protected him from further assault.   *   *   *

Jack Smith, of Company D, is *sui generis*. A brave and gallant soldier, he is yet an inveterate straggler, and is, therefore, not always on hand when the battle is raging, but at Chickamauga he was, and, singularly enough, counted for two.

Another member of Company D is constitutionally opposed to offering his body for sacrifice on the altar of his country, and, when he cannot get on a detail which will keep him out of danger, is sure to fall alarmingly sick. Jack determined to put a stop to this shirking, so, early on the morning of the 19th, he took the fellow under his own protecting and stimulating care, and, attacking him in the most vulnerable point, to the surprise of everybody, carried him into and through the fight of that day. " Come right along with me, Fred, and don't be scared a particle," Jack was heard to say in his coaxing,

mellifluous voice as we began to advance on the
enemy, " for I'll shoot the head off the first man
who points a gun at you. You stick close to me,
fire at everything you see in front of you, and
I'll watch out for your carcass, and after we
have whipped the Yanks you an' me'll finish
them bitters in my haversack." " But I don't
like bitters," protested Fred in a trembling voice.
" I know that, ole feller, an' I don't generally
like 'em myself, but these are made on the old
nigger's plan—the least mite in the world of
cherry bark, still less of dogwood, and then fill
up the bottle with whisky."

Needless to say that after the battle was over
and Jack had brought his protégé safely through
its perils, quite a number of comrades looked
longingly at the bottle. In vain, however; Jack
was loyal to his promise, and he and Fred
were the merriest men in Company D that
night.

Discussing the subject on the picket post the
night General Jenkins interviewed us, and just
before he did, Burges insisted that the influence
which carried Fred into the engagement was a
spirit of patriotism newly awakened in his
bosom, and I gave the credit to Jack Smith's
personal magnetism. But when West insisted
it was the bitters, Burges and I instantly " acknowledged the corn," Burges saying, with a
wink at me,

" You ought to know, West, I reckon, better
than either of us—you carry the same kind of
bitters yourself, don't you? "

Then, not to be outdone in courtesy, West modestly " acknowledged the corn " himself, and thus gave us a chance to repeat our acknowledgments and hope he would never die while he continued as good a judge of liquor, and as liberal in sharing it with his comrades. That was the reason General Jenkins failed to secure an invitation to drink.

XV

CHATTANOOGA, TENN., October 23, 1863.

AMID the many "hair-breadth 'scapes i' the imminent deadly breach " that have fallen to my lot, one that occurred the other day was so amusing, and brought with it such a sense of triumph, that I must relate it. It will prove to you my right to echo the boast of Henry VI., that,

"Thus far our fortune keeps an upward course,
And we are grac'd with wreaths of victory."

When I read those lines to Bill Calhoun yesterday, he fell into improvisation, saying,

"Yes, 'twas a victory in the shape of a hog,
That you brought into camp, suspended from a log,
And was so big and so fat, so juicy and greasy,
As your conscience and stomach, both to make easy."

Appetite comes with eating, to the gourmand, but to the Texans in Bragg's army it comes with fasting. Blue beef and musty corn meal have not only become monotonous, but, as the boys say, "We have soured on 'em." Anyhow, Jim Somerville and I, while on picket together, decided it was a duty we owed ourselves and the Confederacy to "varigate our eatin'," and on the following day we went five miles to the rear, and engaged in a diligent search for quadrupeds of

the porcine persuasion.   Lacking acquaintances
among the citizens, as well as money or credit,
we proposed as a *dernier ressort* a secret impress-
ment, and to effect our purpose with due dispatch one carried a belduque and the other a
gun.   Luck favored us in the search, for about
the middle of the afternoon we found ourselves
in a secluded glade and in near proximity to a
couple of fair-sized and well-fed hogs.   Face to
face with the brutes, my conscience grew tender, and I suggested to my companion that we
should wait for them to begin hostilities—it was
my first experience in that kind of foraging, you
know.   But Somerville was built of sterner
stuff, and crying " Damfido," took careful aim
at the larger and fatter of the two porkers, and
pulled the trigger.

But, alas, for his hopes! How true it is that
" the best laid schemes of men and mice gang
aft agley."   The cap upon which so much depended failed in our time of greatest need, and,
to our chagrin and mortification, neither of us
could find another, look and feel as diligently
as we might in the recesses of our well-worn garments.   Truly it was an exasperating predicament for two hungry Texans to be standing
within twenty feet of the very game for which
they had hunted so long, minus the one thing
needful—a gun-cap.   Even the hogs laughed at
us—that is, if a constant turning up of dirty
noses and a succession of seemingly contemptuous grunts may be called laughing.   Notwithstanding the spasm of honesty which had

prompted me to suggest delay, I felt the disaster so keenly that I lost my temper and began reproaching Somerville for not coming better provided with ammunition; but, paying no heed to me and silent as a sphynx, he continued mechanically the search of his person. Suddenly a rapturous smile lighted up his homely features, and he exclaimed,

" By the great holy Moses, Joe, if I haven't found a cap way down in the corner of this old shirt-pocket, I'll be everlastin'ly derned!"

And so, indeed, he had, and in less than half a minute the body of the larger hog lay lifeless on the sward, and twenty minutes later its carcass, skinned except as to head and feet, was tied up in a linen tent-cloth, and, suspended from a pole, was on the way to camp.

Before setting out on the expedition we had agreed upon our respective qualifications and the part each of us was to perform. Somerville's natural and acquired hog-sense specially adapted him to command in all matters pertaining to search, capture, and transportation. On the other hand, my glibness of tongue and my acquaintance with the ways and habits of the enemy in the case—Captain Scott's provost guard—pointed to me as leader and spokesman in saving the bacon and its captors from confiscation, arrest, and court martial—the last being, now that we were under Bragg, a fate well worth dreading. So when at last the hog was lifted on to our shoulders, Somerville retired to a subordinate position, and I assumed the direction of affairs, and "dressed in a little brief authority," immediately proceeded to commit a grave and inexcusable blunder. Instead of boldly selecting a highway on which to travel, I let timidity govern, and chose a little-traveled route.

As a result, while all went well for a couple of miles, at the first open ground a dozen or more shining bayonets slowly sinking out of view behind a hill over which the road ran, gave warning of danger. As these indicated the presence of provost guards, no sooner did I catch sight of them than I ordered a halt, and, assisting Somerville to deposit our capture on a log, said to him, "What do you think we'd better do, old fellow?" But he was tired, and, having done his part of the directing, was unwilling to assume further responsibility, and between whiffs of his pipe only replied, "Damfiknow." A long silence followed this comforting announcement, and then I asked, "Do you reckon any of those infernal guards saw us?" Rising slowly to his feet, and with a far-away expression in his blue eyes, gazing at the sun just then gliding down behind Lookout Mountain, Somerville again replied, "Damfiknow."

Thus abandoned to my own resources, I decided to stay right there until the provost contingent got out of the way. But when, half an hour afterward, we resumed our journey, we did not cover a mile ere, rounding a point of timber, as unsuspectingly as "the babes in the woods," our little procession ran plump into a squad of the enemy. This wholly unlooked for encounter was terribly demoralizing, and at my wit's end for the moment, I cast an appealing glance across the hog at the stolid countenance of my partner in trouble, but all the reward I got came in a wink which said as plainly as words, " I told you so." Again thrown back upon my own resources, the emergency restored my composure. Recognizing the sergeant of the squad as a First Texas man I had once befriended, I gave him an admirable opportunity to reciprocate. He was not an ingrate, for, after inspecting the pass I handed him, and, although knowing it was a borrowed one, he announced his satisfaction and allowed us ·to proceed. Much relieved, we stepped out for camp at our liveliest lick, and for a while rapidly increased the distance between us and the leisurely moving guard.

Suddenly, though, the sergeant put life into his long legs, and overtaking us, pointed at the swinging carcass, and in a tone of mingled authority and apology said,

" See here, fellows—isn't that hog skinned? If it is, I'll have to take you in out of the wet, or those darned Georgians with me will report me for failing to do my duty."

" Can't you see it isn't skinned? " I asked, pointing to the exposed head and feet, and still relying a little on the sergeant's gratitude.

I was leaning on a broken staff, though. The Georgians had come within hearing, and the sergeant was not in the mind to exchange a soft

berth as a member of the provost guard for hard
service in the ranks of his company, and, with a
provoking smile and in a tone that convinced
me of the necessity of an instant change of
front, he replied,

"You can't work a game of that kind on me,
my friend, and you needn't try to. I have got
to make sure by an examination."

"Well," said I, "as I don't propose either to
lie or to have my pork flavored with dirty hands,
I'll acknowledge straight out that it is skinned.
It takes time to heat water, and we had none to
spare for any such foolishness, even though the
man we bought from offered to help us."

"I'll have to arrest you, then," said the sergeant. "My orders are to arrest every man we
catch toting skinned meat."

"All right," I replied with lofty unconcern,
"obey your orders, then; but, if you want to
reach quarters before midnight, you and your
fellows must do a little of the toting yourselves."

My first thought, when the climax of arrest
came, was to purchase relief by the surrender of
half the hog. But, while debating in my mind
how to broach the subject to the sergeant, I
heard one of his men smack his lips and say to
another, "Great Jiminy, Tom, but won't we fellers waller in good eatin' an' grease to-night!"
Action, look, and speech were so unctiously glut-
tonous and revolting that I resolved to carry my
prize to camp if lying and assurance could win.
Therefore, the moment we reached the provost
guard quarters, I requested Lieutenant Shot-

well, as good and brave a soldier as ever lived, not only to prohibit any interference with the hog, but to accompany me and Somerville at once to the quarters of General Jenkins, a hundred yards distant. The General sat before a fire in front of his tent, reading by the light of a lantern, and as we approached looked up with a pleasant smile. Stepping in front of Shotwell, and respectfully saluting the General, looking boldly and unflinchingly into his eyes—caring not that my hat was torn and slouched, my trousers greasy, and that my big toe protruded conspicuously from the right shoe—anxious, as never before in my life, to combine a respectful *suaviter in mode* with a convincing *fortiter in re*, I began my plea for liberty, saying,

"General, Mr. Somerville and I are members of Company F, of the Fourth Texas, and every officer of that regiment, from the colonel of it down to a corporal, will corroborate my assertion that we are soldiers who never shirk duty in camp, on the march, or in battle. Yet, sir, Lieutenant Shotwell holds us under arrest on the charge of depredating on the property of citizens, the evidence against us being that we have been found in the possession of a partly skinned hog. We come to you for release, sir. When a gentleman—and although we are but privates, each of us claims to be that—buys a hog and pays for it, he has a right to skin or scald it, whichever process he finds most convenient." At this juncture Colonel Harvey Sellers, the adjutant-general of the division, stepped from a tent and approached the fire, and, taking instant advantage of the circumstances, I continued, " Although not personally known to Colonel Sellers, sir, I am sure he knows my people and will testify to their standing, even if he cannot as to mine." Then, turning to that gentleman, I said, " Colonel, my name is Polley, and my father, an old Texan, used to live in Brazoria County, Texas."

" I knew him well," said the Colonel, extending his hand with the utmost cordiality. " And I am glad to make the personal acquaintance of a son of his, whose reputation I know to be that of a gallant and deserving soldier."

Blushing more at this flattering reception than at the bareface attempt in which the Colonel, soldier, gentleman, and Texan to the core, that he was, appeared willing to join, to " pull the wool " over the commanding officer's eyes, I presented such a touching and pathetic picture of modest merit and suffering innocence, that to put me at my ease the General hastened to say,

" I regret exceedingly, Mr. Polley, that you have been subjected to the indignity of an arrest for an offense of which I am satisfied you are innocent. But to refute the oft-repeated charge that Hood's division is depredating on the citizens, right and left, I shall request you and your companion to remain with Lieutenant Shotwell until morning, and then to go with him and show him the party from whom you purchased the hog."

For a second I was fairly cornered; then, gathering my wits together, I replied, "Another day in the country, General, would be very pleasant, but present acceptance of Lieutenant Shotwell's hospitality, sir, would not only compel us to sleep without blankets or discommode him, but would, also, under the peculiar circumstances of the case, affect the reputations of myself and Mr. Somerville as good soldiers. The Lieuetnant will excuse me, I know, for suggesting that a stay in his camp is not considered a distinction worth seeking for. Besides, sir, our comrades are hungry, pork is both scarce and high-priced, and that we have will, I am afraid, spoil unless cut up and salted to-night."

"Oh, well," said the General, after a hearty laugh, "take the meat to camp at once, then, and save your bacon; but come back in the morning and save the good name of the division in the way I have suggested."

It is rarely that a soldier's conscientious scruples interfere with his enjoyment of the fruits of a comrade's enterprise. The advent of that hog marked an epoch in the annals of Company F, and was so timely that, while frying, broiling, boiling, and roasting it, the boys loosened their purse-strings, and in less than half an hour handed me a hundred dollars of Confederate money to be used in satisfying the owner, if he could be found. Next morning at daylight I laid the facts before Captain Kindred, then serving on the staff of "Aunt Pollie," which, you know, is our pet name for General Robertson.

The Captain went immediately to General Jenkins, and, after long wrestling and prayer, argued and persuaded him into a reasonably lenient frame of mind; that is, Somerville and I must find the owner of the hog, pay a fair price for it, and deliver the receipt to Lieutenant Shotwell. That suited us exactly, and, after a long and pleasant ramble, we found the right man and paid him twice the amount he demanded. Then each feeling

> " A peace above all earthly dignities—
> A still and quiet conscience,"

we returned to camp to be heartily congratulated upon the fortunate and hunger-satisfying issue of the adventure.

But both the congratulations and our self-felicitations were " a little too previously premature," as Bill Calhoun took occasion to remark next day. For stimulated to bold and daring deeds by the sight and smell of our hog-meat, he and Holden suffered themselves to be caught by the provost guard, toting a scrawny, insignificant, lean, and lank skinned shoat toward camp. Unable to convince anybody of their innocence, the shoat, too small to divide, and the boys too timid to tackle Jenkins as I had, their plunder was confiscated, and they themselves were sent to camp under guard, for their blankets, and these obtained, carried back to the provost guard-house. Nor was this the sum total of the misfortunes of the day. General Jenkins was " riding a high horse," terribly indignant at this second offense by members of the Fourth Texas, and the guards had orders to rearrest me and Somerville.

Next morning Captains McLaurin and Kindred had a lengthy and stormy interview with the irate General. That distinguished officer's confidence in human nature was at its lowest ebb, and, deeply to my regret, I was the scapegoat on whom he vented the bitterest of his wrathful spleen. McLaurin and Kindred, however, finally talked him into a good humor, and, after admitting he was most humiliated and exasperated at being so completely taken in by me, he washed his hands of both transgressions and delivered the four offenders over to General Robertson with the request that he should administer proper punishment. Aunt Pollie was no sooner made acquainted with the facts and General Jenkins's request, than he put on the sternest look his mild and benevolent countenance was capable of wearing, and turning on us, demanded,

" If you want hog-meat, boys, and must have it, why in the name of common sense and honesty don't you buy it like gentlemen? "

" Now, look here, General," blurted out Bill Calhoun, stepping up closer and looking him squarely in the face, " if you know or can invent any way for a private in this Confederate army to be a gentleman and buy his grub, when he hasn't got the wherewith to pay for a settin' hen, and when the keen pangs of a never-dyin' appetite is a-feedin' on his vitals like a drove of

red ants on a grasshopper, it's your duty to your
Texas constituents, sir, to make her public, and
give 'em a show."

His public spirit thus appealed to, instead of
his question answered, Aunt Pollie forgot both
the request of his commanding officer and the
grave offenses with which the members of his
little audience were charged, and began to abuse
our Confederate Congress for its miserable
makeshift legislation on monetary affairs. I am
something of a politician myself—at any rate, I
became, then, very politic. I followed the General's lead, and for a wonder agreed with him
on every point, and in a few minutes the old
fellow was in the best humor imaginable. Then
Calhoun put in his oar again, saying,

"Look here, General, isn't it about time we
was sorter 'tendin' to the imperative business of
the occasion?"

"Business—business?" repeated Aunt Pollie
in an absent-minded way. "Oh, yes—I had forgotten all about the hog-meat. Well, if Jenkins
and Longstreet and old Bragg think I am going to punish any of my men just for killing a
hog now and then, they'll find themselves mistaken. You boys go right back to camp and
behave yourselves, and the next time you run
across the infernal provost guard, flank the
d——d cusses, or the next time you are caught
I'll have the last one of you court-martialed."

Now, Charming Nellie, please don't draw any
unkind and uncharitable inferences from the fact
that Aunt Pollie had that very morning break-

fasted on broiled spareribs—an officer of high rank deems it beneath his dignity to inquire where the delicacies which appear on his table come from, and I am sure Captain Kindred was too shrewd a man to volunteer information on the point. As for General Jenkins, Captain Mc-Laurin says that, while that officer was most bitter in his denunciations of your humble servant, he eyed with a look of regretful disgust some exceedingly diminutive and wretchedly spare spareribs then being roasted for his breakfast at a near-by fire. Whether he was mentally comparing them with those which a confiscation of mine and Somerville's meat would have furnished his table had I made an earlier confession, is a question I hesitate to decide. Of course, considering that Bill Calhoun's pork was confiscated, his opinion is entitled to little weight, but, when I told him what McLaurin said, he remarked,

"Oh, yes—Mr. General South Carolina Jenkins wanted to confiscate your hog like he did mine, and he'd have done it, too, if you hadn't lied out of it so magnificently. He's in cahoot with the provost guard, I reckon, and his share of the little shoat I brought in wasn't half greasy and juicy enough to suit the fastidious epi-epi-epicurism of his high-mighty-mightiness, and that's what made him look so sour!"

All things considered, it was a grave breach of politeness on my part, not to offer Jenkins a mess of fat pork. Human nature is pretty much the same, in whatever garb it be clothed.

A thick, juicy sparerib, tendered in the proper spirit, has a wonderfully softening effect on an obdurate heart, and in an army whose highest officers are on short commons.

Bill Calhoun did me a wrong when he praised my magnificent lying. As you will see from the foregoing veracious account, I never told Jenkins a single time that I had bought and paid for my hog. That was an inference of his own, as he frankly acknowledged in his interview with the two captains.

XVI

CAMP NEAR CLEVELAND, TENN.,
November 16, 1863.

A PRIVATE on picket duty, under orders to allow no one to pass inside the Confederate lines without giving the countersign, was approached by his brigadier-general, who asked,

"What would you do, sir, were you to see a man coming up that road toward you?"

"I should wait, General," said the private, "until he came within twenty feet of me, and then halt him and demand the countersign."

"Very good, very good," commented the General; "but suppose twenty men approached by the same road, what would you do then?"

"Halt them before they got nearer than a hundred feet, sir, and, covering them with my gun, demand that the officer in command approach and give the countersign."

"Ah! my brave fellow," began the General in his most flattering voice, "I see you are remarkably well posted concerning your duties. But let me put still another case. Suppose a whole regiment were coming in this direction, what would you do in that case?"

"Form a line immediately, sir," answered the private unhesitatingly, and without a smile.

"Form a line? form a line?" repeated the

officer, in his most contemptuous tone. "What kind of line, I should like to know, could a single man form?"

"A bee-line for camp, sir," explained the picket.

Your pictures of Texas home life are so attractive as to almost persuade me to "form a line" myself, but with Texas as the objective point, instead of a hateful camp. Joyfully, indeed, would I say farewell to

> "All quality,
> Pride, pomp, and circumstance of glorious war,"

could I do it without desertion and disgrace. After reading your letter I was for a while inclined to think there was both sense and philosophy in the behavior of a Confederate at Chickamauga. When the battle was at its height and the bullets flying thickest, he stepped behind a tree, and, while protecting his body, extended his arms on each side and waved them frantically to and fro, up and down.

"What in the dickens are you doing, Tom?" asked an astonished comrade.

"Just feeling for a furlough," replied Tom, without a blush, and continuing the feeling process as if his life depended upon it.

While few soldiers actually seek wounds of any character, fewer still regard a parlor wound —that breaks no bones, yet disables one temporarily, and requires time, rest, and nursing to heal it—as any very serious misfortune. Such accidents necessitate furloughs, and these the ladies of the South, by their kindness to both the sick and the well, have made blessings to be hoped for, prayed for, and—within safe and patriotic limits—struggled for.

"Why, sir, that handsome widow and her curly-haired daughter couldn't have been kinder to a son or a brother. They gave me the pleasantest room in the house, brought my meals to it, fed me on chicken and sweet cream with their own hands, dressed my wound half a dozen times a day, and were always ready to play and sing for me, or read and talk to me. I wanted to stay a month longer, but my darned old finger healed in spite of me." That, and a great deal more to the same purport, was said by Lieutenant L—— when he returned to duty after losing half the nail of his little finger at Sharpsburg, getting a furlough on the strength of it, and, fortunately, falling into the hands of a wealthy and patriotic Virginia lady. Can you blame a poor fellow if, after listening to such a story, he is little inclined to " feel for a furlough "?

*　　*　　*　　*　　*

Only Longstreet knows certainly where we are bound, but general opinion favors Knoxville as the objective point, Burnside as the victim. Should these surmises prove correct, you may hear from me next in good old Virginia, for it is whispered confidentially that Bragg and Longstreet are at outs, and that this movement is intended to make their separation permanent.

I have often boasted that the Fourth Texas never showed its back to an enemy, but I am

Mr. and Mrs. W. A. Watson

W. A. Watson

Private, Company H, Fourth Texas Regiment

more modest since that little affair of October
28, known as the battle of Raccoon Mountain.
There the regiment not only showed its back,
but stampeded like a herd of frightened cattle,
it being one of those cases when "discretion is
the better part of valor"; and, instead of being ashamed of the performance, we are merry
over it. Raccoon and Lookout Mountains, you
must know, are separated by Lookout Creek.
Between the creek and Raccoon are half a dozen
high, parallel ridges, whose tops are open and
level enough for a roadway, and whose thickly
timbered sides slope at angles of forty-five degrees into deep, lonely hollows. Hooker's corps,
of the Federal army, coming up from Bridge-
port to reinforce Rosecrans, camped on the night
of the 28th in the vicinity of Raccoon. Imagining that here was an opportunity to win distinction, General Jenkins proposed to Longstreet to march Hood's division to the west side
of Lookout Mountain, and by a night attack
capture "Fighting Joe Hooker" and his corps.
Longstreet, of course, offered no objections; success would place as brilliant a feather in his
cap as in that of Jenkins, while the blame of
defeat would necessarily rest upon the projector
of the affair. As for us poor devils in the ranks,
we had no business to be there if we hesitated to
risk our lives in the interest of commanding
officers.

The plan of operations appears to have been
for Benning's, Anderson's, and Jenkins's brigades to cross Lookout Creek two miles above

its mouth, and, forming in line parallel with the
Tennessee River, force the Yankees to surrender
or drive them into deep water; while Law's
and the Texas brigades should occupy positions
west of the creek, at right angles with the river,
and prevent them from moving toward Lookout
Mountain and alarming Bragg's army.   What
became of the Third Arkansas and First Texas,
I cannot say, every movement being made at
night, but the Fifth Texas guarded the bridge,
across which the Fourth marched and thence
proceeded in the direction of Raccoon Mountain,
climbing up and sliding down the steep sides
of intervening ridges, until brought to a halt on
the moonlit top of the highest, and formed in
line on the right of an Alabama regiment. Here,
in blissful ignorance of General Jenkins's plans,
and unwarned by the glimmer of a fire or the
sound of a snore that the main body of the enemy
lay asleep in the wide and deep depression between them and Raccoon, the spirits of the gallant Texans rose at once to the elevation of
their bodies, and, dropping carelessly on the
ground, they proceeded to take their ease.   But
not long were they permitted thus to dally with
stern and relentless fate.   A gunshot away off
to the left suddenly broke upon the stillness
of the night, and was followed by others in rapid
succession, until there was borne to our unwilling ears the roar of desperate battle, while the almost simultaneous beating of the long roll in the
hitherto silent depths below us, the loud shouts
of officers, and all the indescribable noise and

hubbub of a suddenly awakened and alarmed host of men, admonished us that we stood upon the outermost verge of a human volcano, which might soon burst forth in all its fury and overwhelm us.

The *dolce far niente* to which, lulled by fancied security and the beautiful night, we had surrendered ourselves, vanished as quickly as the dreams of the Yankees. The emergency came unexpectedly, but none the less surely. Scouts dispatched to the right returned with the appalling intelligence that between the regiment and the river, half a mile away, not a Confederate was on guard; skirmishers sent to the front reported that the enemy was approaching rapidly and in strong force. To add to the dismay thus created, the thrilling whisper came from the left that the Alabamians had gone "hunting for tall timber" in their rear. Thus deserted, in a solitude soon to be invaded by a ruthless and devouring horde, the cheerless gloom of an exceedingly great loneliness fell upon us like a pall—grew intense, when, not twenty feet away, we heard the laborious struggling and puffing of the Yankees as, on hostile thoughts intent, they climbed and pulled up the almost precipitous ascent, and became positively unbearable when a dozen or more bullets from the left whistled down the line and the mild beams of the full moon, glinting from what seemed to our agitated minds a hundred thousand bright gun-barrels, revealed the near and dangerous presence of the hated foe. Then and

there, Charming Nellie—deeming it braver to
live than to die, and moved by thoughts of home
and the loved ones awaiting them there—the
officers and privates of the gallant and hitherto
invincible Fourth Texas stood not upon the order of their going, but went with a celerity and
unanimity truly remarkable, disappeared bodily,
stampeded *nolens volens,* and plunged recklessly
into the umbrageous and shadowy depths behind
them, their flight hastened by the loud huzzaing
of the triumphant Yankees and the echoing volleys they poured into the tree tops high above
the heads of their retreating antagonists.

Once fairly on the run down the steep slope,
voluntary halting became as impossible as it
would have been indiscreet. Dark as it was
among the somber shadows, the larger trees
could generally be avoided, but when encoun-
tered, as too frequently for comfort they were,
invariably wrought disaster to both body and
clothing; but small ones bent before the wild,
pell-mell rush of fleeing humanity as from the
weight and power of avalanche or hurricane.
The speed at which I traveled, let alone the
haunting apprehension of being gobbled up by a
pursuing blue-coat, was not specially favorable
to close observation of comrades, but, nevertheless, I witnessed three almost contemporaneous
accidents. One poor unfortunate struck a tree
so squarely and with such tremendous energy
as not only to flatten his body against it and
draw a sonorous groan from his lips, but to send
his gun clattering against another tree. As a

memento of the collision, he yet carries a face ragged enough to harmonize admirably with his garments. Another fellow exclaimed, as, stepping on a round stone, his feet slipped from under him and he dropped to the ground with a resounding thud, " Help, boys, help!" and then, with legs wide outspread, went sliding down the hill, until, in the wholly involuntary attempt to pass on both sides of a tree, he was brought to a sudden halt—a sit-still, so to speak. But adventure the third was the most comical of all. The human actor in it was a Dutchman by the name of Brigger, a fellow nearly as broad as he is long, who always carries a huge knapsack on his shoulders. Aided by this load, he struck a fair-sized sapling with such resistless momentum that the little tree bent before him, and, straddling it and exclaiming, " Je-e-e-sus Christ and God Almighty!" with long-drawn and lingering emphasis on the first syllable of the first word, he described a parabola in the air and then dropped to the ground on all fours, and continued his downward career in that decidedly unmilitary fashion. His was the novelty and roughness of the ride, but, alas! mine was all the loss; for, as the sapling tumbled him off, and essayed to straighten itself, it caught my hat and flung it at the man in the moon. Whether it ever reached its destination, I, am unable to say, for time, inclination, and ability to stop were each sternly prohibited by the accelerating influence of gravitation, and the exigency of the occasion. Anyhow, I am

now wearing a cap manufactured by myself
out of the nethermost extremity of a woolen
overshirt, and having for a frontispiece a generous slice of stirrup leather. Colonel Bane
well deserves the loss he has sustained; he is
not only careless about his saddle, but of his
head as well, on which he still bears a reminder
of the battle of Raccoon Mountain in the shape
of a very sore and red bump.

I enclose some drawings, which, if not artistic,
certainly have the merit of being so graphic as
to leave much to the imagination. In my salad
days at Florence, Alabama, I persuaded Professor Pruskowski to organize and teach a class
in perspective drawing. While refusing to
charge for his services, he reserved the right to
dismiss any member of the class whom he found
lacking in talent. I was the first to advocate
this privilege, also the first and only one of the
class to be dismissed. Then I was satisfied that
he judged correctly, but now I am doubtful.

But, to return to my story. Although I lost
my hat, I neither lost physical balance nor col-
lided with a tree sufficiently sturdy to arrest a
fearfully swift descent, as did many of my comrades. The scars imprinted upon the regimental
physiognomy by large and small monarchs of
the forest are yet numerous, and in some instances were at first so disguising that the wear-
ers were recognizable for the next day or two
only by their melodious voices. " Honors were
so easy " in that respect between the members
of the command, officers as well as privates, that

when they at last emerged from the darkness of the woods, and, taking places in line, began to look at each other and recount experiences, the shouts of laughter must have reached old Joe Hooker.

One poor fellow, though, was too sore, downcast, and trampled upon to be joyful. He was a litter-bearer named D——, six long feet in height, and Falstaffian in abdominal development. His position in the rear gave him the start in the retreat, and his avoirdupois enabled him to brush aside every obstacle to rapid descent. But his judgment was disastrously at fault. Forgetting a ditch which marked the division line of descent of one hill and ascent of the other, he tumbled into it broadcast. The fall knocked all the breath out of him, and he could only wriggle over on his broad back and make a pillow for his head of one bank and a resting place for his number twelve feet of the other, so that his body appeared as the trunk of a fallen tree. Scarcely, however, had he assumed this comfortable position, when Bill Calhoun came plunging down the hill with a velocity that left a good-sized vacuum in the air behind him. Noticing the litter-bearer's body, and taking it to be what it appeared, Bill took the chances of its spanning the ditch, and made such a tremendous leap that he landed one huge foot right in the middle of the unfortunate recumbent's corporosity. The sudden compression produced as sudden artificial respiration, and giving vent to an agonized grunt, D—— sang out, "For the Lord Almighty's sake, man, don't make a bridge of a fellow!"

Bill was startled, but never lost his presence of mind, and shouting back, "Lie still, old fellow, lie still! The whole regiment's got to cross yet, and you'll never have such another chance to serve your beloved country," continued his flight with a speed but little abated by the rising ground before him.

XVII

BEAN'S STATION, TENN., December 21, 1863.
So much has occurred since my letter from Cleveland that two problems confront me: what to mention, and what to leave untold. Skimming over the surface of events—as I must, to keep within the limits of paper supply and your patience—I intentionally omit many things of interest and forget others.   *   *   *

Crossing on pontoons to the north side of the Tennessee River, near Loudon, on the 14th day of November, the Texas Brigade marched and countermarched, advanced, retreated, and halted, much as if a game of " hide and seek " were being played between it and the enemy. From Loudon to Campbell's Station the Yankees offered a very determined opposition to Longstreet's advance, but after complimenting his little army with a few challenging shots from artillery at the last-named place, deemed it prudent to make haste to shelter themselves behind their breastworks at Knoxville. While the Texans had but occasional skirmish fighting to do, their experiences were far from agreeable. The weather had turned bitterly cold; little or no clothing had been issued to them at Chattanooga,

and all were thinly clad and many almost, and
some wholly, barefooted. You can easily conceive their joy, then, when at Lenoir's Station,
late one evening, they were marched into winter quarters just vacated by the enemy, and a
rumor, which had every appearance of truth,
fairly flew about that they were to spend the
winter there. When I saw the neat, well-framed,
and plastered huts, each of a size to cozily ac-
commodate two men, and was led to believe that
within one of them I was to find shelter from
wintry blasts, and comfort and rest for my poor,
hunger-gaunted *corpus,* my heart filled with
gratitude to my adversaries, and had they come
unarmed and with peaceful intent I would gladly
have "fallen upon their necks and wept."

Lieutenant Park and I managed to pre-empt
one of the most elegant of the cabins, and with
almost undignified haste set about to make ourselves thoroughly at home. About nine o'clock
in the evening we were sitting on benches before
a pile of hickory logs that, blazing merrily in
the fireplace, warmed our chilled bodies and
brightened up the walls, and had just lighted
our pipes and begun talking of home, when the
long roll sounded. "Ah! then there was hurrying to and fro," and if not "mounting in hot
haste," a prompt "getting into line"—an end
to quiet smoking and earnest talk of loved ones,
as hurriedly grasping sword, gun, blankets, canteens, and haversacks, we rushed from a para-
dise into a frozen inferno; from warmth into
bitter, stinging cold; from cheering, homelike

firelight, into that of glittering and unsympathizing stars. Little stomach as I have for fighting, I have faced the enemy with far less of reluctance than I left that comfortable little hut; and, worse than all, I never saw its interior again, for, resting upon our arms the balance of the night, we took up the line of march next morning at daylight for Campbell's Station.

> " Oh ever thus from childhood's hour
> I've seen my fondest hopes decay."

One may be ever so philosophical, and yet—especially if he be a Confederate soldier—there will come times when philosophy utterly fails to give strength to bear with becoming fortitude " the slings and arrows of outrageous fortune." This was just such a time to me. I stood manfully in arms that livelong, dreary night, consoled by the thought that morning would carry me back to the little log cabin; but when the order to march gave the lie to hope, fortitude deserted me, and I wished I were a baby, so that I might cry with a show of decency. Nor have I recovered my good spirits altogether yet. And if any one of those gallant warrior friends of yours, whose featherbed patriotism has hitherto bound him irrevocably to the defense of Texas against invasion by water, who stands far inland and gazes fearlessly at the dangerous men of war in the distant offing, who even mocks at danger, and demonstrates his desperate and unquenchable valor by drinking several cups of burning hot coffee in the long intervals between

the flash of the enemy's cannon and the passage
of its shell over the intervening five or six miles
of water and land—if any one of these, I say,
nurses a fond desire for a more active life, for
closer quarters with the enemy, just send him
right here; I will cheerfully and even gladly exchange with the gentleman. He shall have my
gun and all of its attachments, my haversack
and all its varied contents, even the gay and
fashionable garments that adorn my manly person. Indeed, I should insist on his taking the
clothing, for it would furnish him with some
incentives to prompt and vigorous action that,
report says, are yet lacking in Texas. And I
will trade "sight unseen," too; for, while I
should "admire" to do the balance of my soldiering in a neighborhood where there are fair
ladies to sympathize with me in my hardships
and privations, any part of the Texas coast is
preferable to this part of Tennessee.

Since encountering the Western men who fight
under the "star-spangled banner," Longstreet's
corps has somewhat modified its estimate of what
Bragg "might have done" in the way of whipping them. The Yankees who fled before us at
Chickamauga had as little grit and staying
power, apparently, as any we were in the habit
of meeting in Virginia; but Burnside had troops
at Knoxville who not only stood well, but also
shot well. The hardest and most stubbornly
contested skirmish fighting I ever witnessed took
place there, and our lines needed to be frequently
reinforced. On the 23d of November first one

company and another of the Fourth went forward, and finally the turn of Company F came. To reach the line we had to pass around a point of rocks and up the side of a steep ridge, in plain view of and under a galling fire from the enemy. *   *   *   Jim Mayfield and Jack Sutherland, more venturesome than others, sat down behind trees twenty feet farther to the front and began exercising their skill as marksmen. Mayfield grew careless, and, exposing a foot and part of a leg, received a ball which lodged between the bones of the latter just above the ankle. " What will you give me for my furlough, boys? " he exclaimed when the shot struck him. " What will you give me for my furlough, boys? " he asked again, as he came limping hurriedly back, using his gun for a crutch. It was only a " parlor wound," he thought, and, thinking the same, several of us would willingly have changed places with him; I know I would. But there was little time to envy him. The enemy was pressing us hard, and we had forgotten him and his " parlor wound," when, an hour later, a litter-bearer returned from the field hospital with the sad intelligence, " Jim Mayfield is dead, boys; he took lockjaw."

On the evening of November 28 Company F was detailed for picket duty. Three inches of snow lay on the ground and an icy wind, from whose severity we could find little protection, chilled us to the marrow. I went on duty about nine o'clock, my post being at the edge of a high bluff overlooking Knoxville and the valley oppo-

site me, and a half mile away I could see lights
moving back and forth in the enemy's fort on
College Hill. I was growing numb and sleepy
with the intense cold, when the flash and report
of a rifle, followed by a scattering and then a
continuous roar of small arms, awoke and informed me that an attempt was being made by
the Confederates to capture the fort. Out of
the line of firing entirely, I watched the battle
from beginning to end with a strange mingling
of delight and foreboding. Night attacks are
seldom successful, and the fort was not only
well manned, but protected by wire netting and
chevaux de frise. But if terrible while in progress, it was awful when, having been repulsed
with great slaughter, Barksdale's brigade was
forced to withdraw and leave hundreds of its
wounded upon the field, too close to the fort
to be carried off by their friends. After so desperate a night attack it was impossible to ar-
range a truce, and while many of the hurt managed to crawl to help, many more laid where
they fell and froze to death. All through the
long night their voices could be heard calling
for help, both from the Yankees and their
friends, and often screaming with agony as they
essayed to move themselves within reach of it.

*   *   *

About daylight we learned that an advance
would be made that day on our (the east) side
of the river, and immediately began to congrat-
ulate ourselves that, being pickets, Company F
would escape the fighting. But it was a mis-

take, for at sun-up we were relieved by Georgians, and not only ordered to the regiment, but, when the advance began, placed on the skirmish line. It was so cold that, even after running up hill half a mile, the men had to warm their fingers at the fires left by the Yankees before they could reload their guns. Both the weather and the battle grew warmer as the sun climbed higher in the sky. The Federals had made only a slight resistance to the capture of their picket line, but now showed such a bold front against farther advance of the Confederates that it was decided not to attempt it, and until noon we kept our blood in circulation only by incessant sharpshooting. * * *

Old Reub Crigler, the second lieutenant of Company F, never goes into a fight without a gun and a chosen supply of cuss words to fling at the Yankees when he shoots. " There, d——n you! see how you like that," or " Take that, you infernal son of a gun! " fell from his lips that day with an unction and regularity not at all complimentary to the intended victims of his wrath. Captain Martin, though, of Company K of the Fourth, neither draws a sword nor bears a gun in battle, but rubs his hands together and smiles as merrily as if it were the greatest fun imaginable. Not even when he came near me that day and said, his voice choking and the tears standing in his eyes, " They have killed brother Henry, Joe," did the movement of his hands cease or the smile disappear from his countenance.

That evening the Texans learned, as Longstreet had two or three days before, of the defeat of Bragg at Chattanooga, and many were the anathemas hurled against that incompetent, or at least singularly unfortunate, officer by the self-constituted generals and statesmen in the ranks. Of course, he ought to have held the ground against whatever odds, for, given ten days longer, we would have forced Burnside to surrender. But facts were facts, and none less stubborn appeared to Longstreet than the rapid approach from the direction of Chattanooga of two Federal army corps, and the advisability, if he would avoid being caught between two fires, of passing around Knoxville and moving up toward Bristol, Virginia, through the fertile country lying between the Holston and French Broad rivers. The adoption of this course was largely influenced, no doubt, by the considerations that it would insure a permanent separation from Bragg, give Longstreet a longer term of independent command, and enable him to rejoin Lee in Virginia. The last of these appealed so strongly to the Texans that, after getting beyond danger of pursuit on the 4th of December, hundreds of them joined in the chorus, "Oh, carry me back to ole Virginia, to ole Virginia's shore!" with a will and a volume of sound that made the echoes ring for miles around. My melodious voice, however, went up with the mental reservation that I should be privileged to stop this side of the seacoast. Salted shad possesses no allurement to me.   *   *   *

Lest in recounting " the battles, sieges, fortunes, that I have passed "; lest in speaking

" Of most disastrous chances,
Of moving accidents by flood and field,
Of hairbreadth 'scapes i' the imminent deadly breach,"

I have harrowed your gentle heart to the point of swearing

" 'Twas strange, 'twas passing strange,
'Twas pitiful, 'twas wondrous pitiful,"

and expending upon me more sympathy than I deserve, permit me to remark that at this particular juncture in my career I am really " in clover." For—if because of the curtailment of one leg of my pants, because my toes protrude conspicuously from dilapidated and disreputable shoes, and my cap is stained with dirt and grease, my ensemble is scarcely stylish enough to give me a right to the feminine society so liberally and lavishly bestowed on the Toms, Dicks, and Harrys who infest the Texas coast— my canteen is, nevertheless, bulging with the nicest strained honey, my tobacco-pouch and haversack with the very choicest smoking-tobacco; the sweetening being the munificent reward of a moonlight tramp last night over the mountains to Clinch River, the tobacco the product of a raid by Brahan and myself, day before yesterday, on a kind-hearted old farmer. My present state is, in short, the naturally inevitable result of physical satiety, mental and moral plethora, exemption from any duty, writing to you, and a philosophical mind.

XVIII

MORRISTOWN, TENN., December 30, 1863.

THE Texas Brigade left Bean's Station on the morning of the 22d. Jack Sutherland, Green Griggs, and your humble servant determined to do a little foraging, and if possible secure what Bill Calhoun calls the "concomitant ingregents" for a Christmas dinner. Straggling off on a by-road, we tramped about the country all day, slept in a house that night, and next morning—our haversacks filled to overflowing with the good things of life—wended our way, in the best humor imaginable, toward Morristown. Of course we kept a sharp lookout for provost guards, and were not surprised to come upon one of those despised but lordly individuals, complacently standing in the road ahead of us.

Jack and Green proposed to "flank the enemy," but having great confidence in the powers of persuasion and argument which had extricated me from many a predicament, I finally induced them to join me in a bold advance. Giving the fellow no time to make inquiries, I stated to him that we had just been relieved from guard duty, and asked to be directed to the camp of the Texas Brigade. But while politely and

184

promptly furnishing the desired information, he most unkindly arrested us as stragglers.

"We are not stragglers," I insisted. "We left the command yesterday, guarded a private house last night according to orders, and must return to camp at once."

"Maybe so," said the guard, with a provoking smile. "I ain't a-disputin' nothin', but we can't let you pass; orders are to stop everybody that hain't got a pass."

"Call your corporal, then," said I, and that officer appearing, I exercised upon him every blandishment and argument at my command; but alas, without in the least softening his obdurate heart.

"Carry us to the officer of the guard," I demanded; "I reckon he will have a little common sense."

"It isn't common sense or any other kind he's got to have—he has simply got to obey orders," responded the corporal as he led the way to the huge guard fire.

By this time Jack was mad as a hornet, his glances at me lowering, savage, contemptuous; once he sidled up to me and remarked in a tone of withering scorn, "Now, darn your old hide, you've got us in a —— of a pickle by your confounded faith in your ability to out-talk people."

"Wait a while, old fellow," I replied, "no telling what may happen." But I had more misgivings than my words indicated, and I had still more when the lieutenant politely but positively refused to release us.

When the ultimatum fell on his ears, Jack dropped down before the fire with a surly groan, Green looked blue and smiled in a sickly manner, and I felt that my last hope was departing. But *"nil desperandum"* is my motto whenever I get into trouble; I entered at once into conversation with the lieutenant, and learning that he was a Georgian, complimented the soldiers of his State, and especially those of the Eighteenth Regiment, so extravagantly yet judiciously, as to persuade him into a real good humor, and was wondering how to utilize my advantage, when, on the other side of the fire, partly concealed by a blanket, I espied a fiddle and a bow. Like a flash the inspiration came; I stepped around the fire, boldly seized the instruments, and handing them to Jack, said in the most cheery tone imaginable, " Give us some music, old boy."

You never in your life saw such a sudden change as occurred then and there in Jack's countenance. Every shadow and trace of ill-humor disappeared in an instant, and a smile that was absolutely charming irradiated his homely features. He grasped the fiddle and began to tune it, with an eagerness that was surprising, for he is much more fastidious ordinarily about the violin he plays on, than about his eating; neither the landlord nor the quality of the food affects his appetite, but he has an unutterable horror of drawing the bow across the strings of any except his own violin. That has such a sweet and powerful tone, and Jack

J. B. POLLEY

Private, Company F, Fourth Texas Regiment
1862 to 1865

makes such delightful music on it, that Colonel Winkler carries it with his private baggage in order to have it always at hand when its owner is in the humor to play.

Little music as I have in my benighted soul, I discovered at his first scrape of the bow that it was a miserable apology for a fiddle. It did not seem to matter with Jack, though; whether he felt the need of music just then to soothe his own savage breast, or imagined he might use it as a means of securing release from " durance vile," he handled the bow with a deftness and heartiness that made the hills and hollows of East Tennessee echo and re-echo with delicious strains. He put his whole mind to the business as if there was nothing else in the world worth doing, kept time with one foot, wagged his head from side to side for the half beats, and never once forgot to keep his hard-favored countenance illumined with a smile that was both a plea to his captors and a totally unexpected charm to his fellows in misfortune.

The Georgians expected only a little amateur sawing, but Jack had not got halfway through " The Devil's Dream " ere they realized that a master-hand wielded the bow and the highest order of musical genius directed the hand. Entering fully into the spirit of the occasion, some of them began to pat, others to shuffle their feet, and all to nod their heads and show their teeth with delight. Jack was not so overcome by the divine afflatus as to be unconscious of surroundings, and marking the impression made on

his auditors, played, told and acted " The Arkansas Traveler "—changing his voice to mimic
first the strong one of the traveler, and then the
weak, piping tones of the chill-stricken settler, and question and answer given, making
the woods ring with melody from the violin.
*   *   *   You could even hear the traveler
ask, " Where does this road go to, sir? " then
the reply of the settler, " Tain't gone nowhere,
stranger, since we'uns bin livin' in these woods."
Then the first part of the tune—the only part
the settler knew—would be played over and
over again until, interrupted by another question, Jack would stop sawing long enough to answer and then begin again. It is a long story
you know, for you must have heard some old
darky play and act it; but Jack not only told
all of it I ever heard, but a good deal more.
Finally, reaching the place where the traveler
asks, " Why don't you play the balance of that
tune? " Jack, as he repeated the question,
handed me the fiddle and bow, and then answering it, " 'Ca'se I ain't never heard it, stranger—
kin you play it? " personated the traveler by
reaching for the instrument and playing the balance of the tune with a spirit that made a final
conquest of our Georgia captors.

From the " Arkansas Traveler " Jack switched
off suddenly to " Gray Eagle," and as he played,
called all the turns of start, backstretch, home-
stretch and finish of the grand Kentucky race
that was the inspiration of the author in composing the music. Indeed, it was a revelation

of genius, of the wonderful power of a master to extract the sweetest music from an old, weatherbeaten and warworn fiddle, and of histrionic and pantomimic talent, which held the auditors breathless and spellbound.

A radical metamorphosis had taken place in the performer. Generally, we have to beg Jack to play, and, when he consents, it is with the lordly, far-away manner of one who feels he is " casting pearls before swine." He rebukes any request for a particular tune by a forbidding frown or a curt, gruff remark that the instrument is not in tune for it, which says to the offender more plainly than words, " What do *you* know about music that warrants your presumption in selecting a tune for me to play? " But now no longer surly of voice and crusty of manner, he was the most mild-tempered and accommodating of mortals, and let the strings down or screwed them up, at the slightest hint of choice on the part of our hosts, and played every tune called for with an alacrity which demonstrated that it was the very one he was most anxious to play.

How long the music lasted, I cannot say, for captors and captured forgot time, the world and all its sordid cares, as they sat around the big log fires. At last, however, there was a lull, a hush, a silence. Jack laid the fiddle and the bow tenderly on a blanket, brushed from his eyes the tears evoked either by the smoke or the exalted condition of his mind, and reached out for a coal with which to light his pipe; the

Circean spell that enthralled minds and hearts
was broken, and the auditors, drawing long
breaths of sorrow, became once more human beings, " of the earth, earthy."

My tumble from supernal realms was not so
precipitate as to drive from my mind the dire-
ness of our extremity. With the genius of a
great captain, I laid instant hold on the favorable impression made by the music, and rising
to my feet, ready equipped for departure, looked
the lieutenant full in the face with a confident
smile, saying, " Well, gentlemen, we must be
getting on to camp."

Jack looked up at the words, astonishment
depicted in every line of his rugged face; but
when the gallant Georgian smiled kindly back
at me and said, " Yes—you fellows go up the
hill behind the fence to that skirt of timber yonder, then follow the timber down to the road
and you'll get to camp all right;—but of course,
if you are caught again, you will not give us
away,"—the astonishment vanished to be re-
placed by a look of inexpressible relief.

Little conversation was indulged in until, all
points of danger safely passed, Jack turned to
me, and with a disgustingly self-complacent air
said,

" You ain't worth a ——, Joe. You can always rely on me, though, to get out of a bad
scrape. We would be on our way to Captain
Scott's quarters now if I hadn't dazed that lieutenant with the music I gave him."

I felt outraged that the prominent part I had

taken in the happening of the last few hours should be so conceitedly ignored. "The devil you say!" I retorted. "You did draw a good bow, but you lacked the wit, either to hunt for the fiddle, or, after the battle was won, to take advantage of success. It was my unparalleled and sublime conception to pretend that we were mere visitors whose departure would not be opposed. You and Green would have begged for release—I was the Napoleon who seized the golden opportunity and trotted you fellows out of danger into our present safety— wasn't I, Green?"

Thus appealed to, Green looked as wise as an owl, and weighing each word as carefully as if giving an opinion on a question of law, said, "Well, boys, it strikes me this way: Jack can beat all creation a-scrapin' o' catgut, and Joe is —— when it comes to workin' them jaws of his, and sticking the words in pointedly. Betwixt fiddling and chin music, you fellows got away with the lieutenant."

Green's judicious administration of soft soap restored amity.

The first tents of the regiment approached were those of the band. Pausing here to overlook the camp and get its geography, I glanced to the right, and there, fifty yards away, stood Colonel Winkler and Sergeant-Major Brown, looking straight at us.   *   *   *

I picked the old hen and rooster which had fallen to my share, and salted them down for cooking the next day. Just as I finished the job,

Brown sauntered up near me and I asked him what Colonel Winkler said when he saw us coming in. " He just asked where you fellows had been," said Brown, " and I told him you were returning from guard duty." " Did he swallow the lie? " I asked. " Of course not," said Brown, " he is no fool—you got in too late in the day to be mistaken for men relieved of guard duty." * * *

Christmas morning I invited Lieutenant Brahan of Company F—then acting adjutant of the regiment—and Mr. Bunting, the chaplain of the Terry Rangers, to take dinner with me. I promised them a chicken pie, and anxious that it should be a masterpiece of its kind, gave my whole mind to its preparation. I had carried operations to the point where the least carelessness would be ruinous to hopes and pie, when Brahan walked hastily down from the Colonel's quarters, and stopping a hundred yards from me, called out loudly, " Joe, Colonel Winkler wants you to report to him immediately."

Truly, I was in a nice predicament. A fat hen and rooster in the skillet on a hot fire, just at that stage of cookery which required the utmost delicacy of management, and I, the only living person thoroughly capable of giving it, called away at the very culmination of the critical moment. It was enough to provoke a saint —especially when it was a question whether he would be permitted to return to his pie, or be sent to the guard-house.

Judging from their countenances, Jack and

Green felt the same consternation I did. Jack kindly volunteered to take care of the pie, but knowing he had already eaten up his share of plunder, I distrusted him, and requested "Joe Bowers" of Company D, whose true name is John Baker, to watch it. Then in fear and trembling, I went to the Colonel's tent. As I entered, he rose from the adjutant's desk, and saying, "I wish you would sit down here, Joe, and copy this application," handed me three closely written pages of foolscap.

"I'll do it with the greatest pleasure, Colonel," said I, relieved of every apprehension except for the pie; "but see here—I have a couple of chickens on the fire, and I am afraid they will get burnt—can't I do your work after dinner?"

"No," said he, "it is an application to transfer our three Texas regiments to Texas, and a staff officer is waiting at Longstreet's headquarters to carry it to Richmond. You copy it at once, and I'll go down and see after the chickens."

"I'll do the work at once then, Colonel," said I hastily, "but you needn't bother about the chickens—they are in charge of Joe Bowers— the only man in the regiment who won't steal."

The Colonel laughed heartily at my evident doubt of his good faith, and I copied the application in a hurry, and then flew on the wings of hunger and apprehension, to my mess of pottage. The crust was a little burned, the gravy had a flavor of smoke, but the pie was still a toothsome delicacy to hungry Confederates. Better than

all, neither Jack Sutherland, Green Griggs, nor
I have been punished for an offense exactly similar to that which has caused half a dozen of
our comrades to promenade the color line with
a log on their shoulders, for two hours a day,
and will keep them engaged in the pleasant pastime for at least eight days longer.

XIX

MORRISTOWN, TENN., January 15, 1864.
While in the early morn of New Year's Day
I was doing my level best to find both savor and
repletion in the three days' rations of blue beef
and flour made of sick wheat just issued to us,
an order came for the detail of the best-shod
man of each company in the brigade to report at
once to Captain Thrasher of the Third Arkansas. As I happened to be the lucky man of my
company whose footwear was most unimpeachable, the choice fell upon me. Nothing could
have better suited my taste. Four inches of
snow, white, glittering and frozen, lay on the
ground, a stiff breeze, straight " from Green-
land's icy mountains," or some other hyperborean
region, gave a snap and a thrill to the atmosphere that was inspiring and invigorating, and
the sky was cloudless. In truth, it was ideal
weather for a tramp, and in the exuberance of
my joy at release from camp monotony, I turned
over my share of the rations just issued to my
messmates, and when on reporting to Captain
Thrasher he informed me that his orders were to
take a detachment of forty men across the
French Broad River and turn them loose to
wander broadcast over the country as a pro-

tection to foraging parties of quartermasters and commissaries, I was glad I had been so generous. * * *

Crossing the river an hour before sunset, we sought a first night's shelter in a large barn, a quarter of a mile distant from the dwelling house of its owner—a Unionist, and therefore conspicuous by his absence. The house promised the more comfort to a now ravenously hungry soldier, and no sooner after arrival at the barn had I lent the blanket I would not need to a comrade, and placed my gun and accouterments in his charge, than, sure that Captain Thrasher was yet in the barn and was not looking, I made an adroit flank movement and strolled in the direction of the dwelling. Lest, however, the Captain should see me and deem me a little premature in turning myself loose on the country, I pursued a devious route. That proved my undoing, for unfortunately it was the longer way. That plagued Arkansas captain not only got to the house first, but ere I came and put up an eloquent petition for board and lodging for the night, had secured for himself and three members of his regiment all the spare accommodations of the house and every place at the table; and I had to go back to the barn supperless and with little idea where I was to get breakfast next morning. * * *

To describe the good time I had would beggar my powers of description and then leave the half untold. * * * A small and select party of us went thirty miles down the country to the deserted home of Nick Swann, a noted Unionist then commanding a regiment in the Federal Army. All I got for my tramp, though, was a chunk of delicious dried beef that we found in a dark corner of the smoke-house. Next we went over to Pigeon River, to the house of Colonel Jack of the Confederate Army, and while being entertained with music, vocal and instrumental, by his fair daughters, met a straggling party of the Terry Rangers. While the infantry under Longstreet's command have been enjoying their rest in winter quarters in the neighborhood of Morristown, the Rangers and other cavalry have been fighting day and night to keep the Yankees off of them.   *   *   *

I have so little of skirmish and battle to write about that I must perforce resort to story-telling.   *   *   *

A member of the Seventeenth Mississippi related an incident to me the other day that happily illustrates the spirit of the Virginia women as well as the rather rough humor in which a soldier sometimes indulges. The Seventeenth was marching down a street of the historic old town of Williamsburg, seemingly endeavoring to escape the dangers of the battle Longstreet was making against the Federals on the 4th of May, 1862. "A maiden rare, with golden hair," rushed out of a house into the street, and coming to a halt near the moving troops, cried,

"Turn back, Southerners—turn back! Don't you hear the shouts of the captains and the roar of the murderous cannon they and their brave compatriots are facing? Turn back, I beseech and implore you!"

But unmoved by her eloquence, the wearied men trudged stolidly on. Undiscouraged, she took a fresh hold on her voice and shouted,

"Turn back, men—for the sake of the women of the South and all you hold dear and precious, turn back and fight the dastardly Yankees as our forefathers did the red-coats during the Revolution! If your captain won't lead you, I will."

Just at this critical juncture the command ran down the line, "Halt—About face—Double quick!" and as they were being obeyed, a wild, Rebel yell sounded high above the din of the distant battle. Imagining she was being taken at her word and that her appeal had been the cause of the halt and about-facing, the lovely would-be Joan of Arc, her face all ablaze with high and desperate resolve, rushed to the head of the column, evidently intending to lead it. But alas, "pride goeth before a fall!" Her ardor and enthusiasm, fiercely burning as they were, cooled in the next second, and halting in her tracks, she stood mute, motionless and abashed, for having caught her eye, one of the boys said in the tone of one chiding a little sister,

"Don't go with us, Sissie—don't think of going; you might tear your dress."

*   *   *   *   *

Not many of our brigade have ever been captured, and the majority of those that have been have had the luck either to get a quick exchange or to effect an escape. When Bill Givens of my company returned to the command after a sojourn of two months' duration in Fort Delaware, he told an interesting as well as amusing story of his escape. That prison, as you likely know, is in the middle of Delaware Bay, some distance below the city of Philadelphia. Getting tired at last of "durance vile," Bill concluded to risk a swim to the northern shore of the bay, the southern shore being too closely guarded for him to venture in that direction. Once landed, he intended to hide in the tall grasses of the marshes for a day or two, and then make his way around Philadelphia. His voyage from fort to shore had to be made in the night-time on account of the risk of discovery by the many passing vessels. So, one very dark night he evaded the vigilance of the prison guards, procured a plank six feet long and as many inches wide, dropped into the water and struck out for dry land and liberty, and as long as the starlight lasted made good headway and continued hopeful. After midnight, though, a fog came up and he lost his bearings, not being able from the surface of the bay even to see the lights that shone in the fort. This was disheartening, but he kept up his paddling, consoling himself with the reflection that even should he be heading for the Atlantic Ocean, he was at any rate getting further from a hated prison. So on and on he swam, until day beginning to dawn and the fog lifting somewhat, he discovered a vessel within half a mile of him.

" Then, sir," said Bill, " my heroic soul rose to a square level with the direful emergency of the occasion. Never doubting that I was yet in the middle of the cussed old bay, and hopeless of escaping the watchful eyes of the sailors on the deck of the vessel, I resolved, rather than be recaptured, to ' shuffle off this mortal coil,'— in short, to die, to just let myself sink into the vasty depth of the blue waters, and drown. But I wasn't going to be a fool and pass in my checks in advance of discovery. While waiting for that, I remembered having read or heard that drowning was actually a pleasant method of dying, and that the deeper the water the more delightful the sensation, the more comfortable and easy the exit from this vale of tears and trouble. This set me to wondering whether the bay at that point was deep enough to make drowning the picnic it was cracked up to be, and what my first sensations would be. Only by experiment could the weighty problem be solved, and I decided to make it—that is, to sink as deep in the water as I could and stay under long enough to do more or less strangling. Pushing the plank from under me, I pointed the foot end of my corpus toward the center of the earth, and sank. Down, down, down, I expected and intended to go, but I didn't, for the water wasn't even waist deep, let alone deep enough to drown a fellow. I was so amazed and exasperated at finding it too shallow for the test, that for two seconds and a half I forgot to be grateful for my good luck. Then knowing the shore must be near by, I stood up long enough to take a look around me, and discovered land not a hundred yards distant. That I made for it in a hurry you may well imagine—not on my feet though, but, lest I be seen from the vessels, swimming like an alligator, my nose and eyes only out of water. Fortunately I was not seen, and now, thank God, I am here, safe and sound. But I had a mighty close call, boys, for if I hadn't touched bottom I'd have made a martyr of myself, sure, and instead of being able to eat three times the rations I get, would be floating, a cold, pulseless, emaciated and fish-nibbled skeleton, on the blue waters of the ever-heaving Atlantic Ocean."

Here Bill paused, and with his sleeve wiped away the big tear that had stolen down his left cheek. Respecting such evidently genuine emotion, no one spoke for a minute or more. Dansby, always a doubting Thomas, and often irreverent, broke the silence, asking:

"Honest Injin, now, Bill Givens, would you really have had the nerve and the grit to drown yourself?"

Bill's rugged lineaments instantly lost the look of exaltation they had worn, and speaking with a solemnity rather at variance with the savage glance he cast at Dansby, he replied,

"Yes, sir, honest Injun I would have had the nerve and the grit. I was in exactly the frame of mind when life as a prisoner of the infernal Yankees had lost every charm; death, every terror."

"Not a doubt of it," said Dansby, in a tone

of irony; "but go on with your story and tell us
how you circumlocuted around Baltimore?"

"Not to-day—not to-day," said Bill, his voice
shaking with emotion. "When I remember the
small margin of time that was between me and
a briny grave, my heart gets too full for utterance. If you don't stop talking to me I'll go to
downright boohooing."

In the story of the escape from the same prison
of Jim Loggins of Company G of the Fourth
Texas there is a tincture of romance, a flavor of
narrowly averted tragedy. Jim is an exceedingly handsome young fellow, and his pulchri-
tude and captivating ways won him the favoring
regard of a beautiful Philadelphia maiden, a
constant visitor to the fort, and a pronounced
Southern sympathizer. By her he was informed
that if he could manage to outwit his guards,
get into Philadelphia and call on a certain Dr.
B—— there, that gentleman would befriend
him, and send him back to Dixie's Land by the
underground route. How he got out of the
clutches of the guards I do not know, Jim being
very reticent in regard to that part of the adventure. But he got out some way or other,
entered the city, and made the call. Fortunately, Dr. B—— was alone in his office, and
the fugitive had only to say he was a Confederate, to enlist the services of a good Samaritan
in his behalf.

"Sit right down here in my office and wait
until I return," said the old fellow. "I will
step up the street and buy you a suit of citizen's

clothes, and when you have got inside of them, I'll take you to my house and let our mutual friend, Miss ———, know of your arrival."

The voice was friendly and cheering, and it fell most soothingly on Jim's ears. Still, he did not like to be left alone quite so soon, and would much have preferred a bold tramp on the streets by the side of his newly found friend. Dr. B———, however, insisted he should remain in the office, and stay he did. But to diminish the chance of being identified by some caller as an escaped Rebel, he placed his chair in the darkest corner of the room, and seizing on a book pretended to be engaged in its perusal. On his way to the clothing store, Dr. B——— met a compatriot in the person of Dr. Doe, and believing he could safely rely on his discretion, whispered to him, " I left a Rebel in my office who has just escaped from prison. Go and keep him company until I return."

Delighted by the opportunity to serve a Confederate, Dr. Doe rushed into the office where Jim sat trembling with nervous dread of some adverse happening, and noticing that no attention was paid his coming, instantly decided to indulge an inherent fondness for practical joking. Stepping silently to the corner where Jim sat, he laid his hand on the young fellow's shoulder, and in his sternest voice said, " You are my prisoner, sir."

The joke missed fire, its intended victim not being at that moment in the frame of mind to appreciate its humor. Dr. B———'s kindness had inspired him with hopes that the heavy hand and stern voice of the newcomer blasted. Resolving to die then and there, rather than abjectly surrender and be returned to an intolerable captivity, Jim sprang to his feet and between Dr. Doe and the door, and raising a heavy chair threateningly over the bald head of the would-be jokist, exclaimed,

"Make the first motion, you infernal Abolitionist hound, to lay a hand on me, and by the holy Moses, I'll smear the floor with your brains!"

Not a movement made Dr. Doe, nor thought of making one—the moment did not seem auspicious. The resolute tone and look, the unconquerable bearing of the young Rebel, spoke whole volumes of menace, and standing there trembling, he realized that he had sadly mistaken his game. As soon as fright permitted him to use his tongue again, he sought to explain: he was not only an intimate friend of Dr. B——, he said, but was himself a true Confederate; he had come to the office at Dr. B——'s request, and had only intended to play an innocent little joke, and much more to the same purport.

"Well," began Jim, half convinced of Dr. Doe's friendliness, but still indignant at being selected as the butt of such a joke, "if you are as friendly to me and the cause I serve as you make yourself out to be, I reckon you know now that you picked a poor time to play pranks."

"Yes, I know I did," replied Dr. Doe; "and

I humbly beg your pardon for being so thoughtless and inconsiderate. But I'll just step out of doors and see if Dr. B—— is anywhere near."

"Not by a jugful will you step out and do any such thing," quickly interposed Jim. "You will just stay right here in this office till Dr. B—— comes back. Then, if I find you have lied to me, I'll kill you with as little mercy as I would a snake."

And with this possibility staring him in the face, Dr. Doe had no option but to remain; moreover, when Dr. B—— at last returned and demanded an explanation of the obviously strained relations between the fugitive and the gentleman sent to keep him from being lonesome, Dr. Doe had not only to furnish that explanation, but also to accept with meekness a larger measure of chaffing and scolding than such a grave and dignified old gentleman was at all accustomed to. But "all's well that ends well." By the combined assistance of the two physicians and Miss ——, Jim slipped through the lines and is now on duty with his company.

The sun is yet an hour high, I am comfortably fixed for writing, and whether or not you have the patience to read it, have both the time and the inclination to relate the story of another escape. It was told me yesterday, and it is my duty to keep it agoing. The lucky man is a member of the Fifth Texas—his name, I think, Simpson; but whether it be or not, I will call him that. On our way to Maryland in 1862 his chum and messmate, Bob Eddy, said to him:

" See here, old fellow, you are so venturesome
that you are going to be captured some of these
days. If you should be, and can get into the
City of New York, go straight to my father and
he will help you in any way he can. I have
written to him about you. Here is his name and
address on this card."

Simpson took the card and dropped it into
his haversack. Shortly afterward, while out on
a scout, the Yankees gobbled him up and sent
him to a prison on the Delaware coast. A month
later he escaped, boarded a train, and proceeded
to New York City. There his troubles began.
His captors had relieved him of his haversack
and all its contents, and belabor his memory as
he might, he could only remember that the name
of his messmate's father was R. G. Eddy.
When, however, he had recourse to the City Di-
rectory which he found in a leading hotel, and
ascertained that two R. G. Eddys resided on
Chestnut street, he easily identified that as the
street named on the card. One Eddy, though,
lived at 1217, the other at 1310—to which should
he go? At one or the other, assistance awaited
him—at one or the other, the peril of recapture.
Thus far, no notice had been taken of him. To
make inquiries, though, would be to acknowledge
himself a stranger in the city, and perhaps ex-
cite the curiosity of some unfriendly person.
So, jotting down the two addresses, he decided
to call first at 1217. In ante-bellum days tolerably familiar with the city, he had little difficulty in finding, unaided, both street and num-

ber. Tripping lightly up the steps, he rang the
bell, and not caring to attract the attention of
any of the many persons of both sexes then on
their way to church, the moment a servant girl
opened the door sufficiently he stepped inside
and asked for Mr. Eddy. That gentleman happened to be coming down a flight of stairs which
landed in the hall, and, noticing this, the girl
retired. Kindness showed in his countenance,
and he looked enough like the Confederate Eddy
to convince a visitor as sorely in need of help
as was Simpson that he was the father of that
young man, and feeling that at last "his lines
had fallen in pleasant places," Simpson freely
unbosomed himself of his story. Imagine his
dismay when the old gentleman's face lost its
look of benevolence and he said coldly and
sternly,

"You have made a great mistake, sir—you
have come to the wrong place. I am not, thank
God, the father of the Rebel Bob Eddy, but of a
son who is a captain in the Union Army. All
my sympathies are with the Union cause, and
if I do my duty I will have you immediately arrested."

Poor Simpson! A moment ago his heart beat
lightly and buoyantly, now it throbbed slowly
and despairingly, and falling back against the
wall, unable without its support to stand erect,
he stood silent and hopeless. For a minute that
seemed an age to him, not a word was said; then
Mr. Eddy spoke again, saying,

"Yes, it is my duty to have you arrested. But

I can't do as mean a thing as to take advantage
of your mistake in coming here. Just come
along upstairs with me, and we'll see what can
be done."

An hour later Simpson's most intimate friend
would not have recognized him, such was the
transformation that a bath, a clean shave, and
a through change of linen and outer garments
had effected in his appearance. And, *mirabile
dictu,* as many will say who believe that a Northern man cannot be as generous as a Southern,
Mr. Eddy also handed the fugitive a hundred
dollars in greenbacks, and when the latter would
have protested, said,

"It's all right, young man—it's all right, and
don't you bother. I haven't any business to
be helping you at all, but as long as I am doing
it, I am 'going the whole hog' on it. If helping you is treason, I want the treason to be respectable. But it is time you were going. Bob
Eddy's father lives at 1310 on this street, and
in your present disguise you can safely visit him.
But remember, please, that should you and I
meet again it must be as perfect strangers. As
a true lover of my country I ought to wish you
recaptured—as a man, I hope you'll not be."

From the other R. G. Eddy, the father of Bob
Eddy, Simpson received as cordial a welcome
as could safely be given. He spent a month in
the city, frequently meeting his Union benefac-
tor, and then went over into Canada, whence he
made his way back to the South.

XX

BULL'S GAP, TENN., March 25, 1864.

ONCE upon a time, but only by a masterly stratagem, a ragged private secured a seat at a table on which was spread a bountiful dinner which had been specially prepared for a pompous Confederate general. The officer made no objection, but wishing to make sure of the soldier knowing in what distinguished company he was dining, very condescendingly asked,

" Do you know, sir, with whom you are dining? "

" Indeed, I do not," replied the private as he helped himself to half of a roasted chicken; " I used to be very particular about such matters, but nowadays, so the dinner is good and abundant and the company not too fond of blowing his own horn, I don't care a d——n who eats with me."

You would have complimented me on my resemblance to that private had you seen me hobnobbing with General Jenkins, at present commanding the division, last Christmas Eve. There was a symposium that night at his quarters—a feast of reason and flow of soul, under the exhilarating influences of unlimited supplies of apple-jack, and the colonel and inspector-general, for-

209

merly the captain of my company, invited me
and a few others to attend. Although the society promised was higher and more be-barred
and be-starred than we were accustomed to, we
were not such churls as to sulk in our tents while
such festivities were in progress. Not presuming to speak for others, I can only say that after
the third drink a brigadier-general sank in my
estimation to the level of a private, and I sought
and obtained an introduction to my host, General Jenkins. He treated me with distinguished
consideration, talked with me until I became
sober enough to be ashamed of much I had said
to him, and as we parted invited me to call again.
During the conversation I alluded to a former
interview I had had with him at Chattanooga
concerning a hog that had met death and destruction at my hands, but he waived all discussion of the subject, saying with a kindness for
which I am now grateful, " That was official in-
tercourse, sir—this is social and friendly."

Aside from the amusement these incidents may
afford you, I have an object in view. Admitting
my resemblance to the private in the matter of
indifference to the company I dine with, I must
also confess that so she is young and pretty, I
don't care a copper what woman appeals to me
for aid—she is going to have all that is in my
power to offer. It is to call your attention to
the differences between the official and the purely
social and friendly that I have mentioned what
General Jenkins said to me. Hitherto, my letters to you have been quasi-official, and might

be read by anybody you chose to let do so. This communication, though, I wish you to consider confidential, for if our mutual friend gets wind of the adventure I am going to relate, a jealous wrath may tempt her to retaliate. A more prudent person than I might hesitate to reveal it to a living soul, but having the utmost confidence in your discretion and friendship, and feeling that I must tell somebody from whom I may secure a needed sympathy, I will even take the risk.

Three weeks ago and while we were at New Market, Lieutenant Crigler was ordered to take a force of twenty-five picked men and make an effort to capture some Federals who were depredating on our side of French Broad River. Obeying orders, he set out at sunrise, and by 3 o'clock P. M. arrived at a point a couple of miles from the river. There, Crockett and Pengra were sent ahead with instructions not to show themselves, or attack the enemy, and to return as soon as they learned the position of affairs. Giving them twenty minutes start, the rest of us proceeded leisurely forward. About a quarter of a mile from the river, hearing nothing from the scouts, we deployed into a skirmish line with its center on a road that led to the ferry the Federals were in the habit of using, and advanced slowly and cautiously.

To the right of the road, on a hill, and about a hundred yards from the water's edge, stood a large, roomy house inclosed by a plank fence. My position in the line was such that, going straight forward and maintaining proper intervals between myself and comrades to my right and left, I marched directly toward the back door of the house. When within fifty feet of the fence and twice as far from the door, and while I was deliberating whether to go around or through the house, the sound of two rifle shots at the river broke upon my ears. Within a second a volley was fired from the opposite bank, and several of the balls striking the house, and a woman screaming, I sprang forward to the rescue. It was up-hill, though, and speed was as impossible as it was unnecessary, for I had not gone ten feet when a handsome girl of eighteen rushed out of the open door crying, "Save me, save me!" and running to the fence, climbed it with utter and alarming disregard for the planking and other unmentionables, and still crying to be saved, sped down the hill, straight and swift as an arrow, toward me.

You can imagine the predicament I was in, Charming Nellie, as well as I can describe it; but woman that you are, you can never experience or conceive my feelings. Only twenty-three years of age, far away from home and kindred, a sweetheart back in Texas, embarrassed by a gun I dared not drop, and my footing on the rocky and uneven hillside somewhat precarious, I was never in my life as pleased and frightened at one and the same time as when I realized the lovely creature's aim and my duty in the premises. But the faintness of spirit that came over me like a summer breeze, was as short-lived. A

soldier from another State might have taken to
his heels, or at least cleared the way for the
girl to fall in another man's arms. But to me,
a Texan by birth, who had sworn to do his part
in maintaining the reputation for gallantry and
self-sacrificing heroism bequeathed as a priceless
heritage to his State by the patriots who at the
Alamo fought and died that their compatriots
might fight and win at San Jacinto, such un-
manly behavior would have been a disgrace.
Here was the opportunity of my life, both to perform a duty that I owed to the chivalry of my
nature and to secure temporary possession, at
least, of a " thing of beauty and a joy forever,"
and I vowed to myself that it should not pass
unimproved. Therefore, I stood my ground
firmly, resolutely, and unflinchingly, until with
a momentum which nearly carried me off my
feet that one hundred and twenty-five pound in-
carnation of " the true, beautiful and good," in
the guise of exquisitely handsome womanhood,
ran fairly and squarely into arms which opened
to receive the precious and bewitching deposit
as instinctively as they closed to make sure of
it when, coming within their circle, the terror-
stricken maiden threw her own around my neck.

" Save me, save me! " she continued to cry,
even while she clung to me with a tenacity that
would have been alarming had it not been so
comfortably thrilling; and more than willing to
save her, I bent every energy, art, and accomplishment to the task, and drawing her close to
my chivalrous bosom, assured her, again and

again, that she was absolutely safe as long as
she stayed right where she was. Evidently she
believed me—presumably she found as much relief from her fright in clinging to me, as I, comfort and happiness in being stay, support, and
protector, for we stood there in close com-
munion—I, at any rate, unconscious of the passage of time, the proximity of the enemy, or of
anything else less heavenly than the contents of
my arms—until the Yankees retired beyond gunshot and the firing ceased.

The one obstacle and drawback to supreme
felicity was my gun. Too well-trained a soldier
to drop the weapon while an enemy was near at
hand, much as I wanted both hands free I clung
to it to the last. Still, while I might have handled it so awkwardly that it would have puzzled
a military expert to say who held it, or in what
direction it pointed, I am positively sure it was
never between me and my fair companion; it
would have been too much in the way. I frankly
confess, Charming Nellie, that the occasion was
the one time in my career as a soldier when the
enemy's retreat was too precipitate—the one
time when I prayed fervently that the battle
should continue; for as long as it lasted the
maiden seemed to find content, shelter, and
safety within the clasp of my arms, and I forgot my country and, almost, the loyalty I owe
to our mutual friend. Unluckily, and more to
my regret and disappointment than anything
that has happened to me individually since this
never-ending war began, my prayers availed me

not. The enemy retreated, the firing ceased, and the occupant of my arms, alas, awakened to a sense of conventional proprieties and the fact that I was a stranger, and without the least assistance from me, released herself, and left me holding only the cold, insensate, and inanimate gun.

But although she blushed charmingly as she stepped out of my reach, she was no bashful and awkward country miss. The moment she got far enough from me to prohibit whispering, she said,

"Please excuse my behavior, sir. I was so frightened by the shooting that I didn't know what I was doing, and I fear I have not only shocked you by a seeming boldness but also given you a great deal of trouble."

"Pray do not distress yourself by imagining you have done either," I hastened to reply, bowing with a grace that Chesterfield might well have envied. "The incident has given me a delight I would gladly enjoy again." Then noticing she found it difficult to preserve her balance on the steep hillside, I laid my gun down, and pretending a great solicitude, asked, "Are you sure you no longer need support?"—at the same time stepping toward her with extended arms.

"Thank you, but I do not need to trespass again on your gallantry and endurance," she replied, glancing roguishly at me, but blushing like a rose and waving her little hand in further prohibition. "But will you not go to the house and let me introduce you to my mother and sisters and tell them of your kindness to me. I don't know that the latter is necessary, however, for Sis Mary looked out of the door while you had your arms—I mean, while I was most frightened."

I had not seen Sis Mary, for the maid to whom I was giving my whole attention had come at me with such speed that her momentum swung me around and placed me with my back to the house. But still game, I said, " You must introduce me as your lover, then, for that I am, now and forever. You are the captive of my arms, please remember, and I'll not waive a single right or privilege due me as such."

She was of good pluck, too. Her black eyes flashing with mischief, she answered at once, " Well, let us go to the house, at any rate—we can discuss and settle there any rights and privileges you may claim."

As we walked slowly up the hill toward the house, she bore to the right, obviously intending to go around the yard to the front gate. I demurred and suggested returning by the way she had come. But she shook her head in protest, saying,

" No, indeed. Alarmed as I was when I scurried out of the house, I got over the fence with more speed than gracefulness, I fancy. But now that all danger has passed, I will not make another such essay, thank you."

By the time we entered the house—it took us twenty minutes to get to the front door, though

—we learned each other's name and all constraint had vanished. I was duly introduced to the mother and sisters, and they proved to be nice and intelligent ladies, and the wife and daughters of a Baptist minister by the name of Scruggs. But although Sis Mary smiled a trifle significantly as she gave me her hand and the erstwhile tenant of my arms showed her colors charmingly, I do not remember that I felt or betrayed any special embarrassment. But as about that time several of my comrades came in, no reference was made in the general conversation that followed to the recent close engagement between me and Miss Eva. But, alas, time pressed and orders had to be obeyed, even if to obey them almost broke my heart. Much against inclination, I said good-by; not, however, without extending to their late occupant a pantomimic invitation to return to my arms, at which Sis Mary laughed merrily and Miss Eva blushed temptingly, and, I thought, just a little regretfully. Having been too intent on war to learn of my good fortune, my comrades looked puzzled and exchanged wondering glances. Too sad of heart to enlighten their ignorance and thus cause each of them to wish he had been as lucky, I gave Miss Eva's little hand one fond and lingering squeeze, picked up my gun, and with a sigh returned to the stern realities of a soldier's life.

Remember, please, that I relate this incident for your entertainment alone. With naught but a friendly feeling subsisting between us, I know

I can trust you not to communicate it to my
lady. While I have not seen Miss Eva since it
occurred, and bound as we are now, if reports
be true, for old Virginia, never expect to see her
again; and, while I could not with proper regard for my sex and the innate chivalry of my
own nature have done less than I did, my lady
might discover disloyalty in it, and if not content with merely raking me over the coals of her
virtuous wrath, give me the grand bounce.
Really and truly, it is only the second adventure I have had since this cruel war began, in
which a pretty woman has figured. I often
wonder if that lady in the Shenandoah Valley
has yet succeeded in securing either a hoop skirt
or a pair of shoes. I wish I had given her the
gaiters instead of losing them as I did. As a
gift she might have thought them worth a grateful thought—as a loss, they are a disappointment. But she was not as pretty as Miss Eva,
who was in truth and in fact the most thrilling
incident that ever fell to my arms. Hope holds
the word of promise to my lady that the future
will afford me one even more thrilling, but—
well, as there is no saying when or whether I
will get home, I ought to be excused if occasionally I act on the theory that " a bird in the hand
is worth two in the bush." I will bet you the best-
gaited saddle pony to be found in west Texas that
your Tennessee correspondent does likewise whenever opportunity offers. According to my observation and information, not to say experience, the
average Tennessee girl is not only quite handsome,

but is likewise a firm believer in a woman's right to make opportunities, and your fellow is not a man likely to neglect any that come in his way. Fortunately for his and my peace of mind, though, Texas girls are denied the facilities which so abundantly bless the maiden world this side of the Father of Waters. Thanks to the valiancy and watchfulness of the gallant Coast Catamounts, no blustering Yankees are suffered to wander broadcast over the land to frighten timid maidens out of their wits and compel them to " fly to arms " for protection.

XXI

A THIRTY-DAY FURLOUGH

CHARLOTTE, N. C., April 23, 1864.

COMFORTABLY reclining within the ample
depths of a cane-bottom armchair before a cozy
little fire, a mahogany table and writing mate-
rials within easy reach, a carpet under my feet,
wearing neatly blacked shoes lately imported
from England, and a stiffly starched calico shirt
that cost, exclusive of the laundry bill, all of
a ten-dollar Confederate bill, conscience clear,
mind untroubled, digestion excellent, and full
justice recently done to a first-rate dinner—I
feel myself every inch a gentleman. Over my
head a neatly papered ceiling, around me walls
with bookcases filled with elegantly bound literature, looking admonishingly down upon me from
their rosewood frames the portraits of half a
dozen ladies and gentlemen long since dead, a
couple of windows opening into the street,
through which I catch glimpses of well-dressed
people as they pass and repass, on business and
pleasure intent, and a sweet, well-trained voice
in an adjoining room singing to the accompani-
ment of a piano, " Ever of thee I'm fondly
dreaming "—I have to pinch myself to be sure
I am really the same fellow who, a month ago,
wrote you from East Tennessee. Then, ragged,

dirty, and unkempt, I sat on the ground, had
no shelter but the blue sky, wrote on a board
held in my lap, warmed by a fire that filled my
eyes with smoke, looked only upon men as
wretchedly garbed as myself, and heard only
their harsh voices and the martial blare, clang,
and beat of Collin's band.   *   *   *

While encamped on Mossy Creek, down in East
Tennessee, the members of the Texas Brigade
were invited to enlist " for an' indurin' of the
war." In sober and unvarnished truth, it was
enlist or be conscripted, and not the generous
and considerate offer Henry V. made when—
according to the well-thumbed volume of Shakespeare, which, in the absence of other literature,
I have occasionally borrowed, and from which
I have excerpted the poetic gems with which I
have ornamented my letters—he proclaimed:

> " He which hath no stomach for this fight,
> Let him depart; his passport shall be made."

Had it been, it is doubtful whether a single
one of the furloughs—one to every tenth man—
offered as rewards to those re-enlisting, would
have found a taker, but, under the peculiar
circumstances—the adroit mingling of moral
suasion with an implied threat of compulsion—
every mother's son of us stepped patriotically
into line and swore to serve our beloved country,
Providence permitting, for the balance of the
war, last as long as it may. Conscription, you
know, is not a reputable method of earning the
privilege of fighting for one's home and fireside.

Then came the drawing of lots for the furloughs, in which I was unlucky, for of the two
going to my company I drew neither, but schem-
ing and a modicum of filthy lucre accomplished
what chance refused. One of the fortunate comrades found all of his comfort, happiness, and
delight in the fascinating game of poker, and, in
consideration of the wherewithal to enable him
to follow his bent, he readily transferred his
right to a furlough to me. When, after a long
time, the papers finally reached us, the important question of where to go arose, for I had no
citizen friends east of the Mississippi outside
of the Federal lines, except in Virginia, and,
judging from past experiences there, it was not
likely I could find a place far enough away from
the seat of war to be thoroughly pleasant.   I
remained in a quandary but a short while, for
Aleck Wilson, of Company D, proved himself
"a friend indeed" by being "a friend in need,"
and invited me to come with him to this place,
where he has numerous wealthy relatives. Thus
it happens that to-day I am an honored guest in
the house of Judge Wilson, an occupant for the
time being of his library, and an eager and
charmed listener to the delicious vocal and instrumental music of his lovely daughter, whom
to her face and to others I call "Miss Annie,"
but in the gratitude of my heart for her unvary-
ing sympathetic kindness think of only as "Gentle Annie."   To her humanizing influence, more
than to aught else, I am indebted for the larger
part of my self-respect and respectability.

Accustomed all our lives to the simple usages and habits of western Texas people, Aleck and I find it rather difficult to keep ourselves up to the full standard of these North Carolina gentlefolks. There are " F. F's." of North Carolina, just as there are of Virginia. Determined to have all the fun and frolic possible to be enjoyed in our thirty-days' leave of absence, and yet unwilling to cut entirely loose from the exclusive circles of the literary and polished people among whom the relationship of one and the good fortune of the other have thrown us, we lead double lives: one day minding our p's and q's, eating with our forks, punctiliously careful to observe all the proprieties and requirements of the most refined and cultured society—in short, whether walking, dancing, talking, or silent, behaving ourselves absolutely and faultlessly *en regle;* the next day consorting with plain, old-fashioned people, eating with our knives, unmindful of phraseology, romping, dancing, and flirting with the prettiest girls, and as forgetful of prim, mirth-restraining etiquette as a couple of schoolboys. Ample opportunity for the doubleness is afforded, since two other members of the Fourth Texas are here, and their folks, fortunately for us, belong to the great unwashed middle class of people who take life as they find it. Our indulgence of democratic proclivities meets with no direct rebuke, so far as I am individually concerned. Hitherto wholly unknown, I am not likely hereafter to be specially remembered and grieved over as a lost sheep; but Aleck, poor fellow, catches it on all sides from his half-dozen or more handsome lady cousins, each of whom deems it her special duty and privilege to rake him over the coals for every one of his social transgressions. "Where were you last night, Aleck?" one of them will suddenly inquire, looking at him meanwhile with a cousinly tenderness which forbids the least approach to deceit, and drags the truth from him *nolens volens;* and then the sweet creatures pitch into him at a lively rate, and, although pretending to make their remarks entirely confidential, give me the full benefit of them, in spite of the fact that, on hearing the first question, I make a point of engaging the Judge in an argument, from which I invariably emerge outrageously worsted.

* * * * *

When my furlough came to me in East Tennessee, I looked forward to the many and great pleasures anticipated with the keen longing of one to whom for nearly three years social enjoyments have been almost wholly lacking, and the thirty days given seemed to stretch out interminably. Now, looking back at the twenty odd already a part of the past, they seem only so many short and fleeting hours. Only a mere taste of pleasure has come to me, just enough to teach me its flavor and to whet a sharp edge on an always craving and apparently insatiable appetite. Seven days are all that remain of the thirty, and within them I must compress fun and frolic enough to last until the end of the war, however distant and uncertain that may be. I will hardly have the luck to receive a "parlor wound." The Yankees began shooting at my head, and will probably continue the pastime until by some lucky mischance they perforate that member of my body, and thus make it useless as a seat of thought.

Counting up the days of my stay here, and making each give an account of itself, it is easy to calculate in what particulars I have been improvident or neglectful, and failed to extract all the pleasure possible from the best of opportunities and the most favorable surroundings. Retrospection, however, does little good. Time will not " turn backward in its flight," do what I may in the way of praying and grieving. It is not here as in Texas, you know. There, you ladies find masculine game in such superabundance that you have only to choose which you will permit to fall into your traps and nets. Here, though, it is a case of one or two marriageable men a month, and from fifty to a hundred pining maids and widows all the time— the widows, of course, when they are young and pretty and not too largely encumbered with prattling responsibilities, having much the advantage over their fair rivals. I have no right to complain that either class has bestowed many alluring smiles on me. Whatever may have been my hopes and intentions at the outset, of adding a spice of long-wished-for variety to life, they were nipped in the bud by the treachery of my friend Aleck. To make himself the more entertaining to the maid he liked best, he not only informed her that I corresponded regularly with a Texas girl, but when cross-examined was mean enough to deny that I corresponded with any other. This, I suppose, made the conclusion irresistible that I am engaged, monopolized, and appropriated beyond break or recovery; at any rate, while the girls listen kindly to my sentimentalities, they refuse to believe them serious enough to justify even a flirtation with me.

Discussing the situation with Aleck, he suggested I should let one of the darlings read your last letter, and promised, if I would, to confess he was lying when he said I corresponded with anybody but you. That, however, would not do at all, for that particular last letter was the first in which you have acted the part of a true "friend at court," and told me all that I have to hope and fear with respect to our mutual friend.

I wish you would send me a likeness of yourself. There is no telling when I may get a final quietus, and prior to such a distressing event I should like to look once, at least, at the face of the charming correspondent I have never seen in the flesh. Besides, I wish to show the picture to my friend, Lieutenant Grizzle of Company C, to whom I have sometimes read portions of your letters. He swears that he knows you are the prettiest girl in all Texas, and that if he survives the war he will lay his heart at your feet a week after he gets home. I am sure the gallant captain in Bragg's army, whom I suspect of having the first and choicest place in your regard, will not object either to my having the likeness, or to my showing it to the lieutenant. On the contrary, he will likely be glad to have your thoughts drawn away from the stay-at-homes now infesting the Texas coast and slyly but persistently seeking to poach on his preserves. If he is like me, it is the rival who remains always tangible to his sweetheart that he fears—not a poor devil who is taking his chances at a front where fighting is the rule and not the exception.

No words at my command can express the comfort and company that the likeness of our mutual friend is to me. I have had it so long, looked at it so often, and thought and dreamed so frequently of the lady it represents, that it has become a part of myself—an almost constant consciousness. It has been with me in camp and on the march, in every vigil on the picket-post, and in every skirmish and battle, standing between me and every danger that threatened. Although not battle-scarred, it is war-worn, for it has heard the roar of artillery, the rattle of musketry, and the bursting of shells at Eltham's Landing, Seven Pines, Gaines' Mill, Thoroughfare Gap, Second Manassas, Boonesboro Gap, Fredericksburg, Suffolk, Gettysburg, Chickamauga, Raccoon Mountain, Knoxville, Bean's Station, and many minor engagements and skirmishes that will never find place on the pages of history. Of how many more it will be able to speak, God only knows, but, unless we make better headway this year than we did last, and unless the men in blue continue the poor marksmen they have hitherto shown themselves, the number will be doubled, or even trebled. Should the time ever come, as I pray it may, and that very soon, when its original shall fill its place, I am going to put it in a glass case, place beneath it a list of the battles in which it has participated and the marches it has made, and set it where it may be a constant reminder of the past to me and my lady and such little folks as may develop an interest in their father's career as a soldier of the Confederacy.

I have but three days longer to stay here if I would escape punishment for overstaying the time set by my furlough. The parting from the kind friends I have met sits the more heavily on my mind because of the fact that I will have to begin soldiering again the moment I board the train. Counting up my supply of Confederate currency this morning, I discovered that I have not enough left to pay any hotel bills on my way back to the command. Considering that I left my blanket at camp, the sleeping out of doors I will have to do has not a promising look. I have nobody to blame but myself, though—I ought to have been more economical.

Speaking of economy reminds me of Bill Calhoun's last bon-mot. When Hood was made a brigadier-general, the Texas Brigade raised a large sum of money, and investing it in the finest horse to be found in the State of Virginia, presented the animal to him. When he lost a leg at Chickamauga, the brigade raised more money and purchased for him the best artificial limb to be had in the South. When Bill was called upon for his mite toward the last purchase, he fished it slowly and hesitatingly from the cavernous depths of his pocket, then removed a quid of tobacco from his mouth, drew a long, solemn breath, and remarked,

" I ain't got a stingy bone in my body, an' you fellers all know it; but twined round every fiber and filament of my mental caliber is a never-dyin' sperriet o' rigid and uncompromising economy, an' I want yer ter tell ole Hood that hereafter he must slip a curb on the impetuosity of his bravery, and stay farther to the rear. Ole as he is, he oughter know he can't do any good by gettin' close 'nough ter the blamed Yanks ter be shot at. Ef he keeps on doin' like he's been er doin', it'll bust this ole brigade er-buyin' hosses an' legs fur the ole cuss."

But I must close; not, though, because I want to, but only because Miss Annie is calling on me to come into the parlor and help her entertain a squad of maidens who have just called.

XXII

TEXAS IN THE BATTLE OF THE WILDERNESS

IN THE TRENCHES NEAR PETERSBURG,
July 6, 1864.

A LONG, weary time, full of hardship, deprivation, and danger to Lee's army has intervened
since I wrote from Gordonsville. Since then I
have written several letters, but I fear they were
the shadows of a despondent mind—the only
comfort in them to the recipients being the assurance that I was yet living. The present life
in the trenches is the nearest approach to rest
we have had since May 6. Bill Calhoun calls
it "a rest between roasts"; such, he says, as
the unrepentant are sometimes allowed in the
next world. There is much in the situation and
surroundings to warrant the comparison, saying
nothing of the hot sun, whose beams beat relentlessly upon our devoted heads through an
atmosphere as motionless as that said to hover
over the Dead Sea, and of the never-ceasing
"pish," "pish," of bullets, that admonish us
against stiffness of neck and high-headedness.
The Federals are supposed to be undermining
our breastworks, as likely immediately beneath
us as anywhere else. Any day or hour the mine
may be sprung which will send us Texans farther heavenward than many of us ever expect

to get otherwise, and certainly farther than any of us ever have been.   And, yet, were there a certainty—aye! even the half of a hope—that the law of gravitation and the weight of sin with which we are burdened would not interfere, and, arresting our ascent, teach us that "*facilis decensus Averno est*," we are just tired enough of this soldiering, this almost insufferable suspense and monotony, to welcome the change.

Of the battle of the Wilderness I can tell you little beyond what occurred in my own regiment; the character of the ground forbade a general view, even by officers highest in rank. The Texas Brigade broke camp at two o'clock on the morning of the 6th, and, by double-quicking the last two miles, reached the scene of action at sun-up.   Filing to the right, and marching a quarter of a mile down the plank road, it formed into line of battle and loaded.   Then, advancing in a gradual right wheel, it was brought to front the enemy, whose lines stretched across the road.   Our position was on an open hill immediately in rear of a battery.   Within three hundred yards were the Yankees, and, but for intervening timber, we would have been exposed to their fire.   Here General Lee, mounted on the same horse (a beautiful dapple-gray) which carried him at Fredericksburg in 1862, rode up near us and gave his orders to General Gregg, adding, "The Texas Brigade always has driven the enemy, and I expect them to do it to-day.   Tell them, General, that I shall witness their conduct to-day."   Galloping in front, General Gregg delivered the message, and shouted, "Forward, Texas Brigade!" Just then Lee rode in front of the Fifth Texas, as if intending to lead the charge, but a shout went up, "Lee to the rear!" and a soldier sprang from the ranks, and, seizing the dapple-gray by the reins, led him and his rider to the rear. The Yankee sharpshooters soon discovered our approach, and some of our best men were killed and wounded before a chance was given them to fire a shot. At three hundred yards the leaden hail began to thin our ranks perceptibly; four hundred yards and we were confronted by a line of blue, which, however, fled before us without firing a single volley. Across the plank road stood another line, and against this we moved rapidly. The storm of battle became terrific. The Texas Brigade was alone; no support on our right, and not only none on the left, but a terrible enfilading fire poured on us from that direction. Crossing the road, we pressed forward two hundred yards farther, when, learning that a column of Federals was double-quicking from the left and would soon have us surrounded, General Gregg gave the order to fall back. General Lee's object was gained, his trust in the Texans justified, for the ground from which two divisions had been driven was recaptured by one small brigade of whose men more than one-half were killed and wounded. The Fourth Texas carried into the action two hundred and seven men, and lost one hundred and thirty, thirty of whom were killed outright, or died of their wounds.

"Nothing, except a battle lost, can be half so melancholy as a battle won," some writer has said. At sun-up two hundred and seven strong men stand in line of battle; half an hour afterward all but seventy-seven of them are dead or wounded—mangled, torn, and dismembered by bullets, round shot, and shell. Some of the wounded walk back without aid to the field hospital, others are being carried there on litters or in the arms of their friends, and still others are lying on the field of battle, too near the enemy to be safely reached by their compatriots. The dead need neither help nor immediate attention, but next day are buried side by side, as they fought, in a wide, shallow trench, the name of each carved on a rude headboard, while close by the great grave at the side of the plank road is nailed to a wide-spreading, stately oak another board, bearing the simple but eloquent inscription: "Texas Dead—May 6, 1864."

The color-bearer of the Fourth Texas was wounded and sank to the ground, yet he held the flag aloft long enough to hand it to Durfee, of Company B, a brave Irishman, who carried it to a point within a hundred and fifty yards of the enemy's breastworks. There, his hip shattered by a ball, he gave it to Sergeant-Major Charles S. Brown, who, disabled at the moment of receiving it, before sinking to the ground passed it to a fourth man, who held it out of the dust and carried it floating proudly and defiantly in the air back with the regiment. Durfee and Brown, companions in misfortune,

crawled to the foot of the same tree, Durfee
sitting on the side next to the Confederates,
Brown on that facing the Federals. In one of
the lulls of the battle Austin Jones crept out
to them on his hands and knees and offered to
carry Brown in his arms to a place of safety.
The wounded hero refused, saying, " Durfee and
I were wounded together and must leave the
field together." Ten minutes later, when Jones
returned with two litters and their bearers, Durfee was living, Brown dead. He had been shot
in the head, and with it drooped upon his breast
sat there as if sleeping.

The dangers of a battle, and even the presence
of death, never utterly destroy a soldier's sense
of the ludicrous. Among the first men of the
Fourth to be wounded was Jim Summerville. A
bullet struck the buckle of his belt and barely
penetrated the skin, but one's stomach is very
sensitive. Jim dropped his gun, folded his arms
across the front of his corporosity, and, whirl-
ing around a couple of times, gave vent to a long-
drawn, emphatic groan with all the variations
of the gamut in it, which provoked a roar of
laughter from the regiment. It was not insensi-
bility to suffering or lack of sympathy which
caused the merriment, but an irresistible desire
to extract a little comedy out of deadly tragedy.
In such critical emergencies men have no time
to waste in bewailing what has happened; what
may happen is far more important. Sympathy
given every unfortunate would unnerve those on
whose coolness and presence of mind depend the

fate of battle. The wounded soldier has taken his risk and lost; that of his comrade is yet to be run, and who knows but that it may be death?

Bob Murray has a pair of remarkably careless legs, and they often carry him into danger. On this occasion one of them tried conclusions with a Yankee bullet and got the worst of it, being broken below the knee. Two days before, he and I, sitting astride a pine log, were playing our one hundred and thirty-fifth game of "seven-up," and, with characteristic impudence, he "begged," and I "gave him one," when he had "high, low, Jack, and the game" in his hands. It was such an abuse of a friend's confidence that I quit the game in disgust. Now, in identically the same tone in which he "begged" then, he cried out to me: "Dad gum it, Joe, I beg; you and 'Ole Pap' help me to the rear!" Indignation swelled high in my bosom for an instant, and as quickly subsided—the rear was just then infinitely more attractive than the place we were. Placing Bob between us, an arm over each of our shoulders, the Veteran (who is also known as "Ole Pap," because of his age and fatherly ways) and I made for the rear with him. Although not a large man by any means, the venerable comrade has an immense amount of energy, and displayed it on this occasion by an impetuous rush over all the obstacles of undergrowth and fallen timber, Bob's broken limb dangling about with a "go-as-you-please" movement, and wrapping itself around the small bushes, and your humble servant kept altogether

too busy watching out for his feet to hang on to
his sombrero. " Hold on, Morris, and let me get
my hat!" I sang out, as a branch caught and
captured that useful article. " A great time to
pick up a hat!" he responded, without halting.
But he had to stop for breath at the plank road,
and there I found and appropriated a straw hat
which some other unfortunate had lost. Next
day, though, it was claimed by a wounded man,
and if Bob had not been generous I would have
been compelled to administer on the estate of a
deceased Yankee or go hatless.

The 7th was a day of comparative rest and
quiet; also the 8th, on the evening of which day
the brigade moved toward Spottsylvania Court
House and took position behind hastily erected
breastworks. On the evening of the 10th the
Yankees attacked, and, having given no notice
of their intentions, captured and held for a short
time a portion of the line, but were repulsed with
great slaughter. After the fighting ceased, which
was not until sundown, it became necessary to
establish a line of pickets in our front. Details
of two men were accordingly made from each
company, the Veteran Morris and Pokue going
from Company F, and the whole squad being
under command of Captain Mat Beasley. Pokue
is a magnificent specimen of the physical man
—six feet and four inches in height, weighing
nearly two hundred pounds—and noted at home
for courage in personal difficulties. Here in the
army and as a soldier he wins no laurels. While
he keeps in line as long as the advance is con-

tinuous and artillery is not used against us, he never fires a gun. If a shell or round shot hurtles over or through the commands, he lets all holds go and drops broadcast to Mother Earth. If there is a halt, he is so fond of exercise that he runs.

In short, Pokue is as much a noncombatant as any member of Stokes's cavalry. That is a notorious command which pretends to serve the Federals, but dares not fire on Confederates, except from the safety of inaccessible hilltops. Once, when Forrest had surrounded Nashville and was about to open fire on the Union troops holding it, he sent a message to the mayor to remove Stokes's cavalry and the women and children, as he did not want to fire on noncombatants.

That part of the line at Spottsylvania occupied by the Texas Brigade ran along a high ridge, and the dense undergrowth in its front had been so cut down and trimmed as to give a tolerably unobstructed view for a hundred and fifty yards. Beyond this clearing forbiddingly frowned a forest of heavy timber and small growth, a dark and dangerous *terra incognita,* somewhere in whose depths the enemy was presumed to be concealed. Deployed as skirmishers, the pickets made all haste to the cover of these woods, but, arrived there, prudence demanded the greatest caution. It was growing quite dark, not even a guess could be made as to the enemy's whereabouts, and an ambuscade was a thing to be dreaded. Still, it was important to establish the picket line as near that of the Yankees as possible, and slowly and silently the Confederates threaded their way into the obscurity. But someone was careless, and suffered the trigger of his full-cocked gun to be caught by a twig. A loud report broke the awe-inspiring stillness, and a ball came whistling threateningly down the Confederate line. Coming from the front, it would have been expected and returned; coming from the flank, its meaning was serious and demoralizing. "Flanked, boys, flanked!" shouted a soldier of known bravery, and every man, except Beasley and the Veteran, who happened to be near each other, made a rush to the open ground and the breastworks.

Beasley and the Veteran shouted, "Halt! halt!" but there was none; and, deciding it was useless to stay there alone and run the risk of capture, they, too, took to their heels, still shouting "Halt!" as they ran. Few men can beat the Veteran in a foot race, and, as on this occasion he put his whole soul in his legs, he gained rapidly on his retreating comrades, and especially on Pokue, who, however willing and practiced in the art of retreat, is remarkably slow of foot. Hearing the cry of "Halt!" immediately behind him, Pokue, in his agitated condition of mind, imagined it came from a Yankee. Then, just as he looked over his shoulder and caught a glimpse of the Veteran, gun in hand, in swift pursuit, his foot caught under a root and he tumbled headlong to the ground. Rolling quickly over on his back and raising his hands in supplication, he cried, " I surrender, Mr. Yankee! I surrender, sir!" And such was the poor fellow's confusion and fright that not until the light of a campfire shone upon his captor's smiling face did he realize that he had surrendered to one of his own company.

XXIII

FUN IN THE TRENCHES

(Letter of July 6, 1864, Continued)

JUST as I had finished the foregoing, I was handed your letter of June 15, and had scarcely read it, when a sergeant notified me that my turn had come for a little practice at the enemy. The hostile lines are so near each other that picketing is impossible, and, in self-defense, one-third of our command is on watch night and day. Were powder and lead as abundant with us as with the Yankees, we should, like them, keep up a continuous fire during the day, for, while practically useless it would give us employment. Simply peeping over the breastworks, at the risk of our lives, is not the most pleasant pastime in the world. As a compromise between economy and consequent monotony on the one side, and desire for sport on the other, we do shoot some; but rarely except when there is a chance to kill. All through the night firing is maintained from both sides—the Yankees shooting, both to prevent an unexpected attack, and to hide their mining operations; but we, mainly to prevent sudden assault.

Your most amusing account of the fright recently given to the gallant defenders of the

J. F. LOWN
Private, Company H, Fourth Texas Regiment

Texas coast, reminds me of an anecdote told on Roddy's cavalry, a regiment said to be always more ready to run than to fight. Whether there be any truth in this imputation—that particular command serving in the Western army—I simply tell the story as I heard it. It appears that a railroad train passing through Alabama carried a large number of soldiers. One at the front end of a car rose to his feet, gun in hand, and inquired in a loud voice if there was any member of Roddy's regiment on board. No one answering, he repeated the inquiry with a solicitude that demanded response, and immediately a little fellow at the other end of the car arose, and modestly acknowledged himself a member of the regiment. "That's all right, then," said the inquirer, with an air of great relief, as he cocked his gun and poked the muzzle out the window. "I just wanted to tell you not to be scared, honey, for I ain't a bit mad; I'm only gwine ter pop a cap."

But, honestly, Charming Nellie, when I think of those poor Confederate soldiers quartered in the stores and warehouses at Galveston, each mess occupying a room to itself, and their officers boarding around in private families, my tender heart fairly dissolves in its overflow of sympathy. They have a rough time, even if the rations furnished them are supplemented by the daily contributions of citizens, friends, and relatives; and, because of the manly fortitude with which they endure such grievous and disheartening hardships, deserve the plaudits of a grateful country. Should we fellows up here in Virginia and down in Georgia and Tennessee ever succeed in winning Southern independence, they may rely confidently upon me—always provided I am not called upon to be a martyr—to do all in my power to secure them their just deserts. After pampering and petting them so long and assiduously, it would be criminal in the Confederate Government not to continue it. They are not inured to danger and hardship as we are, and should be placed in no position to incur either. Ladies deserve consideration, too, for, if the war continues much longer, there will be an appalling scarcity of men physically capable of bearing their ends of the marriage yoke.

A queer character is Jordan, of Company I, a fast friend of Pokue. He is not a coward by any means, but he is utterly and indescribably lazy. Since the incident of Pokue's capture, both Pokue and Jordan have been objects of intense interest and solicitude to the whole brigade, and scarcely a day has passed that they have not received proof of it. To relieve in some measure the dull monotony of life in the trenches, it has become a custom to call upon them daily for an exhibition of their prowess and marksmanship. Men are only children grown up, you know, and must have amusement. Suddenly the cry arises, "Jordan! Jordan! Pokue! Pokue! Jordan and Pokue!" and, although it starts from one or two, it is taken up by others, until it becomes a volume of sound and an imperative demand upon the parties named. Caring nothing for ridicule, and remarkably good-natured, Jordan sits still and irresponsive. No amount of talking will persuade him to his feet, but, when on them, with a cocked gun laid across the breastworks in easy reach, he always finds the energy to take deliberate aim and pull the trigger; and then, woe betide the bluecoat at whom he shoots! His aim is unerring.

Pokue, however, needs no urging, for he is too proud when out of danger to willingly betray his cowardice. Waiting until Jordan has performed his part of the programme and laughing as heartily as anyone at him, Pokue, with a great show of alacrity and desire to please, lays his gun across the breastworks at an angle that will carry the ball high over the heads of the Yankee in the neighboring works; and, let alone, he shoots at that angle. Our friends across the way are ever on the alert, and send a compliment in the shape of a Minie ball at every head that exposes itself above the safety-line. Pokue is never let alone, but receives cautions and advice from all sides. "Lower the muzzle of your gun, Pokue," one will say; "for you will hit nothing but a quartermaster or commissary that way, and they ain't worth killing." "Take good aim, old fellow," another cries; "ammunition is mighty scarce in these here Confederate States." "But don't wait to see if you get your man," chimes in a third; "it's dangerous." And, anxious to demonstrate his profound appreciation of these and a hundred or more similar remarks, Pokue hugs his gun to his shoulder, and bobs his head and the muzzle of the weapon alternately up and down, like the ends of a seesaw, until, in a sudden access of courage or desperation, rising high enough to catch a glimpse of the top of the enemy's breastworks, he pulls the trigger and sinks back, exhausted, pale, and perspiring, into the arms of his friends, ready to receive their laughing congratulations.

It is not likely you have any definite idea of the trenches. Imagine a ditch eight feet wide and three or four deep, the dirt from which is thrown on the side next to the enemy and forms an embankment just high enough for a man to stand erect and look over. This embankment is the breastworks which protects us from the shots of the Yankees. The ditch extends for miles to the right and left, or, at any rate, as far as there is a necessity for protection. Leading back from the main ditch at acute or obtuse angles, according to the nature of the ground and situation of the enemy's works, and with the dirt likewise thrown on the side next to the enemy, are smaller ditches, called traverses, in which the soldiers sleep and do their cooking, washing, starching, and ironing. Here at Petersburg we found the lines of defense already prepared for occupancy, but until we reached those about Richmond we had to do our own digging; sometimes, too, in an emergency so great that resort was had to bayonets and tin cups, in the absence of spades, shovels, and picks.

Often there was neither time nor inclination to construct traverses, and then men

who objected to sleeping in the main trench, to
be run over and annoyed by wanderers, dug
square, shallow holes in the ground just back
of the main line. At Cold Harbor our brigade
worked all night with only bayonets, cups, two
or three picks, and as many shovels to throw
up a breastwork, and next day several of us
excavated sleeping-places in the rear. When
night came on, in a cloud of almost palpable
darkness, I groped my way out to mine, and
in a little while was fast asleep—if one can be
that while dreaming. Whether the fancies which
flitted through my passive mind were grave or
gay, tender or savage, of home or of war, has escaped my memory; but I do know that "a
change came o'er the spirit of my dream" with
alarming suddenness when a belated straggler
going up the line landed one of his huge feet
fairly and squarely on the side of my head. My
first thought was that it was one of the immense
hundred-pound shells which the Yankee gunboats occasionally shoot at us, and, expecting
an instant explosion, and strangely unwilling
to be buried in a grave of my own digging, I
sprang to my feet with a celerity not at all usual
with me. Then, discovering the truth, I gave
a loud and appropriate expression to my
wounded feelings in language not fitting, I am
sorry to say, to be repeated to a lady. But,
seemingly conscious he had offended beyond
hope of forgiveness, my assailant waited not to
apologize. On the contrary, he went stumbling
on up the long line of sleeping soldiers; and,

judging from the innumerable cuss words that for the next ten minutes broke the silence of the night, and even attracted the attention of our Yankee friends across the way, must have made stepping-stones of the heads and bodies of every man along his tortuous route. The print of a nail that was in the heel of the shoe which dropped down upon me shows yet on my left ear.

Bill Calhoun always finds some compensation for an injury inflicted upon him by the Yankees in a joke on a Confederate. Some weeks ago a bullet buried itself in the fleshy part of his thigh, and, after gouging it out with his fingers, he limped back to the rear. There encountering a surgeon new in the business of attending to gunshot wounds—in fact, a gentleman whose practice at home had ceased to be lucrative enough to support him, and who had recently decided to take pay from the Confederate Government for the exercise of his limited abilities —Bill thought it prudent to have the wound examined. The surgeon probed here and cut a little there, until patience, fortitude, and silence ceased to be virtues.

"What the —— are you carving me up so for, doctor?" inquired the victim.

"I am searching for the ball," explained the doctor.

"Searching for the ball?" exclaimed Bill with inimitably sarcastic inflection of voice, as, diving with one hand into a pocket, he produced a battered piece of lead and held it out. "Here it is, if that's all you want."

Proud of being a Texan, I rejoice exceedingly
that I am " to the manner born," a native Texan.
Being that, I am foolish enough to arrogate to
myself an extra modicum of consequence when
I remember that the impress of a star was first
used as the seal of an independent nation at
the house of my father in Brazoria County.
Governor Henry Smith—a near neighbor, by the
way—happened to be there on the day he signed
the first official document which required such
an authentication.   Whether it was at his own
or the suggestion of another person, I know not,
but it is a fact that he detached from his coat
a button on which was stamped in relief a five-
pointed star, and with it and old-fashioned seal-
ing-wax furnished the design for the seal, first
of the Republic and then of the State of Texas.

Yet, proud as I am of these mere accidents, I
am more proud of being a member of a brigade
which, inspired by the memory of the Alamo
and San Jacinto, has added luster to the " lone
star " on many a hard-fought field of battle, but
never displayed greater soldierly qualities than
at Bermuda Hundred on the 17th of last month.
Occupying an old and abandoned line of works
in a hollow, the privates of the brigade discovered that by an immediate attack they could
recover from the Yankees a portion of the line
from which, that morning, the Confederates had
been driven; and, waiting not for orders, sprang
forward with one simultaneous impulse and accomplished the undertaking.   " Now's our time,
boys," shouted a private, so unconsciously and

involuntarily that not a soul remembers who it
was, and then away the boys went. Halfway
between the two lines Colonel Winkler did manage to overtake them and cry "Forward!" but
it was a useless expenditure of breath; every
man of the brigade was already running forward
at the top of his speed. Reaching the works, it
was discovered that the Yankees had leveled
them almost to the ground, and that to be ten-
able they must be reconstructed. Scarcely two
hundred yards beyond frowned a Federal fort,
and the gaping mouths of twenty or more huge
cannon, and from sundown until twilight deepened into the blackest of darkness, round shot,
grape, canister, and shells rained upon us so
fast and furiously that "we wished we hadn't."
And when the terrible and demoralizing fire
ceased, and orders came for us, the gallant captors, to do the reconstructing, the wail of regret
for our hastiness would have melted even the
war-calloused hearts of your gallant coast-guard
friends, Tom and Johnnie, could they have
heard it; for the order meant not only the most
laborious toil, but working in the dark—the
Yankees would not suffer lights used. There
was no escape, and, putting our whole souls
into the business, we finished the job by daylight. Then, just as we began to feel good over
the day's rest certainly in store for us, the order
came to march, and that day, the 18th, we came
to Petersburg, the sleepiest and weariest set
of "Cornfed" mortals imaginable.

XXIV

PHILLIPS HOUSE, VA., September 27, 1864.

JUST now we are on the north side of the
James, about eight miles below Richmond, taking our ease something in the manner of the old
planter's darkies down in Alabama. When they
came from the field to dinner, he was accustomed to say to them, "Now, boys, while you
are resting, suppose you hoe the garden." Thus
General Lee said to us when we reached this
place, "Now, gentlemen, while you are resting
at the Phillips House, suppose you watch Beast
Butler's negroes." At any rate, that is what we
are doing, and not grumbling at the task, either
—the darkies, so far, appearing devoid of bel-
ligerent propensities, and picket duty, conse-
quently, being very light. It breaks in somewhat
upon our *otium cum dignitate* and *dolce far
niente,* but it would not only be unmilitary and
insubordination to refuse, but dangerous in the
double sense of exposing us to a court-martial
and to being suddenly and unexpectedly gobbled
up by Mr. Butler and his Ethiopian cohorts.
We have well earned the small privileges
granted, for from May 1 of this year until arrival here the brigade has been constantly on

duty—marching, fighting, and, what is infinitely worse, lying in the trenches under a broiling sun, and starving.

In some of the days to come, when peace has spread her white wings over the land and I have pacified the craving of my inner man with a "God's lavishment" of good and wholesome food, I may be able to find pleasure in the recollection of the hunger experienced at Petersburg. Not that rations enough were not issued to keep body and soul together and maintain strength at a maximum, but the quantity was so distressingly disproportioned to the appetites and capacities of the recipients. As three days' rations for fifteen men the commissary-sergeant of the company usually drew seven pounds of rancid bacon. You would have been amused to see him distribute it. Impossible to do it fairly by weighing on scales—which marked only pounds and fractions of pounds, and not ounces and pennyweights—he would cut it up into as nearly equal shares as possible, and then, requesting a comrade to turn his head, call upon him to say who should get this or that pile. I said it would have amused you, but I retract the assertion. *We* are used to such tragedies, and can laugh and joke over them; but *you,* a tender-hearted woman, would have cried, for you would have seen behind the laugh and the joke, and detected the almost ravenous hunger of the gaunt and ragged men, who, like dogs for a bone, waited and watched so earnestly for their portions. The sole relief was in imagination, half a dozen of us getting together and describing the dinner we should like to have.

The morning we left the trenches at Petersburg I got a twenty-dollar gold piece from my good old mother in far-away Texas. Three of us—Brahan, Wiseman, and I—determined to have a feast, and had it in the shape of apple dumplings and a sauce made of sugar and butter, buying the ingredients in Petersburg at a cost, all told, of eighty-seven dollars (Confederate). And we had Colonel Bane to dine with us, too, for nowadays regimental officers of the highest rank are on the same footing as privates with respect to rations; and the Colonel was not only as nearly famished as either of us, but also out of money. My gold I sold for four hundred dollars in Confederate money, and now it is all in the hands of the hucksters. As long as it lasted I bought everything I could find that was eatable and for sale. Now, since it is gone, I manage to live on the rations issued by the commissary. I ought not to have spent it so lavishly, you think? Why, Charming Nellie, what lease had I on life? To be a little Irish, I should feel like a fool were I killed with money in my pocket; shroud, coffin, and funeral cost nothing up here in Virginia; one's friends, should they find you and have time, will always bury you in a shallow grave; and, if they don't, perhaps the enemy will. No, no, the only sure way for a soldier in Lee's army—one of " Lee's miserables "—to get the full worth of his money is to spend it for grub and eat what he buys in a hurry. Diogenes made light of his rags as long as people kept out of his sunshine, but he found no comfort in philosophy for an empty stomach, and neither can I.

Delighted as we were to escape the breast-works at Petersburg, we came near "jumping from the frying-pan into the fire," for the very next morning after the dumpling banquet the brigade was ordered around to the left of our line to support Hoke's division in an assault upon a Yankee fort. Most fortunately, there was a change of plan, and we had only a ter-rific shelling to endure for an hour or more. During this General Beauregard, and one of his staff whose spick and span, brand-new uniform shone resplendent with gold braid, sat down in a shallow ravine very near a pine tree, the safe side of which I was hugging. "A fellow feel-ing"—especially of fear—"makes one wondrous kind," and notwithstanding his rank and finery, the aide kindly lent his cigar to light the pipe of a ragged Texan who sat near him. Embold-ened by this act of condescension, the Texan asked what command would support us when we moved forward. This was a step too far, and with freezing hauteur the officer replied, "That's the business of your commander, sir; not yours," and turned to the General as if for commendation. And he got it, but as the boys say, "over the left"; for, casting a stern glance at him and saying, "That is not the way to answer veteran soldiers, Captain; they have a right to know the truth on an occasion like this," General Beauregard courteously gave the desired information, and then entered affably into conversation with the inquirer. Two hours afterward we boarded the cars, and by sundown were camped in the pine woods five miles north of Richmond. Between daylight and sunrise next morning we heard the loud explosion at Petersburg which announced that the Yankees had at last sprung their much-talked-of mine. Supposing it was dug beneath the part of the line so recently vacated by us, expressions of mutual congratulations were frequent and earnest. Bill Calhoun voiced the sentiment of all when he said, "Well, fellers, it's a d——d sight more comfortabler to be standing here on good old Virginia *terror firmer* than to be dangling, heels up and head down, over that cussed mine, not knowing whether you'd strike soft or hard ground." We expected for a time to be recalled to Petersburg, but in the evening learned that the projects built upon the mine had resulted in a grand and ridiculous *fiasco* and that the Yankee loss had been far in excess of ours.

My admiration for General Wade Hampton was always large, and became immense when, taking the place of Stuart, he adopted the tactics of General Forrest and transformed the Virginia cavalry into mounted infantry. The two legs of a man are difficult enough to manage on the battlefield, but when they are supplemented by the four of a horse, the six have a singular tendency to stray absolutely beyond control. Liking, however, changed to dislike when, one of the warmest days of August, he persuaded us to hold the bag while he drove a brigade of Yankee cavalry into its open mouth. The trouble was the Yankees were too wary to fall into the trap, and in our efforts to induce them to do so the location of the bag had to be changed so often that our infantry lost more men by sunstroke than Hampton's cavalry did by fighting. Still, just before sundown, we not only got within range of the Federal rear-guard, but cornered them as well, and killed and wounded a few, captured quite a number, and drove the balance into the Chickahominy Swamp; and of those who unwisely sought that miry refuge we captured a dozen or more, pulling them and several splendid horses out of bog-holes into which they had sunk until only their heads were visible.

On the evening of August 18 the brigade was at New Market Heights, occupying a line of breastworks from which it could look down with lofty contempt, scorn, and defiance upon the enemy in the open valley below. To prevent the force in our immediate front from dispatching reinforcements to their troops on the left, then being pressed by Hampton's cavalry, several Confederate batteries were brought forward, and began a vigorous shelling. Two guns were placed within fifty feet of where I sat with my back against the breastworks, writing in my journal. Well accustomed to such small demonstrations, and securely protected from danger, I felt neither curiosity nor fear. But Lieutenant

Eli Park and Pat Penn, of Company F, having nothing else to occupy their minds, stood up and peeped over the works to watch the effect of the shells, Pat almost touching me, and Park just beyond him. The firing continued perhaps ten minutes, when Pat stepped back, ejaculating, " Oh, pshaw! " in such a peculiar tone as to attract my attention. Looking up, I saw that Park's head had dropped forward and rested on the top of the embankment, some sharpshooter away off on our right having sent a ball through it. It was a sad and most unexpected ending of a vigorous and promising young life. He had applied.for a transfer to Texas, in order to be near his widowed mother, and not half an hour before the fatal shot, spoke of his application and expressed a wish that it might come back, approved, before the detail for picket duty was made, for he knew he would be the officer detailed. Although he made but the one application, two transfers came " approved " before the sun set—one from an earthly commander to Texas, the other from his God to another world —the last, alas! first.

Dr. Jones, the surgeon of the Fourth, is from west Texas. When first appointed assistant surgeon of the regiment the boys said it was a shame—he was entirely too young either to prescribe for the sick, or carve and saw on the wounded; and, besides, he neither looked nor acted like a doctor. At Eltham's Landing the objectors were altogether too excited to notice where he was; at Seven Pines they didn't get

enough in danger to care where he was; but at
Gaines' Mill, our first baptism of fire, when it
was discovered that he followed close behind the
line into the very thick of the battle, and, reckless of his own peril, remained sufficiently cool
and collected to bind up a wound, stanch the
flow of blood, and to do the right thing at the
very moment it was most needed, the sentiment
changed, and to-day Dr. J. C. Jones is the
standby and dependence of both the sick and
wounded of the Fourth. Asked once why he did
not stay farther in the rear, he answered, " Because it is the duty of a regimental surgeon to
go where he can do the most good. Many a brave
man has died from loss of blood, which by a
minute's work at the critical time a surgeon
could have arrested."

The Fourth Texas was the happy recipient
the other day of a box of clothing sent by the
ladies of middle Georgia, the section of the State
from which came the Eighteenth Infantry. An
open-air meeting of the regiment was immediately called, Colonel Winkler elected to the
chair, and a committee of five, of whom I was
proud to be " one of which," appointed to draft
resolutions expressive of our gratitude. The
committee repaired to the spring, and its members, stretching themselves at full length around
upon the green grass, proceeded to discuss the
work before them. Scarcely, however, was a
general outline of it agreed upon, when Jim
Cossgrove and Bill Burges drifted off into an
argument concerning the battle of Waterloo;

and, as Burrel Aycock and Lieutenant Grizzle at once became deeply interested in the dispute, the manufacture of the resolutions devolved wholly upon your humble servant, who " gave his whole mind to it " as completely as did the dandy to the tying of his cravat. He fell short, I fear, of literary excellence, yet contrived to frame half a dozen resolutions that were warmly applauded and accepted without amendment. Then my friend Grizzle sidled up to me and in a confidential way asked me to write some special resolutions for him to one of the ladies, as he was engaged to her, and she had sent him a lot of nice things in addition.

XXV

HOT SKIRMISHING—WOUNDED

HOWARD GROVE HOSPITAL, RICHMOND, VA.,
November 10, 1864.

WHEN I was devoting my whole mind and
more spare time than I knew what to do with
to the composition of my letter to you from the
Phillips House, down below Richmond, it never
once occurred to me that just nine days later
I would fight my last battle for the Confederacy. It has so happened, though, for unless persuaded by the song, " If you want a good thing,
jine the cavalry, jine the cavalry," into tender-
ing my services to that branch of the service,
my career as a soldier is ended. Through " our
mutual friend," to whom I wrote as soon after
I got here as I was able to hold a pen, you have
doubtless learned that I am a cripple for life,
having lost my right foot in an engagement with
the enemy on the 7th of October. Whether or
not I should regard the loss as in the least de-
gree a misfortune, depends entirely on the way
one looks at it. My enjoyment of the only furlough I have had since I left Texas was marred
by the thought that I must soon return to the
front and offer myself as food for powder, but
I could not help remaining a combatant. Now,

however, being *hors de combat* as far as service
in the infantry is concerned, I am inclined to be
a noncombatant in the largest sense of the word.
While the cause of the South is inexpressibly
dear to me—more so than ever, since I have
made this sacrifice for it—my whole being yearns
for the safety, the rest, and the happiness which
misfortune and love promise me—the latter held
out to me in a letter I read half a dozen times
a day to convince me it is a reality and not a
dream. It is human nature, I reckon, and I
do not think I need be ashamed of it. That I
do not deserve any very great amount of happiness, I am only too well aware, but now that
it seems to be coming my way, why should I
refuse to accept it?

That letter from the Phillips House was dated
the 27th of September and finished the 28th. I
remember the dates distinctly, for, while writing on the 28th, the Veteran came in from the
picket line and intimated a suspicion that some
movement was on foot among the Yankees. Being an optimist, and knowing him to be fond
of looking on the gloomy side of everything, I
laughed scornfully at the idea. Next morning,
however, when he came with a triumphant " I
told you so! " I acknowledged him a true
prophet. Hostilities had begun on the picket
line at three o'clock, and at daylight the Texas
Brigade, in position behind half-dismantled
works running across the valley of a little creek,
was busily engaged in slaughtering negroes for
breakfast. All that could be seen through the

dense fog enveloping us was what appeared to
be a moving black wall a hundred feet away;
yet in five minutes' time the four regiments of
the brigade killed one hundred and ninety-four
non-commissioned officers and privates, and
twenty-three commissioned officers. Those are
the figures given by the New York *Herald* of the
next day, which is very creditable work, I think,
for a brigade numbering scarcely six hundred,
all told. Besides, quite a number of the darkies
who "played possum" to escape our fire surrendered after the retreat of their comrades.
Given the choice of going to the Libby or saying
"master" to their respective captors, most of
the poor devils chose the latter alternative, and
while I remained with the regiment I had a
likely young negro always at my beck and call.

We had barely recovered our breath after this
little flurry, when an order came to double-
quick to the right if we would save Fort Harri-
son from capture, and ourselves from being cut
off from Richmond. Simply to rescue the fort
we would not likely have made much of an effort,
but to be cut off from the Confederate capital
was to be forced to surrender or "die in the
last ditch," and Texas pride and manhood re-
volted at either alternative. So, girding up our
loins, we set out for the fort, which was a mile
and a half away, at as lively a gait as apprehension, legs, and patriotism could carry us.
Luck was against us; the Yanks got there first,
and all we could do was to move around its
rear and take position behind a line of works

half a mile nearer Richmond, and, defended only by a battery of heavy artillery in Fort Gilmore. Here, by dint of racing up and down the trenches to meet the partial and desultory attacks of the enemy, we managed, unaided, to hold the enemy in check until the middle of the afternoon brought us reinforcements from the south side, and put a quietus to General Ord's "On to Richmond!" Had he moved forward early in the morning with his whole force, the city must inevitably have been lost. The Yankee papers admit he had a force of forty thousand under his command; and, until reinforcements came, the Texas Brigade, Benning's brigade, half a regiment of cavalry, and the artillerists in Fort Gilmore—not exceeding two thousand in all— were the only Confederate troops which stood in his way.

A brigade of negroes, supported—or, rather, urged forward—by white troops, made an assault on Fort Gilmore, but the artillerists there were game, and, by the help of half a hundred Georgia and Texas infantry, easily repelled the attack. Death in their rear as surely as in their front (the prisoners taken declaring that they would have been fired upon by their supports had they refused to advance), the poor darkies came on, for a while, with a steadiness which betokened disaster to the Confederates. But suddenly the line began to waver and twist, and then there was a positive halt by all, except perhaps a hundred, who rushed forward and, miraculously escaping death, tumbled headlong and pell-mell into the wide and deep ditch surrounding the fort.

"Surrender, you black scoundrels!" shouted the commander of the fort.

"S'rendah yo'seff, sah!" came the reply in a stentorian voice. "Jess wait'll we uns git in dah, eff you wanter." Then they began lifting each other up to the top of the parapet, but no sooner did a head appear than its owner was killed by a shot from the rifles of the infantry.

"Less liff Cawpul Dick up," one of them suggested; "he'll git in dah suah"; and the corporal was accordingly hoisted, only to fall back lifeless with a bullet through his head.

"Daw now!" loudly exclaimed another of his companions; "Cawpul Dick done dead! What I done bin tole yer?"

Yet, notwithstanding the loss of Corporal Dick, it was not until the inmates of the fort threw lighted shells over into the ditch that the darkies came to terms and crawled, one after another, through an opening at the end of the ditch, into the fort. *   *   *

Alford is a good soldier, but is a trifle weak-minded. Tried in Texas once for the abduction of a slave, riding behind whom on the same horse he was caught within ten miles of the Rio Grande, the lawyer defending him found little difficulty in convincing the jury that the negro was the abductor, Alford the abducted. A loyal friend and messmate of Ed Crockett, who was on picket the night of the 28th, Alford deemed it his bounden duty to bring from the Phillips

House a quart cup half full of beans intended for his friend's breakfast. Not once during all the danger and excitement of the day did he release his hold on the cup, for to set it down and turn his head away for a half minute was to risk its confiscation. Cooked beans are as much contraband of war to a hungry Confederate, as the negro to the Yankees. As a necessary consequence, Alford for the first time shirked duty, and until noon remained a non-combatant. Then a large body of the enemy advanced, and we began firing at them. Noticing that Alford hung back in the rear, doing nothing, Lieutenant Brahan ordered him to take his place in the ranks. Too good a soldier to disobey this positive command, Alford stepped forward, set the cup on top of the breastworks within six inches of his face, and cocked his gun and leveled it at the enemy. But alas! before he could take aim and pull the trigger there was an ominous clatter. A ball had struck the side of the cup, overturned it, and splashed its savory contents over its owner's bearded face. It was the straw too much for the poor fellow's fortitude. Uncocking his gun and stepping back to the middle of the trench, the beans dripping from his huge beard in a saffron-red stream, he looked reproachfully at Brahan, pointed impressively at the unfortunate quart cup, and in a voice faltering with genuine emotion exclaimed, " There now, Lieutenant! just see what you have gone and done, sir! Crockett's beans is all gone to ——, an' he'll swar I eat 'em up."

Pat Penn, whom I mentioned in relating the manner of Lieutenant Park's death at New Market Heights, was one of the noblest and most gallant soldiers of the regiment. If he had faults, they were contempt of danger and recklessness in exposing himself to it. When other men stooped their heads he held his erect, and laughed at the suggestion that he might be killed. Being detailed for picket duty on the night of the 29th, his messmate said to him, " Come along, old fellow, and help us."

Pat shook his head in refusal.

" Oh, come along! " urged the other, " and don't be so lazy. We'll have a heap of fun driving the Yankees back."

" Well, I believe I'll go then," said Pat, rising to his feet; and, going, he went to his death. While half bent over a stump, incautiously peering into the gathering darkness to locate the position of a fellow who appeared to have a special spite against him, a bullet struck him in the top of the shoulder; and, although he walked back to the field hospital laughing, next day he was a corpse.

The newspapers mentioned the affair of October 7 on the Darbytown road, and history will likely call it a reconnaissance in force; but to me and fifty or a hundred others of the Texas Brigade who lost their lives or were wounded, it was a desperate assault by a small force upon well-manned earthworks, approachable only through open ground, and protected by a *chevaux-de-frise* made of felled timber. Hoke's

division was to have supported us by engaging
the enemy on our right, but they made such a
poor job of it that the Yankees had abundant
leisure and opportunity to concentrate their
strength against us. The fire from the works
was terrific, and in climbing under, over, and
around the tree-tops our folks lost their alignment and scattered. A bullet struck my gun,
and, glancing, passed between the thumb and
forefinger of my left hand, barely touching the
skin, but, nevertheless, burning it; another bored
a hole in the lapel of my jacket. Catching sight
of the Fifth Texas flag to my left and fifty yards
or so ahead of me, and taking it for that of the
Fourth, I made for it with all possible dispatch.
But before I reached it its bearer cast a look
behind him, and, finding himself alone in the
solitude of his own impetuosity and bravery,
prudently sought protection from the storm of
lead behind a tree scarcely as large around as
his body, and within sixty yards of the breastworks. First one and then another of the
Fourth and Fifth dropped in behind him, until
seven or eight of us were strung out in single file,
your humble servant, as last comer, standing at
the tail-end. Discovering that I gained no benefit from the tree, that our little squad could not
hope to capture the breastworks without aid,
and that our comrades in the rear seemed loath
to reinforce us, I hurriedly stated the last two
conclusions to my companions, who, without a
dissenting voice, sensibly agreed that an instant
and hasty retreat must be made. In this move-

ment my place at the tail-end of the file gave
me the start of the others, but I had not gone
thirty feet when a bullet struck me in the foot,
which at that critical moment was poised high
in the air, and I dropped to the ground with a
thud which I thought resounded high above the
roar of battle.

> " 'Twas ever thus since childhood's hour
> I've seen my fondest hopes decay."

If either wounded or killed, I always wanted
it to be in a big battle. Wounded there, I could·
boast of it in this world; killed there, the fact
might give me a standing in the other, superior
to that which I can now hope will be accorded
me.

"Help me out, Jack!" I shouted, as Jack
Sutherland, the adjutant of the regiment, was
about to pass me in his stampede to the rear.
Not abating his speed in the least, he pointed
expressively to a bleeding shoulder.

"Help me out, Ford!" I shouted to that valiant member of Company B. Never hearing the
plaintive cry, he plunged into a tree-top, whence
he emerged half a minute later minus the tail of
his long, light-colored coat.

Thus abandoned, I did some rapid thinking.
If I lay there I was sure to be shot again, for
the enemy's bullets were striking the ground
on both sides of me with dangerous viciousness.
If I rose to my feet, the risk would be increased.
While many balls struck the ground close to me,
the air above was resonant with the music they

made. That was the dilemma between the horns
of which I wavered, for say, half a minute;
and then, patriotically resolving either to die for
my country or live for it,—but infinitely pre-
ferring the latter alternative,—I sprang to my
feet, and, my heart in my mouth and every ounce
of my energy in my legs, ran for the regiment,
a hundred yards away. Much to my surprise,
the wounded foot made no protest until I got
within twenty feet of Colonel Winkler. He immediately ordered a litter brought forward, and
in less than five minutes I was being carried
to the ambulances upon the broad and high
shoulders of Wallingford, Aus Jones, and Jim
Cosgrove, and the equally broad, but one foot
lower, shoulders of my friend the Veteran—
three corners of the litter high in the air, and
the other so low that I had to cling with a death-
grip to its side-bars in order to avoid being
spilled out. I was never so scared in all my life
as on that little jaunt. Six feet above the
ground, lying with my head to the enemy, and
the bullets still whistling vengefully around me,
I begged imploringly to be laid on the ground
until the firing ceased. While I knew no guns
were being aimed at us, every shot at the brigade
endangered our lives. But the Veteran would
hear to no such foolishness, and you may well
believe I drew a sigh of relief when at last we
got behind the walls of a fort, where the ambulances were.

When a fellow is helpless kindly acts touch
him deeply. I shall never forget or falter in

my sincere gratitude to the comrades who befriended me that day. Wallingford, Jones, Cosgrove, and the Veteran; Buchanan, the ambulance driver, who, in carrying me to the field hospital and then to Howard Grove Hospital, in Richmond, was so solicitous for my comfort; Will Burgess, of Company D, who made me a pallet at the ordnance wagons and walked a mile for morphine to allay my pain; Dr. Jones, who humored my wish to take chloroform before the wound was probed, and amputated the foot so skillfully that I have had little suffering to endure; and last, but not least, Charley Warner and his fellows of the band, who, after the operation, carried me to their tent, placed me on a pile of blankets, and, after I awoke from the sleep into which I instantly fell, gave me a cup of pure, delicious, invigorating coffee—each and every one of them will be gratefully remembered as long as I live. Honestly, I doubt if any wounded general ever received more genuine and timely kindness and consideration than was extended to me, a private.

I know you will pardon the seeming egotism of this letter. Although we have never looked into each other's faces, I am sure that our long continued correspondence has served to make you my friend, and that you take an interest in all that concerns my welfare.

I want to go home as bad as ever one did in the world, but the surgeon tells me I cannot for two or three months—that I must take a furlough, and go out in the country where I can recuperate my wasted strength and let the work of healing complete itself. My friend Mrs. Allen, a lady whose folks live near us in Texas, and who married a Virginia lawyer and came here with him at the beginning of the war, has kindly invited me to spend my furlough at the home of her father-in-law, Judge Allen, with whom she lives, and I am going to do it. Before I can leave Virginia I must apply for retirement, and as that will take more or less time I will hardly be ready to start to Texas until about the first of March of next year. Once on the way, nothing but sickness, high water, or other unavoidable calamities will stop me. I ought to deliver myself first to my good and loving mother, but knowing she will pardon me, I shall make the first delivery by submitting myself to the tender mercies of a lady who says she will marry me if only I take to her " body enough to contain my soul." Fortunately, I have not only body enough for that, and to spare, but also a pair of arms that are longing for exercise, and a pair of lips that are hungering for the toll due by your friendship and her love. *Verbum sat sapienti.*

XXVI

LUXURIATING IN FEASTS AND FEATHER BEDS

BOTETOURT COUNTY, VA., December 20, 1864.

Is it a dream, or have I really been a soldier for the last four years? is a question I frequently ask myself nowadays; for here in this old Virginia country home of genuine kindness and hospitality—where I take my place three times a day at a bountifully provided table; sleep on a feather bed, between clean, white sheets; hear the chatter and laughter of little children; and may, when I choose, listen to the low, sweet voices of refined and cultured women, or to the music evoked by skillful fingers from a melodious piano—there is little to remind me of the cruel war except a pair of crutches, my missing limb, and the empty sleeve of my genial host, Captain John J. Allen. The crutches are " out of mind as soon as out of sight "; my wound has healed nicely and gives no pain; the Captain is post-quartermaster at Buchanan, and always there during the day—and so, whether talking with the ladies in parlor or library or (he taking snuff and I smoking a long-stemmed pipe) sitting with Judge Allen, of the Court of Appeals of the State, in his cozy little law office in the yard, and thinking lazily of a future that is always to be happy, I can easily—too easily, perhaps—forget my comrades of brigade, regiment, and even company, who are struggling and suffering in the cause of the South.

It is the most selfish of selfishness, but I can not help it. This peace and plenty, rest and content, are too pleasant and soothing to mind and body to be disturbed by thoughts of either my own past or the hardships of my dearest friends.

> "Trust no Future, howe'er pleasant!
> Let the dead Past bury its dead!
> Act, act in the living present!
> Heart within and God o'erhead!"

may have been, when written, good advice to the civilians of that day, but is not applicable in its entirety to a fellow in my situation. "Let the dead past bury its dead" is doctrine to which I willingly submit, but *I must trust the future,* for in it lie all my hopes and ambitions. As for acting "in the living present," that is so diametrically opposed both to bodily condition and to feelings that I absolutely refuse to obey the injunction. I want and I need repose, and nowhere can I find it in such perfection as among these kind and thoughtful friends here in the mountains of Virginia. I speak of home so seldom that young Mrs. Allen expressed surprise the other day at my apparent apathy.

"Why, Miss Lizzie," said I, addressing her by the name I used to call her when, as a callow youth two years her junior, and she a young lady out in society, I claimed her as a sweetheart, "I am so sure of going home that I am just luxuriating in the first feeling of certainty permitted me since June, 1861!"

"That statement is not very complimentary to your sweetheart," said she. "Don't you want to see her?"

The question placed me fairly on the horns of a dilemma—the one, natural gallantry; the other, regard for truth. To add to my embarrassment, Miss Eva, the Captain's sister, entered the room in time to hear the question, but not the prelude to it, and she also insisted on an answer. I hemmed and I hawed, tried the efficacy of a joke I have never known to fail, and went off at a tangent on half a dozen other subjects, but all in vain; the ladies held me relentlessly to the inquisitorial rack, and in self-defense, and to escape a lie, I had to reply, "No; not a bit more than to see my mother and sisters. She is as much a certainty as they."

"Maybe not," mischievously remarked Miss Eva; "ladies change their minds sometimes."

"My sweetheart is not of that sort," I proudly replied. Don't you think I am right?

Whether because of previous long fasting or the keen, invigorating air of these mountains, my appetite has become a veritable tyrant, so insatiate in its demands as almost to ignore the law of physics that no two bodies can occupy the same space at the same time. In camp my grievance was not getting enough to eat; here, it is inability to eat enough of the plenty I get, either to satisfy the cravings of the corporeal system or the hospitable solicitude of entertainers. As the last forkful of meat on my plate starts to reinforce its predecessors the Judge lifts another slice of ham, corned beef, or turkey from the dish, and, if not warned to desist, lays it silently before me. The other folks at the table are equally attentive.

Just before I left Richmond to come up here the Veteran came to see me, and, as he had been considerate enough to bring his rations along, I could afford to ask him to dinner. Ravenous as was my appetite, the provender furnished by the hospital was barely sufficient for one grown man, let alone two. We had a jolly day of it, for he brought both the latest news and the latest jokes from camp. One of the jokes was on Jim Cosgrove, who helped me off the field on the day I was wounded. Cosgrove is fond of fun and excitement, plays a practical joke on a comrade whenever he can, and is always making himself heard. One day when rations were slenderest and he hungriest, he said to his messmate, " I would eat anything in the world— snails, frogs, grasshoppers, dogs, rats; anything but cats. I draw the line at those cussed, sharp-clawed, treacherous creatures."

" I helped eat a cat once," remarked Babe reminiscently, with a far-off look in his hungry eyes, " and it was good too; and I shouldn't object to the leg of one right now."

" But I would," protested Cosgrove. " Just remember that, please; and if you ever have cat for breakfast, dinner, or supper, count me among

the missing. Why, I'd—I'd eat a buzzard
sooner than a cat, any day."

Babe made no reply, but a bright idea struck
him; Cosgrove would be on picket that night,
and when he came back next day was sure to be
too famished to be inquisitive, and he might be
taught that cat was not bad eating, after all his
antipathy to it. Luckily for Babe's plans, an
old bachelor citizen lived near camp, whose most
cherished pet was a half-grown, fat, and sleek
pussy, that was in the habit of taking a nightly
stroll through the camp. That night Babe lay
in wait for it, and next morning its remains
swung from the rafters of its captor's little cabin,
and later in the day became the principal in-
gredient of a "rabbit" pie, so called in deference to Cosgrove. The intended joke would be
too good for one man, besides Babe didn't care
to be alone with Cosgrove when the truth was
revealed to him, and so he invited a friend to
dine with them.

"What have you got in the skillet to-day, old
man?" asked Cosgrove when, released from
duty, and standing before the mess fire, he
caught a whiff of savory odors.

"The fattest little cotton-tail rabbit you ever
saw," responded Babe, with a childlike smile.

"It smells good, anyhow," remarked Cosgrove approvingly. "Isn't it most done?"

"Yes," answered his messmate; "get off your
traps, and take a fair start with us."

Soon the three were seated around the skillet,
busily consuming its contents.

"Umph!" grunted Cosgrove as he closed his teeth on a juicy morsel; "if this isn't good enough eatin' for General Lee! Where'd you get it, Babe?"

"Out of a hollow stump," answered his comrade, with his mouth almost too full for utterance.

The skillet was soon sopped clean enough to bake a cake in. Then, with his feet high up on the jamb of the fireplace, Jim folded his hands across his corporosity and said in his mellowest tone, "Lord! Lord! Lord! how good that mess was, and how peaceful I feel! Why, Babe, a five-year-old child could play with me now, and I could be amiable even to a Yankee."

Babe looked at Jim a moment, took his stand in the doorway, and, discovering that retreat was possible, remarked, "I thought you didn't like cat, Jim?"

"Cat?" shouted that suddenly surprised gentleman; "cat? Is it a cat I've been eatin'?"

"Of course it is," said the guest; "and it's powerful good eatin' too."

Cosgrove turned pale as a ghost, and endeavored to get rid of the portion of the animal he had appropriated, but in vain. His digestion had not been worked to its limit for a long time, and it clung successfully to its prey. Then he got mad, but Babe Metcalf was out of sight and hearing, and the guest could not be held responsible for any deception, and so poor Cosgrove had to stomach both the cat and the joke.

"But," said the Veteran, "you'd better not

say 'cat' to him when you meet; he has already
thrashed one fellow within an inch of his life
for just mewing like one."

As you will perceive, I have made a change
in my quarters since inditing the foregoing.
Dry Kindred, the captain of my company, had
the good fortune while I was at Charlotte to
persuade a very handsome lady into double har-
ness with him, whose father, a wealthy Balti-
morean, has an elegant home at this place and
insists on keeping his daughter with him until
the war is over. Wounded the same day I was,
the Captain got out of the hospital as soon as
he could, and flew "on the wings of love" up
here, to be nursed and petted by his wife. Not-
ing how kindly and unwearyingly she does it,
and how the Captain seems to enjoy it, I feel
like kicking myself for not being a Benedict
myself. I might get a course of the same medi-
cine.   *   *   *

While I do not feel as much at home here as
I did at Judge Allen's,—young Mrs. Allen being
so nearly kinfolks to me,—I get along tolerably
well, considering. The genuine Virginia girl de-
lights in being a sister to every wounded Southern soldier lucky enough to get within her reach,
and as there are three of them here who have
got beyond short dresses, I get more sistering
than somebody in Texas might behold with
equanimity. All of them are refugees from the
lower Shenandoah Valley. Miss Laura K—— is
a beautiful girl whose black curls hang below her
waist; but as she is mourning the fall of the

E. F. KINDRED
Captain Company F, Fourth Texas Regiment

cavalryman to whom she was engaged, she is
not as sisterly to me as her sister, Ida, and her
cousin, Sallie Sowers. Neither of these over
eighteen, and both high-spirited, frolicsome, and
most pleasantly compassionate, it would amuse
you to hear them quarreling over which one of
them shall sit next to me on the sofa and do the
most for me. To balance the sofa problem equi-
tably, I usually crowd myself in between them
and extend my arms along the back of the seat.
They never let me use my crutches at all in the
house,—they wear out the carpet, they say,—
and so I do all my moving about, inside doors,
between the girls, an arm around the neck of
each. It is certainly a pleasanter method of
locomotion than hobbling around on a pair of
inanimate sticks. When I showed them somebody's picture and warned them I was pre-
empted,—which I did, I assure you, the day after
I got here,—they said they were glad of it—
that they had been actually pining for a fellow
in my fix on whom to expend their sur-
plus sweetness without risk of being flirted
with. * * *

Talking over some of the incidents of our
long stay at the Phillips House, Captain Kindred explained the cause of an alarm down there,
for which I never could account. In order to
be near her husband, a field officer in the brigade, Mrs. ——, a six months' bride, was staying at the house of a bachelor uncle of hers,
half a mile in rear of our regiment. That day,
the 20th of September, she took a notion about

10 o'clock A. M. to have a swim in an immense bathtub on the place. The darkies filled it nearly full of water from a spring that is icy even in the heat of summer. Not dreaming how cold it was, but longing for instant refreshment, the lady no sooner got rid of every garment that a wetting would endanger, than she tumbled broadcast into the tub with an abandon that submerged her, head, foot and corpus—the corpus weighing fully a hundred and sixty pounds and being as plump as a partridge. Rising to the surface, she gave vent to the emotions of her shivering anatomy by a scream that reached our camp, and made such a hasty, ill-considered effort to climb out of the tub that it tilted completely over, and not only submerged her again, but caught her lower limbs beneath it. Then of course she screamed again and again. Such a yelling you never heard, especially as it was immediately joined in by the lady's maid, and a negro man who thought the Yankees had come. The moment it was heard at camp there was a hurrying to and fro, a grabbing at guns, haversacks and canteens, and the regiment was almost in line and ready to rush to the rescue, when the news came that the whole rumpus was caused by a lady finding the water in a bathtub too cold for her to stay in.   *   *   *

This letter, I reckon, will close my correspondence with you from Virginia. Of course we may write to each other many times hereafter, but a part of the charm and romance to me will be gone. Never having seen you, and a description of your personality as persistently denied me as a picture of yourself, I have had to depend on imagination entirely, and have often wondered whether your eyes are black or blue— your hair, red or brown—your nose, Roman, straight, or with a heavenward tilt—your hand and foot, small or large, and whether you are short or tall, angular or plump, fleshy or bony. That you are graceful in every movement, good-natured and with ample variety of mood and manner to make you as charming and fascinating as your letters have always been to me, I am sure.   But once we have met, I will have no more fun guessing how you look.   Besides, when I leave Virginia I will leave behind me all the exciting and amusing incidents of the camp and the march, the skirmish and the battle, that have furnished me subjects.   *   *   *

XXVII

FANNIN HOUSE, HOUSTON, TEXAS,
March 23, 1865.

DEAR DICK: Condemned by high water to
a three days' delay at this dead old town, and
too near homefolks that are and homefolks soon
to be, to write to them, I have decided to inflict
upon you the letter I promised. While I hope
it will entertain you, I am not writing as much
for that purpose as to rid myself of the
"ongwee" of which Bill Calhoun is so fond of
complaining, when his spirit is too dull to afford
a witticism. I have it bad, hence resort to my
pen for relief—that much of a camp habit still
clinging to me. I never knew how much I
loved you boys of the company, regiment, and
brigade until I had told you all good-by, and
remembered that to some of you it was a last
good-by. Just to stay with you and share your
hardships and risks, and hear you jest and laugh
in the midst of all the dangers and trials of
soldiering under Lee, I would cheerfully have
destroyed my retirement papers but for the conviction that a cripple would be a burden to you.
As it is, I am here in Texas, on my way to home
and happiness—feeding high, dressed as comfortably if not as stylishly as these Trans-

Mississippi fellows, sleeping on mattresses under rain-proof roofs, and free to go wherever high water and mud will permit me—while you fellows are yet in Virginia, and though ragged, hatless, shoeless, starving and freezing day and night, and sleeping in huts and dug-outs, are still undauntedly and resolutely facing a well-fed, well-equipped Federal army outnumbering you three to one. If it is patriotism that holds the Yankees in the field, how much more noble, self-sacrificing, and enduring must be the conviction which keeps the Confederates there?   *   *   *

I stopped at Charlotte, as I promised Aleck Wilson I would, and Miss Annie, his sweet little cousin, cried over my crippled and emaciated condition as though I had been her brother. When the time came to take the train again, she walked to the depot with me, and when I had told her good-by and was on the car, had a darky, who unknown to me had followed us, pass up to me a basket containing a ham, a turkey, a bottle of scuppernong wine, and as much bread as could be crammed in it. I had wanted to kiss her before that, but dared not. But when the basket was handed me, I got right off the train and not only dared, but succeeded, taking her completely unawares. She blushed charmingly, but to show she was not offended, said,

" You might have done that before you got on the train, bu—bu—but you didn't seem to care to."

"To show you how much mistaken you are," said I, hobbling toward her, "I'll take another."

"No, sir," said she, retreating. "The picture you carry proves you have a sweetheart, and as I have one too, I can't afford to risk the jealousy of both—it'll be double poaching, you know."

* * * * *

At Branchville it was reported that a part of Sherman's army had torn up the track ahead of us, and no train would be run to Augusta. So Hugh Davis and a Virginian on his way to marry a Georgia girl, tempted no doubt by the basket of grub Miss Annie gave me, went back with me to Orangeburg. There a couple of good Samaritans in the guise of old maids hunted up a darky who for a large consideration agreed to haul me and the plunder of the party as far as we could go in three days. * * *

As it would have been barbarous to make the old darky haul me any farther, Hugh and the Virginian impressed a horse for me, and on him I rode five miles to the railroad, where we found a hand-car in good running order. Confiscating it, we ran it down the road about six miles. Then Hugh and the Virginian gave out. Fortunately, a carriage driven by a darky came along in the nick of time, and we impressed it and were carried to its owner's home. Thence, next morning, we were sent into Aiken, where we learned that communication between it and Branchville had not been interrupted and that had we remained but an hour longer at Branchville we might be now half way to the Mississippi.   *   *   *

Coming within five miles of the wide swath of destruction marking the passage of Sherman and his army of marauding patriots (?), I had to take a stage, and as the inside of the vehicle was jammed and crammed with women and babies, climbed up to a seat by the driver. All night long and for thirty odd miles we traveled through a once thickly settled and prosperous country without seeing a house standing, and without getting out of sight of the charred and often still burning timbers of comfortable homes from which the inmates—women and children and an occasional old man only—had been driven, in many instances in their night clothes, and refused permission to take even bedding for their sick ones. Could General Lee have foreseen such inhumanity, I doubt if he would have made us behave so well in Pennsylvania. Thank God, though, we Confederates have never warred on women and children, and never will.   *   *   *

At Montgomery I had to wait two days for a boat to carry me down the river to Selma, and there I had a startling adventure. The night before I left, the clerk at my hotel told me that an old gentleman at another hotel would be glad to have me call on him. Not dreaming who it was, I went, and to my surprise and consternation found it was the very respectable but stiff-mannered gentleman who, if he behaves himself and a certain dear one does not go back on her promise, will in the near future have the honor of being my daddy-in-law. His bearing toward me was so distant—caused, I reckon, by a well-founded suspicion that I contemplated robbing him of the one precious ewe-lamb of his flock—that I could not at once muster courage to inform him of the honor I designed him. And alas, before I did, he let his emotions affect his breathing to such an extent that he was compelled to bid me a hasty good night and go to bed for relief.

I would have been glad to sound his views with respect to his daughter and myself, but, as the boat started at an early hour next morning, was compelled to defer the undertaking. However, I called at his hotel on my way to the landing, and told the clerk to explain the whys and wherefores, and express my regrets and condolences. It would be funny, though, if the old gentleman held the latter to refer to the future. * * *

From Selma I came to Jackson, and thence to Hazlehurst, the present terminus of the railroad. There I fell in with Isaac Stein of Company B, our regiment. He minus an arm, and I, a foot, we formed an alliance, offensive and defensive—he to do all the walking—I, all the hugging that might be necessary to speed our journey. Hiring a darky to drive us to Dr. January's in a wagon drawn by a couple of scrawny little mules, we advanced six miles and broke an axle. A noble-hearted citizen, Dr. Applewhite, came

to our rescue, kept us all day Sunday, and on
Monday sent us on to a Mr. Duncan's in his
carriage.   Mr. Duncan, though, could only obey
the first half of Sage Homer's rule, " Welcome
the coming, speed the parting guest," and so we
were compelled to impress the good old doctor's
team, carriage and driver, for transportation
twelve miles farther.   *   ,   *   *

Learning that every skiff in ten miles of us,
and its darky owner, had been pressed into the
service of the cavalry, we went down to the place
where they were.   Having but one arm, and all
his earnings as a sutler invested in the silver
watches and spoons with which his valise was
crowded, Stein hesitated to make the fifth man
in a boat. I did not, though.   *   *   *

In the skiff were the oarsman, three cavalry-
men, each holding the reins of a swimming horse,
and myself.   Thus overloaded, our progress
across was painfully slow.   Twice a horse ceased
swimming, and to inspire him to renewed exer-
tion had to be ducked, at the risk of capsizing
the frail craft and tumbling its cargo into the
water.   When we were a little more than two-
thirds of the way across, a gunboat rounded a
bend two miles above us, and came puffing down
toward us, and, inspired by the emergency, the
darky oarsman bent to his oars with such a will
and energy as threatened to break them, but
nevertheless carried us to the shore in a hurry.
The margin of lowland, fifty feet or more wide,
between water's edge and the levee, was a bog
strewn with drift, large and small; but driven to

haste by fear of capture, I plunged into and through the mud and mire, and over huge logs and piles of drift, with a speed and recklessness which took me behind the levee just as the gunboat got abreast of me.   *   *   *

Half a mile from my landing-place I came to a rail causeway which spanned a narrow, shallow part of Bruin Lake, and gave access to the island. At the farther end of the causeway, the beams of the setting sun shining upon his gray wool and bringing his weazened ebony face into bold relief, sat an ancient darky astride of as ancient a mule, whose ears, also gray and touched by the sunlight, seemed to be tipping me a cordial welcome. Approaching this strangely harmonious pair, I asked the distance to the house.

" Jest up hyar, a li'l' piece, Master," replied the human being, as, removing his battered old hat, he descended with an effort from the back of his patient confrère. " Just git up on dishyere old mewel o' mine, suh, an' hit'll fetch yer dar, suh, 'mejitly."

Black though his skin was, his heart was that of a gentleman, and though as well able to walk as he, I accepted his offer rather than pain him by refusal.   *   *   *

On the broad piazza of the dwelling, busily engaged cutting out garments for the darkies, stood a middle-aged lady, and near her sat a personage in blue uniform, who no sooner saw me than he hurried out to the gate, and, extending his hand, said,

"My name is Johnson, sir—Captain Johnson, of the United States Navy."

Convinced by his uniform and insignia of rank that he was what he claimed to be, and determined not to disgrace my colors by denying them even if I had fallen among Unionists, I grasped his hand with every appearance of pleasure and replied,

"And mine, sir, is Polley—Private Polley, late of the Confederate States Army under General Robert E. Lee, but now retired on account of wounds and on my way to Texas. Can I find quarters for the night with you?"

"I am but a guest at this hospitable mansion," he answered. "You will have to consult the lady of the house, who is now on the piazza; but I shall be glad, if it becomes necessary, to add my entreaties to yours, for as you are just from the seat of war you can probably give us later news than any we have."

*　　　*　　　*　　　*　　　*

Later in the evening mine host kindly gratified my curiosity concerning Captain Johnson. It appears that a week or so ago General Dick Taylor wanted a gunboat worse than General Hood did down at Suffolk when Bill Calhoun sat down on him. Doubting his ability to secure one by capture, he decided to follow Bill's plan as proposed to Hood, and buy one, and immediately entered into negotiations with Captain Johnson, then in command of one of the best on the Mississippi River. But while willing to betray the trust reposed in him by the

Federal Government, the Captain must have managed badly. At any rate, after the trade was made and all details arranged as to time and place of delivery, he let his purpose be suspected by his subordinate officers. Learning that his intended treachery had been reported, to avoid arrest he took advantage of a dark night to climb over the side of the vessel, drop into a boat, and deliver himself to General Taylor. But although crazy for a gunboat, that officer had no use for a naval commander of the Captain's kind, and hence the traitor is now hiding from the Federals, and under suspicion by the Confederates.

＊　　＊　　＊　　＊　　＊

My favorite steed at home being a spirited calico, I took the paint pony, hoping he would be as spirited, paying for him and a buzzard-nest old saddle fourteen hundred dollars in Confederate promises to pay after the war. Mounting him, and taking Stein's valise—it did not weigh less than seventy pounds, I am sure—up on the saddle before me, I started, Stein walking.

After five miles whipping and kicking to make the lazy beast keep pace with Stein, I came to the conclusion that he had far the best end of the bargain—his walking being easier than my riding, and no huggings, so far, having come to me, or being in sight, this side of Texas. But I held to the horse and his valise until night found us at a plantation on the Tensas. There he bought a horse, and managed somehow to ride

him, carry his valise, and keep ahead of me, and
my Lazy Rosinante.   *   *   *

At Alexandria we had the luck to overtake
Captain Haggerty and an Irish beef-drover
named Murphy, who was well acquainted with
the route ahead of us.   Together, we set out for
Mr. Taylor's, thirty miles distant, Murphy be-
guiling the way by recounting *Mr.* Taylor's adventures and exploits as a Confederate scout.
You may judge of my surprise when, arriving
at his house, I discovered him to be a quadroon,
his wife the same, and the couple free, and own-
ers of twenty odd coal-black niggers—Taylor,
it is said, never buying any other kind than the
coal blacks.   At our meals Taylor, his wife, and
daughters waited on us; when we had eaten
they sat down to the same table and were waited
on with every show of deference by their slaves.
It was an odd condition of affairs, I thought.
Murphy, who knows General Dick Taylor well,
told me that he and our host were half brothers,
and except in color looked the counterpart of
each other.   *   *   *

At Lewis' Ferry on the Angelina River my
steed came to the end of his row, and I gave him
and the saddle to a man who furnished me a
tiptop animal to ride to Livingstone in Polk
County, and on Trinity River.   There I took stage
to Liberty.   Ten miles out the team ran away,
and for a mile I wondered if I had gone through
a dozen battles just to come back to Texas
and be killed by a pair of mules.   At Liberty I
boarded a steamboat which carried me to Galves-

ton. There I ran afoul of Ireland's company of Hobby's regiment. Theirs is indeed a sad fate. Although empty store and dwelling-houses are abundant, no private is given a room to himself, but is compelled to share that assigned him with the members of his mess; and they have to live on ham and eggs, fish, oysters, turtle soup, poultry, pure coffee, and a whole lot of other things so new in my experience that I came near foundering myself just tasting them to see if they were good. * * *

I got here at noon day before yesterday, and found John Wheeler of Company B, who is minus an arm, you know, delayed by high water. That evening as he and I sat in front of the hotel, Colonel Gaines, of Brazoria County, sat down between us and inquired our names and where we were from, etc. When we had told him and conversed a while, he opened a pocket-book crammed with five-dollar gold pieces, and holding it out to us told us to help ourselves to all we needed. "You have been fighting for me, boys," he said. "Give me a right to feel that I have been working for you."

"Your age excuses you for not being in the army, sir," said Wheeler, his voice trembling, "and your offer is proof that you have been doing all you could to aid us. If I needed money I would take it as willingly from you as from a father—not needing it, I must decline taking any."

"I think as my comrade does, Colonel," said I. "We take the will for the deed, sir." And so the matter ended. But the old fellow actually went away hurt by our refusal to either take as a gift or borrow from him.

A while later, looking over the hotel register, I discovered that Miss Dora P—— of Richmond, Texas, was stopping here. She was the last woman to tell me good-by in 1861, and resolving she should be the first to welcome me back to the State, I sent up my card, and five minutes later had her little hand in mine. If—but that is a contingency so improbable that it is not worth mentioning, and I will content myself with the remark that she is pretty and charming enough to heal the broken heart of any gentleman she takes the right kind of liking for. Next morning a note was handed me by the clerk from a Miss Emma M—— that was, a Mrs. Scott that is, a wife of three months' experience. The first time I ever saw her she was up a peach tree under which I was about to pass. I do not know what caused me to look up, but I remember distinctly that she had not then arrived at the dignity of long skirts, and that I got from under the tree and out of sight in one time and movement. In the note she asked me to call on her and her widowed sister, Pheny, whom I had once tilted into my arms by suddenly running the wheels on her side of the buggy up on to an elevation. Of course I went, and being so well-known to both, got a kiss from the wife, but none from the widow. I tell you these incidents in which ladies figure, just for revenge —to harrow your feelings. I have not forgot-

ten how you and Captain Jim Hunter appropriated two girls each, up in the Valley, and
would not introduce me to either.   *   *   *

Give the old boys a heart full of love from me.
Tell Jim Cosgrove that if his fondness for cats
continues to hurt him he had better come here
to Houston as soon as he can. We have what
is called rabbit pie, for dinner, every day at this
hotel, but as there is an abundance of cats running round, I think it is cat pie.   *   *   *

Yours as ever,

J. B. POLLEY.

XXVIII

MARLIN, TEX., June 27, 1903.
THE following paper by General J. B. Polley
was read this afternoon:

No braver soldiers fought in the war between
the States than the Virginia Confederates; their
survivors are good fellows—none better. The
perfection of human nature, though, has not yet
been attained by them, for some of these good
fellows have betrayed an undue greed for military laurels. Not satisfied with hailing from a
State distinguished as the birthplace of Washington, Jefferson, Stonewall Jackson, and that
grandest of all the grand, Robert E. Lee; not
content with the glory won at Gettysburg by Virginians in a charge whose equal in soldierly daring and heroic endeavor the world has never witnessed, these yet hungry ones made the startling
discovery, thirty-six years after the event, that
to Pickett's brigade belonged the honor of being
the first Confederate command to break the
Union lines at Gaines' Mill, on the 27th day of
June, 1862.

A tardy but clamorous champion of that renowned brigade, Adjutant Cooper, entered the

controversial lists in the October number, 1898, of the *Confederate Veteran.* In succeeding issues of that admirable publication the contention waxed warm. Comrades Vidor, Schadt and Todd of the First Texas, other Confederates, and one or more Federals who participated in the engagement and believed they knew " who struck Billy Patterson " the first crushing blow, came generously and gallantly to the aid of the Fourth Texas Regiment of Hood's Texas Brigade—laying on most doughtily not only with quotations from the official reports of distinguished Confederate generals, but as well with their own personal recollections of the events of that memorable day, forty-one years ago. Although prompt to take notice of the controversy and not unwilling to " fight the battle over " on paper, I did not get ready to do any firing until the incident seemed, in diplomatic parlance, " to be closed."

It should remain closed, but for the fact that many persons have read only the Virginia side of the case and are so constituted as to accept loudness of assertion as convincing evidence of statements not specifically denied and disproved. Such people are so plentiful that each member of the Fourth Texas may well exclaim:

> " I see my reputation at stake;
> My fame is shrewdly gor'd."

For, if Adjutant Cooper and his corporal's guard of followers are in the right—if Pickett's brigade and not the Fourth Texas was first to

break the Federal lines at Gaines' Mill and
convert what was almost a disastrous defeat of
the Confederate Army into a glorious victory—
the concurrent, contemporaneous statements of
Lee, Jackson, Hood and Whiting, each of whom
gave the credit to the Fourth Texas, are untrue,
and the stories which members of the Texas
brigade have told their sweethearts, wives, and
children are figments of the imagination, base-
less dreams, memories unsupported by any foundation of fact.   If Pickett's brigade is entitled
to the honor, the Fourth Texas never was, and
its survivors and those of its companion Texas
regiments should bend their mighty minds, immediately, to the reconstruction of the long and
lovingly cherished legend that as between the
three regiments "honors are easy"; since, although the "H—ll-roaring Fourth" was the
first Confederate regiment to break the Union
lines at Gaines' Mill, the "Bloody Fifth" routed
and practically annihilated the Zouaves at Second Manassas, and the "Ragged First" held the
cornfield at Sharpsburg against Hancock's whole
corps, losing in that heroic achievement more
heavily than any other regiment, Confederate or
Federal, did at any one battle during the four
years of war.

Texans might safely rely upon the statute of
limitations to bar the claim of Pickett's brigade.
However little they are inclined "to want the
earth and the fullness thereof," it is unreason-
able to suppose Virginians would wait thirty-
six years to present a just claim.   If they ever

had a shadow of right on their side, it is charitable to presume they would have sought to establish their pretensions while it was possible to amend official reports. Instead of doing that they remained silent—so silent, indeed, that until Adjutant Cooper raised his voice not even well-informed Confederates of his own State dreamed of the existence of such pretensions. At any rate, when in 1896 Mr. Corbin Warwick and Colonel Maury of Richmond, Virginia, kindly accompanied me to the battlefield of Gaines' Mill, neither of them mentioned it. Both had been Confederate soldiers and had participated in the seven days' fighting—Colonel Maury having commanded a Virginia regiment and Mr. Warwick being the brother of Lieutenant-Colonel Warwick of the Fourth Texas, who was mortally wounded on the field. Notwithstanding we discussed the battle, and, old soldier-like, I boasted, time and again, that the Fourth Texas was the first command to break the Union lines there, not a word did they say about Pickett's brigade, except, perhaps, to mention that it fought half a mile to the right of the Texans.

In the agitation of mind produced by a long delayed and startling presumed discovery, Adjutant Cooper and his party have overlooked the topography of the ground and the situation as it was on the day of the battle. The Federal line of intrenchments along the south side of Powhite Creek was several miles in length. The Watts house—behind and to the left of which the artillery, captured by the Fourth Texas, was posted—stood about the middle of the line; and the Federals had artillery not only behind the Watts house, but also at other points, and each battery or section of artillery was likely supported by cavalry. In truth and fact, the Federals employed enough artillery and cavalry that day for both Pickett's brigade and the Fourth Texas to have captured cannon and repulsed mounted enemies. To this abundance as well as to the passage of time and a natural, if not altogether excusable, forgetfulness of details is largely due, no doubt, this controversy between Confederate commands. The survivors of Hood's Texas Brigade cannot in justice to themselves and their posterity afford to ignore the claim made by the Virginians, and by silence acquiesce in its justice. The past, and whatever of honor it gave the Lone Star, should be held by secure and unimpeachable title, not a breath of suspicion or boast tarnishing its luster. To remove the last lingering shadow of that cast by Adjutant Cooper and his party is the purpose of this paper.

The following facts, all of them undisputed, I think, should be borne in mind. The final and successful attack upon the enemy's works at Gaines' Mill began at 7 o'clock P. M. The sun set that day in the latitude of Virginia at 7.30. In the assault the Confederates moved to the southeast, the Federals faced to the northwest, and Powhite Creek ran between the two armies, a triple line of breastworks, each occupied by

Federal infantry, skirting the southeastern bank of that stream.

Having, as already stated, revisited the battlefield at a time when it presented a strictly peaceful aspect—when the only music to be heard was the lowing of cattle and the songs of birds, and when no death-dealing missiles hurtled through the air to the disturbance of one's composure—I can speak with approximate accuracy concerning the distances between salient points. From the crest of the ridge immediately north of Powhite Creek it is barely a quarter of a mile to the Watts house. From the Watts house to the artillery it is about three-eighths of a mile.

Most of the statements made by the Virginia writers concerning the movements of Pickett's brigade on the day in question may be accepted as absolutely correct. At present, let us follow the Fourth Texas. All day long, Porter's brave men had held the Confederates at bay at Gaines' Mill. To break their lines here meant overwhelming disaster to the Union arms, glorious victory to the Confederate. General W. C. Whiting, who commanded the division composed of his own and the Texas brigade, approached Hood and said to that gallant officer, pointing in the direction of the guns in rear of the Watts house,

"General, those guns over there ought to be silenced, but I have tried to do it and failed."

"I have a regiment that can do it," replied Hood.

"Try it then," ordered Whiting, and immediately Hood took personal command of the Fourth Texas and led it forward.

Halting in a stretch of low ground a hundred yards short of the crest of the ridge, long enough to form line of battle, the Fourth Texas without further delay advanced to the crest, passing over, just before reaching it, a long line of prostrate Confederates who had sought shelter from the infantry fire of the Federals in a kind of swag extending along the north side of the ridge. At the crest the regiment came within sight and range of the Federal infantry occupying the triple line of breastworks beyond the creek— these breastworks, by the way, so constructed along the hillside that one line fired over the heads of another. Reckless, though, of the storm of bullets which decimated its ranks, the Fourth Texas neither wavered, hesitated nor halted, but fixing bayonets at the command of the gallant Hood, rushed down the slope of the ridge, into and across the little stream at its foot, through timbered bottom and *chevaux de frise,* and at the enemy in the first line of entrenchments. Dismayed, apparently, by the impetuosity and vigor of the attack upon them, these stood not upon the order of their going, but fled at top speed, carrying the two lines of soldiery in their rear with them. Following fast and furiously, loading and shooting as they went, the Texans pushed on directly up the slope of the ridge on that side of the stream and never came to an instant's halt in the resolute and rapid advance until the last armed Federal infantryman in their immediate front was either killed, captured, or driven out of sight in the lowlands of the Chickahominy valley.

The pursuit carried the Texans a hundred yards or so beyond the Watts house, the left of the regiment, in its advance, almost brushing the walls of that historic building. They halted, for the first time, on the eastern edge of a peach and pear orchard, where they reformed their line, facing, now, diagonally to the left in such a manner as to front the fourteen pieces of artillery stationed in rear of the Watts house, which were then hurling round shot and shell, grape, canister and shrapnel by the wholesale at the daring band. The halt, therefore, was not a long one; in the face of such a fire, even the bravest desire to move quickly. The line reformed—and not five minutes was consumed in the effort—Hood ordered the charge, and at the word and by common impulse, the Texans swept forward and captured the guns, in their charge upon them descending a slope which led into a deep ravine, and after struggling across the ravine, climbing a steep ascent to the top of the elevation on which the guns were posted. Quite a while after they seized the guns they were attacked by a squadron of cavalry, one of its companies being that in which Hood had served as a second lieutenant in Texas, previous to the beginning of hostilities between North and South. Its captain—Chambliss, I think his name was—was severely wounded, and General

Hood hunted him up and saw that he received surgical attention.

Placed *hors de combat* at a point west of the Watts house, the writer failed to reach the peach and pear orchard. Yet, although worse frightened than hurt, and possessed of a yearning longing for the peace and safety of the rear, he distinctly remembers seeing the Fourth Texas in line at the edge of the orchard, General Hood standing a few paces in its rear, holding aloft in his right hand a sword whose bright blade reflected the level beams of a sun still above the horizon.

He recalls with the same distinctness that when Austin Jones and himself—Mr. Jones had also been wounded—faced northwest on their way to the rear, the sun shone in their faces. These recollections are sustained by the testimony of the majority of his regimental comrades with whom he has had an opportunity of talking on the subject. Those who remember anything about the sun declare emphatically that it yet shone above the horizon when the Fourth Texas reformed for the culminating desperate charge upon the artillery, and that it was yet shining when the guns were seized and silenced. Add to such statements that of General Stephen D. Lee in the letter which follows, and the proof appears positive that the Texans had possession of the guns at sunset.

Every presumption and probability favors the contention. The general advance of the Confederates began, according to the official reports, at seven o'clock in the evening. It is a fair presumption that, having been selected as a forlorn hope to silence those terrible guns, the Texans were given a slight precedence in point of time. Other commands to its right and left must naturally have waited a little while to see what the Fourth Texas accomplished. At quite a leisurely gait men can cover five-eighths of a mile—eleven hundred yards—in a half hour. The emergencies of the occasion, though, not only invited but imperatively demanded rapidity of movement. Hood was as ambitious as he was brave and daring. The stars of a major-generalship hung in the near perspective. Like Henry of the Wyand in the combat between the clans Chattan and Quhile, he " fought for his own hand."

Not a Texan there, whether by birth or adoption, but shared his spirit and resolved to maintain the reputation for bravery won for the " Lone Star " by the heroes who at the Alamo fought and died that their compatriots might at San Jacinto fight and win. Therefore, they moved rapidly—so rapidly, indeed, that ere the sun set they had accomplished the undertaking they had set out to perform, and had silenced and taken possession of the artillery in the rear of the Watts house.

Where was Pickett's brigade all this while; when did it begin its advance, and when did it drive the enemy from the breastworks in its front? According to General Longstreet, it occupied a position in the Confederate line to the

right of that occupied by Anderson's brigade.
That position placed its left flank at least half
a mile to the right of the Fourth Texas. The
Virginia writers do not state at what time it
began the advance, but they do fix the time at
which it made the assault upon the breastworks
—it was after sunset. Adjutant Cooper says, in
the October (1898) *Veteran:*

" The sun shone brightly and the atmosphere
was clear, and every move that Lee's troops made
could be plainly seen by the enemy. Pryor's
line advanced to the attack, and in a short time
was almost annihilated. Pickett, with his five
regiments, went in on a double-quick, and, being
hid by the smoke of the battle, approached to
within thirty or forty yards of the first line of
intrenchment, where in the intense heat and the
dense smoke they involuntarily threw themselves flat upon the ground and commenced firing. The roar of musketry was so terrific that
it was impossible to hear anything else. The
men knew, however, that heavy work was intended, as each man had his eighty rounds of
ammunition. This continuous firing was kept
up, neither side knowing the proximity of the
other on account of the smoke. Finally the firing of the enemy somewhat slackened, and the
sun set, as it were, in blood, with neither side
having gained any advantage. At the slight
lull in the enemy's fire, General Pickett ordered a charge, to which his brigade responded
promptly."

Such explicitness of detail is commendable. From it we learn that after Pryor's brigade was almost annihilated, and while the sun shone brightly, Pickett's brigade went in on a double-quick, and, hid, most fortunately, by the smoke of battle, approached within thirty or forty yards of the enemy and " involuntarily threw themselves flat upon the ground," and that they remained thus flatly recumbent until " the sun set, as it were, in blood." Add to these facts the significant circumstance mentioned, that each man carried a double supply, or eighty rounds, of ammunition, and the inference in the absence of positive denial by an officer presumed to know the truth, is as plain as irresistible, that General Pickett's object was not to carry the works in his front, but simply to pour such a continuous and heavy fire upon the Federals there as might prevent them from reinforcing other points of their line. Troops ordered to assault and capture a strong position do not ordinarily carry an extra supply of ammunition. But be that as it may, the fact stands out in bold relief that not until after sunset did Pickett's brigade carry the fortifications in its front. That true, and it also true that the Fourth Texas carried the works in its front before sunset, and stood in line of battle in the peach and pear orchard while the sun was still shining, how was it even possible for the Virginia command to precede the Texans in the capture of the guns in rear and to the left of the Watts house?

To say that the Texans waited for the Virginians—that they stood passive, inactive, until after sunset, under such a fire as fourteen well-handled guns could pour upon them from an elevation not seven hundred yards distant, is an absurdity. To say that the Virginians, late as they started, overtook and actually passed the Texans, is nonsense. To do that Pickett's brigade must have been endowed with race horse speed and have wheeled to the left and passed squarely across the front, commanded by Anderson's South Carolinians. That gallant command, though, has never complained that its advance was retarded by such a maneuver; nor, although it was just to the right of the Fourth Texas, and for that reason might with greater plausibility than Pickett's brigade claim, at least, to have aided in the capture of the guns, it has never done so in the writer's knowledge. If, as claimed and believed, the guns were captured by the Texans before sunset, their capture from the Federals by Pickett's brigade was an impossibility—that command was not ubiquitous. It could not have engaged in the capture of artillery while it lay recumbent, a good long mile away, and waited for the enemy's fire to slacken.

Time is an important consideration in military movements. Minutes and even seconds count when a battle is on. The official reports and the testimony of the living support the contention that the Confederate advance began at seven o'clock P. M. Almanacs will show that in the latitude of Virginia the sun set on the 27th day of June, 1862, at 7.30 P. M. The Texans made no halt whatever before penetrating the Federal lines—the Virginians did halt within thirty or forty yards of those lines, and not only halted, but " threw themselves involuntarily flat upon the ground," and waited for the firing in the front to slacken. That this did not take place until the Texans had broken through the lines in their own front and gained the crest of the ridge south of Powhite Creek is evident from the circumstance that when they got that far and glanced back to their right and left rears they saw the Federals in those directions just beginning to retreat. Whether those to our right were moved by the expenditure of the eighty rounds of ammunition the Virginians had supplied themselves with, or, seeing that the Texans had broken the lines, made a change of base from motives of expediency, is an open question. Those in our left rear delayed their retreat simply because, owing to the nature of the ground over which the Eighteenth Georgia, Hampton's Legion, and the First and Fifth Texas struggled, it was impossible for those commands to keep abreast of the Fourth Texas.

While disclaiming the least desire to rob Pickett's division of a single one of its justly won laurels, let me condole with it in its misfortunes, the chief of which, in my humble opinion, is such a reckless eulogist as Adjutant Cooper. One who rushes into print, thirty-six years after an event, should have better foundations for his assertions concerning it than his own memory. Company and regimental officers and the privates they command see little of a battle except that immediately before them. General officers have opportunity for more extended observation. Stonewall Jackson, W. H. C. Whiting, and John B. Hood wrote history in their official reports, and elsewhere, as accurately as it was made by the troops they commanded.

Stonewall Jackson wrote: " In this charge, in which upward of a thousand men fell, killed and wounded, before the fire of the enemy, and in which fourteen pieces of artillery and nearly a regiment were captured, the Fourth Texas, under the lead of General Hood, was the first to pierce these strongholds and seize the guns."

General Whiting wrote: " The battle was very severe, hotly contested, and gallantly won. I take pleasure in calling special attention to the Fourth Texas regiment, which, led by Briga-dier-General Hood, was the first to break the enemy's lines and enter his works."

General Hood, after stating that he took command of the Fourth Texas and led it in the charge, says: " At quickened pace we continued to advance, without firing a shot, down the slope, over a body of our soldiers lying on the ground, to and across Powhite Creek, when, amid the fearful roar of musketry and artillery, I gave

the order to fix bayonets and charge. With a
ringing shout we dashed up the steep hill,
through the abatis and over the breastworks,
upon the very heels of the enemy. The Federals,
panic-stricken, rushed precipitately to the rear
upon the infantry in support of the artillery.
Suddenly the whole joined in flight toward the
valley beyond. I halted in an orchard beyond
the works and dispatched every officer of my
staff to the main portion of the brigade in the
wood to the left, instructing them to bear the
glad tidings that the Fourth Texas had pierced
the enemy's lines, and to deliver orders to push
forward with the utmost haste.   *   *   *
Meantime, the long line of blue to the right and
left wavered, and finally gave way as the Eighteenth Georgia, First and Fifth Texas, and
Hampton's Legion gallantly moved forward
from right to left, thus compelling a grand left
wheel of the brigade into the very heart of the
enemy. Simultaneously with this movement
burst forth a tremendous shout of victory, which
was taken up along the whole Confederate line.
I rode forward and found the Fourth Texas and
Eighteenth Georgia had captured fourteen pieces
of artillery, while the Fifth Texas had charge
of a Federal regiment which had surrendered
to it."

I have not access to the official report of Generals Lee and Longstreet, but as the latter, in
1866, complained that Lee had overlooked his
report of the battle of Gaines' Mill, and been

guided by that of Jackson, it is safe to presume that Lee was so guided. For other obvious reasons, it is equally safe to assert that in writing "The Memoirs of Robert E. Lee," the author, General A. I. Long, Lee's military secretary, was guided by Lee's report when he wrote:

"The day was now drawing to a close, and Lee decided to end the conflict by a charge of the whole line. The word 'charge,' as it passed along the line, was responded to by a wild shout and an irresistible rush on the Federal position. The Texas Brigade, led by the gallant Hood, was the first to penetrate the Federal works."

President Davis, in his book, "Rise and Fall of the Confederacy," says of the battle: "The dead and wounded marked the line of their intrepid advance, the brave Texans leading, closely followed by their no less daring comrades."

General Stephen D. Lee has written as follows:

"COLUMBUS, MISS., May 27, 1899.
"GENERAL J. B. POLLEY:

"MY DEAR COMRADE: I have your letter of May 22, with reference to Hood's Texas Brigade breaking the Federal lines at Gaines' Mill, June 27, 1862. In reply, will state your recollection of the conversation at Houston, Texas, is in the main correct, excepting as to my being with

General Lee. I will state the facts as I recall them. It is the first time I have ever heard that any command other than Hood's Texans broke the Federal lines about sundown at Gaines' Mill, nor do I believe that any such claim can for a moment be sustained. On the afternoon of the day the lines were broken I was across the Chickahominy on what was known as the Nine-Mile road out of Richmond, and had some guns at the Garnett House overlooking the field on the other side of the creek, and the great battle in progress, distant some two and a half miles or thereabouts. Just before sundown I was on the top of the house with my glass, and President Davis (not General Lee) was in the yard, a most anxious observer, and asking questions as I reported progress. General D. R. Jones also came up about that time on the housetop. I reported our lines advancing and carrying the Federal lines. General Jones took my glasses and in an instant, in a joyous voice, reported, ' Yes, our troops have driven the Yankees, and they are flying in great disorder towards the Chickahominy.'

" The President was delighted and overjoyed. Soon after, and before he left, messengers came across the river and said Hood's Texans had swept everything before them, piercing the lines and driving the enemy before them in the greatest disorder. Of course, I could not distinguish at the distance what troops did the work, but the messengers said the Texans had done it. I heard nothing else to the contrary till your let-

ter was received. I feel sure the official reports
will sustain the fact that the honor belongs to
the Texans. I have always so stated it myself,
as I did to your Texas Brigade at Houston.

" I have not the time now, but if you will ex-
amine the reports the matter can be cleared up
without the shadow of a doubt, in my opinion.
If I can further aid you it will give me pleasure.
My post office address is Columbus, Miss.

" Yours truly,
" S. D. LEE."

Judge John H. Reagan, the sole surviving
member of the Confederate Cabinet, has written
as follows:

" AUSTIN, TEXAS, June 6, 1899.
" GENERAL J. B. POLLEY,

" Floresville, Texas.

" DEAR GENERAL: I am in receipt of your
letter of 3d instant, in which you call my attention to the claim which has been made that to
Pickett's brigade of Virginians, and not to the
Fourth Regiment of Hood's Texas Brigade, belonged the credit of being the first Confederate
soldiers to break the enemy's lines at Gaines'
Mill on the evening of June 27, 1862.

" As I was not on the field of battle I can only
speak from hearsay and the current understanding at that time and since, and from having more
than once, soon after that battle, gone over the
battlefield with officers who were in the battle.
My information and understanding was then,
and has been at all times since, that General

Lee had ordered our troops forward once or oftener, and that they had fallen back under the fire of the enemy; and that when Hood's brigade came up they moved forward, and that the Fourth Texas Regiment went through the abatis on the creek and drove the enemy from their partially fortified lines on the steep hillside, and drove the enemy's artillery from the crown of the hill, passing on to a depression in the field beyond where a Federal cavalry brigade charged them and was repulsed, and going a little farther on they captured a battery of artillery. In the mean time, the Fifth Regiment of Texans, Hood's brigade, commanded by Colonel J. B. Robertson, broke through the Federal lines, to the left of where they were broken by the Fourth Texas, and that together they returned to find the Federal lines closed behind them by a New Jersey regiment, which they made prisoners.

"I have always understood that the Fourth Texas Regiment of Hood's brigade was the first to break through the enemy's lines at Gaines' Mill, and I think the charge of that regiment on that occasion one of the most remarkable in the history of wars, taking into consideration the strength of the enemy's position, the abatis to be passed through, the three lines of infantry to be driven from their partially fortified lines, protected by artillery which crowned the hill beyond them, going into the battle with about eight hundred men and coming out of it with less than two hundred and fifty, its colonel killed,

its major mortally wounded, and its lieutenant-
colonel badly wounded in the early part of the
engagement. " Yours respectfully,
" JOHN H. REAGAN."

General Longstreet, Lee's " Old War Horse,"
tried and true, and, in the writer's judgment,
more " sinned against " than " sinning," has
been *persona non grata* to Virginians since he
dared to doubt the infallibility of a chief not
less mortal than himself. As, however, he offered a crumb of comfort to them in a letter
addressed to me in 1899, which I have mislaid,
I quote it from memory. I wrote to him asking
what command first broke the lines at Gaines'
Mill. He replied with a brevity that was non-
committal: " The victory at Gaines' Mill was
won by the combined efforts of the Texas, Anderson's, and Pickett's brigade." That was all he
wrote. Against it, read the following from
Volume III. of Confederate Military History,
beginning on page 290, prepared by Major Jed.
Hotchkiss, a Virginian himself, and, therefore,
not likely to fail in giving a Virginia command
its every due:

" The forests and the condition of the country
occupied by Lee's lines prevented the use of
much artillery in this battle of Gaines' Mill,
but braver, daring, and more heroic endeavor
was never made by patriotic soldiers than on
that day, all along the lines, especially by Hill's
North Carolinians and Virginians, Lawton's

Georgians, and memorably by Hood's Texans, who stormed the heights of Turkey and Mc-Gehee's hills, sweeping across fences and ditches, through fallen timber and abatis, and over intrenchments which blazed with sheeted fire from infantry and artillery from the entire Federal front, leaving well-nigh half of their comrades dead or wounded on the way, and rolling back in a sullen tide of defeat both the regulars and the volunteers of Porter's corps, and becoming masters of the heights they had so bravely stormed. As it ever did, Jackson's 'Stonewall Brigade' pushed into the thickest of the fight, across the path of Ewell, and bore its full share in winning this glorious victory."

Comment is almost superfluous. Major Hotchkiss is too just a man, not to say too loyal a Virginian, to suffer himself influenced while writing history by any bias or prejudice. Had Pickett's Virginians taken any notable or conspicuous part in that grand final charge of the day, the fact that it belonged to Longstreet's division would not have prevented the Major from giving it its proper meed of praise. But he not only does not mention it, but emphasizes that omission by special mention of the Virginians under Hill and Jackson who fought to the left of the Texans.

And why should he say "memorably Hood's Texans," if they did not in some way distinguish themselves? When he was writing the lines quoted it is not likely he was engaged in showering bouquets around indiscriminately and without regard to merit.

Holding Adjutant Cooper as the accredited representative and spokesman of Pickett's brigade—his gallantry and efficiency as a soldier, his merits as a gentleman, *sans peur et sans reproche,* having been vouched for by his old commander, now, alas, gone to join the great majority—I have not deemed it necessary to notice statements made by others in behalf of that command. Each of the other writers patted the Adjutant on the shoulder and encouraged him in his heroic but audacious effort to cast discredit on the statements of Lee and Jackson and to reverse the long-rendered verdict of history, that the Fourth Texas was the first Confederate command to break the enemy's lines at Gaines' Mill. No other command, brigade, or regiment aided in that—the Eighteenth Georgia overcoming the difficulties in its path only in time to assist the Fourth in the capture of the fourteen guns. Possibly one or two more companies of the right wing of the Eighteenth went through the line abreast of the Fourth— the ground in their front being also quite open. Doubtless, too, there was a sprinkling of Alabamians, Mississippians, North and South Carolinians, and even Tennesseeans, moving along with the Texans. If so, they were adventurous spirits who, surmising that Hood would give the regiment of which he had once been the colonel the first opportunity to win distinction, straggled to the front.

But if any of Pickett's brigade went forward with the Fourth Texas, or got with it in time to assist in the capture of the guns, they came from the line of recumbents over which the Fourth passed before attaining the crest of the ridge and getting under fire.

What troops these were, was then and has ever since been a profound mystery. General Whiting said of them that " he didn't know who they were, and didn't want to know." Some of them claimed to be Virginians, and considering only Adjutant Cooper's admission that his brigade sought safety on the very bosom of Mother Earth, previous to making an assault upon the breastworks, this might appear plausible. Not so, though, when it is remembered that the Adjutant carries his command within thirty or forty yards of the works before the involuntary prostration began. These troops were fully two hundred yards from the works. Besides, Pickett's brigade fought half a mile to the right of the Fourth Texas.

No special mention is made of Hampton's Legion, and the First and Fifth Texas, comrade regiments of the Fourth Texas in the brigade. It would be in bad taste to apologize for the omission, since neither will feel aggrieved. Given the same opportunity, either would have done as well as the Fourth Texas—denied it, not one of them begrudges, or ever has begrudged, to the Fourth the honors it so gallantly and fairly won. Their advance was across heavily timbered and marshy ground, and it was therefore impossible for them to keep abreast of the Fourth Texas. Besides, it is not likely they began their advance quite as early as that regiment, for it took time to communicate orders in the dense undergrowth of swampy Virginia woodlands, especially in the month of June, when every tree and shrub was in full foliage.

END

INDEX

319